W9-BIS-422

*The Faber Book of
Popular Verse*

The Faber Book of
POPULAR
VERSE

*Edited by
Geoffrey Grigson*

faber and faber

LONDON · BOSTON

First published in 1971
by Faber and Faber Limited
3 Queen Square London WC1N 3AU
This edition published 1974
Reprinted 1986

Printed in Great Britain by
Whitstable Litho Ltd., Whitstable, Kent
All rights reserved

Introduction and this selection
© Geoffrey Grigson 1971

This book is sold subject to the condition that it shall not, by way of
trade or otherwise, be lent, re-sold, hired out or otherwise circulated
without the publisher's prior consent in any form of binding or cover
other than that in which it is published and without a similar
condition being imposed on the subsequent purchaser

ISBN 0 571-10606 4

To Adey Horton, who likes such things.

Contents

Introduction

This is a book of poems, in a broad sense, not of folklore, or anthropology or social history, so I do not have to enlarge on difficulties of origin or definition which are so troublesome when people write, for example, about folksongs or about ballads, that special class of folksong, or about nursery rhymes. Popular verse is a large box. Popular, it may be asked at once, with whom? With everyone? With all classes of curiosity or concern? Not necessarily. I include a few macaronic songs, for instance, without supposing that the shepherd out on the Long Mynd or the churl working in the common field would have been singing '*Inducas, inducas*' to himself, or 'I feel *puerum movere.*' Either song, though, might have been sung by a scholar in an Oxford hall. Which is to say that there have always been different layers, different circles of popularity, separate or overlapping. It would not do to make popularity through all speakers of a language a condition of exclusion or inclusion.

There are negative tests. Popular verse is not 'literary', it is not egoistic or private, or – except by corruption sometimes – obscure: it does not share qualities, I mean, of much other good verse. It does not deal with the exceptional, its vocabulary is not idiosyncratic, its images are few and immediate in appeal, its forms are uncomplicated. All of this, in any climate of the 'literary', especially today's climate, offers some rest or relief; as well as some instruction in the nature of language and poetry.

The lightest play or the most piercing incantation, popular verse does arise, too, from the common measure of experience and legend and belief, no less than from the common measure of language as our way of communication; which explains why few good poets have been other than sympathetic to their country's mainly anonymous accumulation of popular verse,

9

or to the best of it. Think of Skelton, Shakespeare, Fletcher, Herrick, Blake, Burns, Coleridge, Wordsworth, Clare, Morris, Christina Rossetti, Yeats, de la Mare, Graves, Auden, Louis MacNeice, in our own tradition. (And the late T. S. Eliot, was on occasion heard to sing 'Frankie and Johnny'.)

Those who write about folksong (popular verse, tunes apart, of a particular kind), or ballads, are often, it does seem to me, shifty and mystical, or sentimental, or in some cases politically sentimental, about the 'folk', and about transmission. Of course the folksong they write of, is both tunes and words (which do merit consideration on their own account). Both have changed, both have been subject to 'communal re-creation' (or incremental or substitutional invention), and in this the tunes have done better than the poems. To a good tune you can still sing words – as long as they fit – which have turned half or absolutely into nonsense. The evidence suggests to me that as far as the verse, the words go, 'communal re-creation' is often synonymous with communal corruption; it does, in the long run, more harm than good. I have seen it suggested that the ballads, the older ballads as we have them, owe more than many of us would like to think or more than we can actually be sure of, to emending and polishing by eighteenth century poets who were in sympathy with the traditions of folksinging. More recent collector-poets have done the same, evidently, in America. Now-a-days, when a song is recovered, scientific scruples take charge, and its acquired imperfections are made sacrosanct; which is a pity, perhaps.

Still, as I say, some things are to be learnt from all that happens, in time and through repetition, to a set of appealing verses. Years ago Cecil Sharp spoke of qualities acquired by a folksong in its passage through the centuries. Its 'individual angles and regularities', he said, were rubbed or smoothed away just as the pebble on the shore gets itself 'rounded by the action of the waves.' A popular poem, spoken or sung, a squib of locality, a riddle, or a successful song which has spread from the theatre, may certainly lose what does not quite fit the language or the changes in the language. A poem may even lose everything except the one striking memorable stanza which persists on its own.

This is very true of what we have learnt, in an unfortunate way, to call nursery rhymes (as if most children had ever had nurseries or nursery-maids). 'Misty-moisty was the morn' (page 37), for example, lives on, in different brief versions, from a long, otherwise tiresome printer's ballad, 'The Wiltshire Wedding' (*Roxburghe Ballads*, Vol. VII) of the late seventeenth century, the first, the one, good stanza out of fifteen.* Or one may see the process of abstraction beginning in the famous quatrain of the 'Westron Wind' (page 118). Someone, between 1500 and 1550, wrote out in his manuscript, now in the British Museum, songs, pieces of music, tablatures for the lute, etc., including, with the tune, these four lines, the best piece of the words of a song which was not recovered – with the quatrain rather debased (see page 341) – until 1905.

Again, because transmission has corrupted them, or because we have forgotten the circumstances in which they originated, the words of a song will lose their meaning, on the surface at any rate, and yet remain powerfully fascinating. The famous 'Dilly Song', for instance (page 28). Here the words enumerate group after group of mysterious persons who wouldn't have been mysterious at all to a schoolboy of 1530 learning the commonplaces of medieval cosmology. Or consider how the New Year Water song (page 297) and 'Sunny Bank' (page 300) have declined – is 'declined' the word? – into the extremely suggestive and intriguing.

Often the mystery goes to the head of commentators (see the note in this book on the 'Corpus Christi Carol', page 358), eager against reason sometimes to promote traces of 'old heathen practices' and what they call 'the Old Religion.' Yet popular verse does hint that, in spite of the offended *amour propre* and the remonstrance of poets, the best of poetry may after all be the occasional quatrain, the occasional couplet or line, which compels wonder in the mind, the rest of the poem in which it occurs being dross or draff. It does hint that basically the arts *are* irrational.

Reverting to Cecil Sharp's image of the pebble on the beach, I would give it more colour, more variety, at the risk of being too poetical. The sea (extend and interpret 'sea' as you like)

* See the *Oxford Dictionary of Nursery Rhymes.*

11

washes up and rounds, in pebble shape, different substances, differently coloured, of varying density, texture, and attraction. It transforms a piece of green or blue bottle glass into a kind of jewel. It smoothes – not, it is true, with a polished surface – scraps of amber, gabbro, onyx, agate, jet, chalcedony, anthracite, fossilized bone, old battery carbon, wood, and red brick. So various is the nature of popular verse. Yet every piece of it is, good or bad, a nodule of the life, the pleasures, the distresses, the common fantasies of man, between childhood and dying.

The popular poems or fragments in this selection run from the thirteenth century to the twentieth. They seem to be best arranged by our concerns between the cradle (rather than that nursery of the moneyed classes) and the coffin; in which, naturally, poems about love are the most numerous. Limericks I have excluded, partly because of their monotony. Lavatory wall verse I do not despise –

> Wise people come here just to shit,
> Others come to show their wit.

Below, in another hand:

> By writing this, you miserable arse,
> You include yourself in the latter class –

but even its masterpieces do not mix well with most of these poems. Longer ballads, old or modern, I have generally excluded, on account of their length and their accessibility in so many collections. Much else of the very familiar I have also omitted, sometimes with regret. But the very familiar is not always the best.

I must warmly thank A. L. Lloyd for directing me to many obscure sources.

GEOFFREY GRIGSON

1 · Childhood, Some Children's Rhymes, and Game Rhymes

Hush-a-ba, Burdie

Hush-a-ba, burdie, croon, croon,
   Hush-a-ba, burdie, croon.
The sheep are gane tae the siller wid,
   An the coos are gane tae the broom, broom.

An it's braw milkin the kye, kye,
   It's braw milkin the kye,
The birds are singin, the bells are ringin,
   An the wild deer come gallopin by.

Hush-a-ba, burdie, croon, croon,
   Hush-a-ba, burdie, croon,
The gaits are gane tae the mountain hie,
   An they'll no be hame till noon.

Hush and Baloo

Hush and baloo, babbie,
   Hush and baloo.
A the lave's in their beds –
   I'm hushin you.

Bonny at Morn

The sheep's in the meadow,
The kye's in the corn,
(Thou's ower lang in thy bed),
Bonny at morn.
      Canny at night,
      Bonny at morn.
      (Thou's ower lang in thy bed),
      Bonny at morn.

The bird's in the nest,
The trout's in the burn,
Thou hinders thy mother
In many a turn.
Canny at night,
Bonny at morn.
(Thou's ower lang in thy bed),
Bonny at morn.

We're all laid idle
Wi' keeping the bairn,
The lad winnot work,
And the lass winnot lairn.
Canny at night,
Bonny at morn.
(Thou's ower lang in thy bed),
Bonny at morn.

The Miller's Wife's Lullaby
(Orkney)

Kenst doo hoo
Dae dogs gaed tae dae mill,
Trill, trill, trill!

Ap aboot dae clappars,
An doon aboot dae happars
Dae dogs gaed tro dae mill.

First in dis man's meal-poke,
An dat man's meal-poke,
An in dae millar's meal-poke,

An hame again!
Emly-amly, emly-amly,
Fill, fill, fill!

Go to Bed First

Go to bed first,
A golden purse.
Go to bed second,
A golden bezant.
Go to bed third
A golden bird.

Don't Care

Don't Care didn't care,
  Don't Care was wild,
Don't Care stole plum and pear
  Like any beggar's child.

Don't Care was made to care,
  Don't Care was hung.
Don't Care was put in a pot
  And boiled till he was done.

Some Riddles

i

Four and twenty white bulls
  Sate upon a stall,
Forth came the red bull
  And licked them all.

(*The teeth and the tongue*)

ii

Black within and red without,
Four corners round about.

(*A chimney*)

iii

Fatherless an' motherless,
   Born without a skin,
Spok' when it ca'ame into th' wo'ld
   An' niver spok' sin.

(A fart)

iv

Long legs and crooked thighs,
Little head and no eyes.

(A pair of tongs)

Jack the Piper

As I was going up the hill
   I met with Jack the Piper,
And all the tunes that he could play
   Was 'Tie up your petticoats tighter.'

I tied them once, I tied them twice,
   I tied them three times over,
And all the songs that he could sing
   Was 'Carry me safe to Dover.'

The Nut-Tree

I had a little nut-tree,
   Nothing would it bear
But a silver nutmeg
   And a golden pear.

The King of Spain's daughter
   Came to visit me,
And all for the sake
   Of my little nut-tree.

What's in the Cupboard

What's in the cupboard? says Mr. Hubbard.
A knuckle of veal, says Mr. Beal.
Is that all? says Mr. Ball.
And enough too, says Mr. Glue,
And away they all flew.

Come, let's to Bed

Come, let's to bed,
Says Sleepy-head;
Sit up awhile, says Slow;
Hang on the pot,
Says Greedy-gut,
Let's sup before we go.

Crosspatch

Crosspatch,
Draw the latch,
Sit by the fire and spin.
Take a cup
And drink it up,
And call your neighbours in.

Fire, Fire

Fire! Fire! says the town crier.
Where? Where? says Goody Blair.
Down the town, says Goody Brown.
I'll go and see't, says Goody Fleet.
So will I, says Goody Fry.

Dips or Counting Out Rhymes

i

Ex and squary,
Virgin Mary,
Vick, vock,
Little stock,
O – U – T, etc.

ii

Dip, dip, dip,
My blue ship
Sailing on the water
Like a cup and saucer,
Dip, dip, dip,
You – are – not – it.

iii

Eachie, peachie, pearie, plum,
Throw the tatties up the lum.
Santa Claus got one on the bum,
Eachie, peachie, pearie, plum.

iv

I saw a doo flee our the dam
Wi' silver wings an golden ban.
She leukit east, she leukit west,
She leukit fahr t' light on best.
She lightit on a bank o' san'
T' see the cocks o' Cumberlan'.
Fite puddin,
Black trout,
Ye're oot.

v

Zeenty, peenty, heathery, mithery,
Bumfy leery over Dover.
Saw the King o' Heazle Peasil
Jumping o'er Jerus'lem Dyke.
  Black fish, white troot,
  Eerie, oorie, you're oot.

vi

Dip, dip, allebadar,
  Duck shee shantamar,
  Shantamar allebadar,
  Duck shee shantamar.

vii

Hickety pickety i sillickety
Pompalorum jig,
Every man who has no hair
Generally wears a wig,
One, two, three,
Out – goes – he.

viii

Did you ever, ever, ever,
In your leaf, life, loaf,
See the deevel, divil, dovol,
Kiss his weef, wife, woaf?
No, I never, never, never,
In my leaf, life, loaf,
Saw the deevel, divil, dovol,
Kiss his weef, wife, woaf.

21

Starting Rhymes for Hide-and-Seek

i

The cock doth crow, the wind doth blow,
I don't care whether you are hidden or no,
I'm coming!

ii

Green lady, green lady, come doon for thy tea,
Thy tea is a' ready an' waiting for thee —
Coo-ee!

The Merry-ma-Tanzie

(Verses for a marrying game)

Here we go the jingo-ring,
    The jingo-ring, the jingo-ring,
Here we go the jingo-ring,
    About the merry-ma-tanzie.

Twice about, and then we fa,
    Then we fa, then we fa,
Twice about and then we fa,
    About the merry-ma-tanzie.

Guess ye wha's the young goodman,
    The young goodman, the young goodman,
Guess ye wha's the young goodman,
    About the merry-ma-tanzie?

Honey is sweet, and so is he,
    So is he, so is he,
Honey is sweet and so is he,
    About the merry-ma-tanzie.

He's married wi a gay gold ring,
　A gay gold ring, a gay gold ring,
He's married wi a gay gold ring,
　About the merry-ma-tanzie.

A gay gold ring's a cankerous thing,
　A cankerous thing, a cankerous thing,
A gay gold ring's a cankerous thing,
　About the merry-ma-tanzie.

Now they're married I wish them joy,
　I wish them joy, I wish them joy,
Now they're married I wish them joy,
　About the merry-ma-tanzie.

Father and mother they must obey,
　Must obey, must obey,
Father and mother they must obey,
　About the merry-ma-tanzie.

Loving each other like sister and brother,
　Sister and brother, sister and brother,
Loving each other like sister and brother
　About the merry-ma-tanzie.

We pray this couple may kiss together,
　Kiss together, kiss together,
We pray this couple may kiss together,
　About the merry-ma-tanzie.

How Many Miles to Babylon?

How many miles to Babylon?
Threescore miles and ten.
Can I get there by candle-light?
Yes, and back again.
If your heels are nimble and light,
You may get there by candle-light.

Who goes round my Pinfold Wall

Who goes round my pinfold wall?
Little Johnny Ringo.
Don't steal all my fat sheep!
No more I will, no more I may,
Until I've stoln 'em all away,
Nip, Johnny Ringo.

London Bridge

London Bridge is broken down,
Dance o'er my lady lee,
London Bridge is broken down,
With a gay lady.

How shall we build it up again?
Dance o'er my lady lee,
How shall we build it up again,
With a gay lady.

Build it up with silver and gold,
Dance o'er my lady lee,
Build it up with silver and gold,
With a gay lady.

Silver and gold will be stole away,
Dance o'er my lady lee,
Silver and gold will be stole away,
With a gay lady.

Build it up again with iron and steel,
Dance o'er my lady lee,
Build it up again with iron and steel,
With a gay lady.

Iron and steel will bend and bow,
Dance o'er my lady lee,
Iron and steel will bend and bow,
With a gay lady.

Build it up with wood and clay,
Dance o'er my lady lee,
Build it up with wood and clay,
With a gay lady.

Wood and clay will wash away,
Dance o'er my lady lee,
Wood and clay will wash away,
With a gay lady.

Build it up with stone so strong,
Dance o'er my lady lee,
Build it up with stone so strong,
With a gay lady.

Huzza! 'twill last for ages long,
Dance o'er my lady lee,
Huzza! 'twill last for ages long,
With a gay lady.

Green Grass

A dish, a dish, a green grass,
A dish, a dish, a dish,
Come all you pretty maidens
And dance along wi' us.

For we are lads a roving,
A roving through the land,
We'll take this pretty fair maid
By her lily white hand.

Ye sall get a duke, my dear,
An ye sall get a drake,
An ye sall get a bonny prince
For your ain dear sake.

25

And if they all should die,
    Ye sall get anither,
The bells will ring, the birds will sing,
    And we'll clap our hands together.

We are Three Brethren come from Spain

We are three brethren come from Spain,
    All in French garlands.
We are come to court your daughter Jean,
    And adieu to you, my darlings,

My daughter Jean she is too young,
    All in French garlands,
She cannot bide your flattering tongue,
    And adieu to you, my darlings.

Be she young, or be she old,
    All in French garlands,
It's for a bride she must be sold,
    And adieu to you, my darlings.

A bride, a bride, she shall not be,
    All in French garlands,
Till she go through this world with me,
    And adieu to you, my darlings.

Then you shall keep your daughter Jane,
    All in French garlands,
Come once, we come not here again,
    And adieu to you, my darlings.

Come back, come back, you courteous knights,
    All in French garlands,
Clean up your spurs, and make them bright,
    And adieu to you, my darlings.

Sharp shine our spurs, all richly wrought,
   All in French garlands,
In towns afar our spurs were bought,
   And adieu to you, my darlings.

Smell my lilies, smell my roses,
   All in French garlands,
Which of my daughters do you choose?
   And adieu to you, my darlings.

Are all your daughters safe and sound?
   All in French garlands,
Are all your daughters safe and sound?
   And adieu to you, my darlings.

In every pocket a thousand pounds,
   All in French garlands,
On every finger a gay gold ring,
   And adieu to you, my darlings.

To-Morrow's the Fair

To-morrow's the fair,
And I shall be there,
Stuffing my guts
With gingerbread nuts.

Lemonade

Lemonade
Made in the shade
Stirred with a spade
By an old maid.

He that ne'er learns his ABC

He that ne'er learns his A, B, C,
For ever will a blockhead be;
But he that learns these letters fair
Shall have a coach to take the air.

The Schoolmaster

Mr. Rhind is very kind,
He goes to kirk on Sunday.
He prays to God to give him strength
To skelp the bairns on Monday.

The Dilly Song

I'll sing you one O.
  Green grow the rushes O.
What is your one O?
  One is one and all alone
  And ever more shall be so.

I'll sing you two O.
  Green grow the rushes O.
What are your two O?
  Two, two the lily-white boys,
  Clothed all in green O.
  One is one and all alone
  And ever more shall be so.

I'll sing you three O.
  Green grow the rushes O.
What is your three O?
  Three for the rivals,
  Two, two, the lily-white boys,
  Clothed all in green O.
  One is one and all alone
  And ever more shall be so.

I'll sing you four O.
   Green grow the rushes O.
What is your four O?
   Four for the Gospel makers,
   Three for the rivals,
   Two, two the lily-white boys,
   Clothed all in green O,
   One is one and all alone
   And ever more shall be so.

I'll sing you five O.
   Green grow the rushes O.
What is your five O?
   Five for the symbol at your door,
   Four for the Gospel makers,
   Three for the rivals,
   Two, two, the lily-white boys,
   Clothed all in green O,
   One is one and all alone
   And ever more shall be so.

I'll sing you six O.
   Green grow the rushes O.
What is your six O?
   Six for the six proud walkers,
   Five for the symbol at your door,
   Four for the Gospel makers,
   Three for the rivals,
   Two, two, the lily-white boys,
   Clothed all in green O,
   One is one and all alone
   And ever more shall be so.

I'll sing you seven O.
   Green grow the rushes O.
What is your seven O?
   Seven for the seven stars in the sky,
   Six for the six proud walkers,
   Five for the symbol at your door,

Four for the Gospel makers,
Three for the rivals,
Two, two, the lily-white boys,
Clothed all in green O,
One is one and all alone
And ever more shall be so.

I'll sing you eight O.
Green grow the rushes O.
What is your eight O?
Eight for the eight bold rangers,
Seven for the seven stars in the sky,
Six for the six proud walkers,
Five for the symbol at your door,
Four for the Gospel makers,
Three for the rivals,
Two, two, the lily-white boys,
Clothed all in green O,
One is one and all alone
And ever more shall be so.

I'll sing you nine O.
Green grow the rushes O.
What is your nine O?
Nine for the nine bright shiners,
Eight for the eight bold rangers,
Seven for the seven stars in the sky,
Six for the six proud walkers,
Five for the symbol at your door,
Four for the Gospel makers,
Three for the rivals,
Two, two, the lily-white boys,
Clothed all in green O,
One is one and all alone
And ever more shall be so.

I'll sing you ten O.
Green grow the rushes O.
What is your ten O?

Ten for the ten commandments,
Nine for the nine bright shiners,
Eight for the eight bold rangers,
Seven for the seven stars in the sky,
Six for the six proud walkers,
Five for the symbol at your door,
Four for the Gospel makers,
Three for the rivals,
Two, two, the lily-white boys,
Clothed all in green O,
One is one and all alone
And ever more shall be so.

I'll sing you eleven O.
Green grow the rushes O.
What is your eleven O?
Eleven for the eleven who went to heaven,
Ten for the ten commandments,
Nine for the nine bright shiners,
Eight for the eight bold rangers,
Seven for the seven stars in the sky,
Six for the six proud walkers,
Five for the symbol at your door,
Four for the Gospel makers,
Three for the rivals,
Two, two, the lily-white boys,
Clothed all in green O,
One is one and all alone
And ever more shall be so.

I'll sing you twelve O.
Green grow the rushes O.
What is your twelve O?
Twelve for the twelve apostles,
Eleven for the eleven who went to **heaven,**
Ten for the ten commandments,
Nine for the nine bright shiners,
Eight for the eight bold rangers,
Seven for the seven stars in the sky,

31

Six for the six proud walkers,
Five for the symbol at your door,
Four for the Gospel makers,
Three for the rivals,
Two, two, the lily-white boys,
Clothed all in green O,
One is one and all alone
And ever more shall be so.

2 · The Seasons

The Zodiac Rhyme

The Ram, the Bull, the Heavenly Twins,
And next the Crab, the Lion shines,
    The Virgin and the Scales,
The Scorpion, Archer and He-Goat,
The Man that carries the Watering-pot,
    The Fish with glittering tails.

Wassail Song

We have been a walking
    Among the leaves so green,
And hither we are coming
    So stately to be seen.

    With our wassel,
    Our jolly wassel,
    All joys come to you
    And to our wassel bowl.

Good Master and good Mistress,
    As you sit by the fire,
Remember us poor wassellers
    That travel in the mire.

Our bowl is made
    Of the mulberry tree,
And so is your ale
    Of the best barley.

Pray rise up, master Butler,
    And put on your golden ring,
And bring to us a jug of ale,
    The better we shall sing.

Our purse it is made
    Of the finest calves skin,
We want a little silver
    To line it well within.

Good Master, good Mistress,
 If that you are but willing,
Send down two of your little boys
 To each of us a shilling.

We'll hang a silver napkin
 Upon a golden spear,
And come no more a wasselling
 Until another year.

Snow

Snaw, snaw, coom faster,
White as allyblaster.

Feathers of Snow

The men of the East
Are picking their geese,
And sending their feathers here away, there away.

Riddles of the Weather

i

A white bird featherless floats down through the air
And never a tree but he lights there.

(*Snow*)

ii

White bird featherless
Flew from Paradise,
Pitched on the castle wall.
 Along came Lord Landless,
 Took it up handless
 And rode away horseless
To the king's white hall.

(*Snowflake and sun*)

iii

Arthur O'Bower has broken his bands
And he's come roaring owre the lands.
The King o' Scots and a' his power
Canna turn Arthur O'Bower.

(*A high wind*)

iv

Banks fou, braes fou,
Gather ye a the day,
Ye'll no gather your nieves fou.

(*Mist*)

v

White sheep, white sheep, on a blue hill,
When the wind stops, you all stand still.
When the wind blows, you run away slow,
White sheep, white sheep, where do you go?

(*Clouds*)

vi

Trip trap in a gap,
As many feet as a hundred sheep.

(*Hail as it falls*)

Misty-Moisty was the Morn

Misty-moisty was the morn,
Chilly was the weather;
There I met an old man
Dressed all in leather.

Dressed all in leather
  Against the wind and rain,
With How do you do? and How do you do?
  And How do you do? again.

March

March yeans the lammie
  And buds the thorn,
And blows through the flint
  Of an ox's horn.

The Borrowing Days

March said to Averil,
I see three hoggs on yonder hill,
And if you'll lend me dayis three,
I'll find a way to gar them die.
The first o' them was wind and weet,
The second o' them was snaw and sleet,
The third o' them was sic a freeze,
It froze the birds' feet to the trees.
When the three days were past and gane,
The silly poor hoggs came hirpling hame.

Which is the Bow?

Which is the bow that has no arrow?
(The rainbow, that never killed a sparrow)
Which is the singer that has but one song?
(The cuckoo who singeth it all day long).

More Riddles

i

Red and blue and delicate green,
The king can't catch it and neither can the queen.
Pull it into the room and you can catch it soon.
Answer this riddle by to-morrow at noon.

(The rainbow)

ii

On yonder hill there is a red deer,
The more you shoot it, the more you may,
You cannot drive that deer away.

(The rising sun)

iii

I washed my face in water
That neither rained nor run.
I dried my face on a towel
That was neither wove nor spun.

(Dew and the warmth of the sun)

iv

In Mornigan's park there is a deer,
Silver horns and golden ear,
Neither fish, flesh, feather, nor bone,
In Mornigan's park she walks alone.

(The moon)

I See the Moon

I see the moon
    And the moon sees me,
God bless the priest
    That christened me.

39

Sumer is Icumen in

Sumer is icumen in,
Lhude sing cuccu!
Groweth sed and bloweth med
And springeth the wode nu.
Sing cuccu!

Awe bleteth after lomb,
Lhouth after calve cu,
Bulluc sterteth, bucke verteth.
Murie sing cuccu!
Cuccu, cuccu,
Wel singes thu cuccu.
Ne swik thu naver nu!

Sing cuccu nu, Sing cuccu!
Sing cuccu,
Sing cuccu nu!

The Rural Dance about the Maypole

Come lasses and lads,
Take leave of your dads,
And away to the Maypole hey;
For every he
Has got him a she
With a minstrel standing by;
For Willy has gotten his Jill,
And Jenny has got his Jone,
To jig it, jig it, jig it, jig it,
Jig it up and down.

Strike up, says Wat,
Agreed, says Kate,
And I prithee, Fiddler, play,
Content, says Hodge,
And so, says Madge,
For this is a holiday,

For every man did put
His hat off to his lass,
And every girl did curchy,
Curchy, curchy on the grass.

Begin, says Hall,
Aye, aye, says Mall,
We'll lead up Packington's Pound;
No, no, says Noll,
And so, says Doll,
We'll first have Sellinger's Round;
Then every man began to foot it round about,
And every girl did jet it, jet it, jet it in and out.

Y'are out, says Dick,
'Tis a lie, says Nick,
The Fiddler played it false;
'Tis true, says Hugh,
And so, says Sue,
And so, says nimble Alice;
The Fiddler then began to play the tune agen,
And every girl did trip it, trip it, trip it, to the men.

Let's kiss, says Jane,
Content, says Nan,
And so says every she;
How many, says Batt,
Why three, says Matt,
For that's a maiden's fee;
But they instead of three did give 'em half a score,
And they in kindness gave 'em, gave 'em, gave 'em
    as many more.

Then after an hour
They went to a bower
    And played for ale and cakes,
        And kisses too
        Until they were due,

The lasses held the stakes.
The girls did then begin to quarrel with the men,
And bid 'em take their kisses back, and give 'em their
    own agen.

Yet there they sate,
Until it was late
    And tired the Fiddler quite,
        With singing and playing,
        Without any paying
    From morning until night.
They told the Fiddler then they'd pay him for his play,
And each a 2 pence, 2 pence, 2 pence gave him and went
    away.

The Mayers' Song

Remember us poor Mayers all,
    And thus we do begin
To lead our lives in righteousness
    Or else we die in sin.

We have been rambling all this night,
    And almost all this day,
And now returned back again
    We have brought you a branch of May.

A branch of May we have brought you,
    And at your door it stands,
It is but a sprout, but it's well budded out
    By the work of our Lord's hands.

The hedges and trees they are so green,
    As green as any leek,
Our heavenly Father he watered them
    With his heavenly dew so sweet.

The heavenly gates are open wide,
    Our paths are beaten plain,
And if a man be not too far gone
    He may return again.

The life of man is but a span,
    It flourishes like a flower,
We are here to-day, and gone to-morrow
    And we are dead in an hour.

The moon shines bright and the stars give a light
    A little before it is day,
So God bless you all, both great and small,
    And send you a joyful May.

The Padstow Night Song

(for May Day)

Unite, unite, let us all unite,
For Summer is a-come unto day
And whither we are going we will all unite
    On the merry morning of May.

The young men of Padstow they might if they would,
For Summer is a-come unto day.
They might have built a ship and gilded her with gold
    On the merry morning of May.

The maidens of Padstow they might if they would,
For Summer is a-come unto day.
They might have made a garland of the white rose and the red
    On the merry morning of May.

Up Merry Spring, and up the merry ring,
For Summer is a-come unto day.
How happy are those little birds that merrily do sing
    On the merry morning of May.

The Pretty Ploughboy

As I was a-walking
    One morning in spring
I heard a pretty ploughboy,
    And so sweetly he did sing;

And as he was a-singing O
    These words I heard him say,
'There's no life like the ploughboy's
    In the sweet month of May.'

There's the lark in the morning
    She will rise up from her nest,
And she'll mount the white air
    With the dew all on her breast.

And with the pretty ploughboy O
    She'll whistle and she'll sing
And at night she'll return
    To her nest back again.

Under the Greenwood Tree

In summer time when leaves grow green
    And birds sit on the tree,
Let all the lords say what they can,
    There's none so merry as we.
There's Jeffrey and Tom, there's Ursula and Joan,
    With Roger and bonny Bettee,
O how they do firk it, caper and jerk it
    Under the greenwood tree.

Our music is the Choir Pipe,
    And he so well can play;
We hire him from Whitsuntide
    To latter Lammas Day:
On Sundays and on holidays
    After even song comes he,
And then they do firk it, caper and jerk it
    Under the greenwood tree.

Come play we Adam and Eve, said Dick.
    What's that? quoth Choir Pipe.
It is the Beginning of the World,
    Thou most illiterate wight.
If that be it, then have at all,
    And he plays with a merry glee,
And then they did firk it, caper and jerk it
    Under the greenwood tree.

Then in comes Gaffer Underwood,
    And he sits him on the bench,
With his wife and his daughter Mary,
    That pretty round-fac'd wench;
There was Goodman Chuck and Habbacock,
    And all sit there to see
How they did firk it, caper and jerk it
    Under the greenwood tree.

We must not forget my Lord's son,
    For he's full of merry conceits,
And brake a jest among the maids
    And he capers, leaps and sweats,
And he gives them a flap with his fox-tail,
    And he thrust it in, to see
How they did firk it, caper and jerk it
    Under the greenwood tree.

And then we went to Sir Harry's house,
    A rich old cob was he,
And there we danc'd a round, a round,
    But the devil a penny we see.
From thence we went to Somerton,
    Where the boys be jolly and free,
And then we did firk it, caper and jerk it
    Under the greenwood tree.

Hollin, Green Hollin

Alone in greenwood must I roam,
　　Hollin, green hollin,
A shade of green leaves is my home,
　　Birk and green hollin.

Where nought is seen but boundless green,
　　Hollin, green hollin,
And spots of far blue sky between,
　　Birk and green hollin.

A weary head a pillow finds,
　　Hollin, green hollin,
Where leaves fall green in summer winds,
　　Birk and green hollin.

Enough for me, enough for me,
　　Hollin, green hollin,
To live at large with liberty,
　　Birk and green hollin.

The Ripe and Bearded Barley

Come out, 'tis now September,
　　The hunter's moon's begun,
And through the wheaten stubble
　　We hear the frequent gun.
The leaves are turning yellow,
　　And fading into red,
While the ripe and bearded barley
　　Is hanging down its head.

All among the barley
　　Who would not be blithe,
While the ripe and bearded barley
　　Is smiling on the scythe.

The wheat is like a rich man,
    It's sleek and well-to-do.
The oats are like a pack of girls,
    They're thin and dancing, too.
The rye is like a miser,
    Both sulky, lean, and small,
Whilst the ripe and bearded barley
    Is the monarch of them all.

      All among the barley
        Who would not be blithe,
      While the ripe and bearded barley
        Is smiling on the scythe.

The spring is like a young maid
    That does not know her mind,
The summer is a tyrant
    Of most ungracious kind.
The autumn is an old friend
    That pleases all he can,
And brings the bearded barley
    To glad the heart of man.

      All among the barley
        Who would not be blithe,
      While the ripe and bearded barley
        Is smiling on the scythe.

The Yule Days

The king sent his lady on the first Yule day
A papingo-aye:
Who learns my carol and carries it away?

The king sent my lady on the second Yule day
Three partridges, a papingo-aye:
Who learns my carol and carries it away?

The king sent his lady on the third Yule day
Three plovers, three partridges, a papingo-aye:
Who learns my carol and carries it away?

The king sent my lady on the fourth Yule day
A goose that was gray,
Three plovers, three partridges, a papingo-aye:
Who learns my carol and carries it away?

The king sent his lady on the fifth Yule day
Three starlings, a goose that was gray,
Three plovers, three partridges, a papingo-aye:
Who learns my carol and carries it away?

The king sent his lady on the sixth Yule day
Three goldspinks, three starlings, a goose that was gray,
Three plovers, three partridges, a papingo-aye:
Who learns my carol and carries it away?

The king sent his lady on the seventh Yule day
A bull that was brown, three goldspinks, three starlings, a
    goose that was gray,
Three plovers, three partridges, a papingo-aye:
Who learns my carol and carries it away?

The king sent his lady on the eighth Yule day
Three ducks a-merry laying, a bull that was brown,
Three goldspinks, three starlings, a goose that was gray,
Three plovers, three partridges, a papingo-aye:
Who learns my carol and carries it away?

The king sent his lady on the ninth Yule day
Three swans a-merry swimming, three ducks a-merry
    laying, a bull that was brown,
Three goldspinks, three starlings, a goose that was gray,
Three plovers, three partridges, a papingo-aye:
Who learns my carol and carries it away?

The king sent his lady on the tenth Yule day
An Arabian baboon, three swans a-merry swimming,
Three ducks a-merry laying, a bull that was brown,
Three goldspinks, three starlings, a goose that was gray,
Three plovers, three partridges, a papingo-aye:
Who learns my carol and carries it away?

The king sent his lady on the eleventh Yule day
Three hinds a-merry hunting, an Arabian baboon,
Three swans a-merry swimming,
Three ducks a-merry laying,
Three goldspinks, three starlings, a goose that was gray,
Three plovers, three partridges, a papingo-aye:
Who learns my carol and carries it away?

The king sent his lady on the twelfth Yule day
Three maids a-merry dancing, three hinds a-merry hunting, an
    Arabian baboon,
Three swans a-merry swimming,
Three ducks a-merry laying,
Three goldspinks, three starlings, a goose that was gray,
Three plovers, three partridges, a papingo-aye:
Who learns my carol and carries it away?

The king sent his lady on the thirteenth Yule day
Three stalks o' merry corn, three merry maids a-dancing,
Three hinds a-merry hunting, an Arabian baboon,
Three swans a-merry swimming,
Three ducks a-merry laying,
Three goldspinks, three starlings, a goose that was gray,
Three plovers, three partridges, a papingo-aye:
Who learns my carol and carries it away?

Yule's Come, and Yule's Gane

Yule's come, and Yule's gane,
    And we hae feasted weel,
Sae Jock maun to his flail again,
    And Jenny to her wheel.

3 · Living Things

The Hart Loves the High Wood

The Hart loves the high wood,
  the Hare loves the hill,
The Knight loves his bright sword,
  the Churl loves his bill.

I Have Twelve Oxen

I have twelve oxen that be fair and brown,
And they go a-grazing down by the town.
  With hay, with howe, with hay!
Sawest thou not mine oxen, thou litill pretty boy.

I have twelve oxen and they be fair and white,
And they go a-grazing down by the dyke.
  With hay, with howe, with hay!
Sawest thou not mine oxen, thou litill pretty boy.

I have twelve oxen and they be fair and blak,
And they go a-grazing down by the lak.
  With hay, with howe, with hay!
Sawest thou not mine oxen, thou litill pretty boy.

I have twelve oxen and they be faire and rede,
And they go a-grazing down by the mede.
  With hay, with howe, with hay!
Sawest thou not mine oxen, thou litill pretty boy.

Cat at the Cream

Jean, Jean, Jean,
The cat's at the cream,
Suppin wi her forefeet,
And glowrin wi her een!

The Cat's Song

Dirdum drum,
Three threads and a thrum,
Thrum gray, thrum gray.

My Father Kept a Horse

My father kept a horse and my mother kept a mare,
My brother kept a dog and my sister kept a hare,
Had a ride from the horse, a foal from the mare,
Pleasure with the dog and sport with the hare.

My father kept a bull and my mother kept a cow,
My brother kept a boar and my sister kept a sow,
Had beef from the bull and a calf from the cow,
Had bacon from the boar and pigs from the sow.

My father kept a buck, my mother kept a doe,
My brother kept a tup, my sister kept a ewe,
Had venison from the buck, fawn from the doe,
Had mutton from the tup, lamb from the ewe.

My father kept a cock, my mother kept a hen,
My brother kept a robin, my sister kept a wren,
Had chickens from the cock, eggs from the hen,
Had young ones from the robin, fed by the wren.

My father kept a cat, my mother kept a mouse,
My brother kept a flea, my sister kept a louse,
Had a scratch from the cat, had a squeak from the mouse,
Had a nip from the flea, had a bite from the louse.

Old Gray Mare

Oh, the old gray mare, she ain't what she used to be,
Ain't what she used to be, ain't what she used to be.
The old gray mare she ain't what she used to be,
    Many long years ago.
Many long years ago, many long years ago,
The old gray mare, she ain't what she used to be,
    Many long years ago.

The old gray mare she kicked on the whiffletree,
Kicked on the whiffletree, kicked on the whiffletree.
The old gray mare she kicked on the whiffletree,
    Many long years ago.
Many long years ago, many long years ago,
The old gray mare, she ain't what she used to be,
    Many long years ago.

The False Fox

The false fox came unto our croft,
And so our geese full fast he sought.
With how fox, how! With hey fox, hey!
Come no more unto our house to bear our geese away.

The false fox came unto our sty,
And took our geese there by and by.
With how fox, how! With hey fox, hey!, etc.

The false fox came into our yerde,
And there he made the geese aferde.
With how fox, how! With hey fox, hey!, etc.

The false fox came unto our gate,
And took our geese there where they sate.
With how fox, how! With hey fox, hey!, etc.

The false fox came to our hall-door,
And shrove our geese there in the floor.
With how fox, how! With hey fox, hey!, etc.

The false fox came into our hall,
And assoyled our geese both great and small.
With how fox, how! With hey fox, hey!, etc.

The false fox came unto our coop,
And there he made our geese to stoop.
With how fox, how! With hey fox, hey!, etc.

He took a goose fast by the neck,
And the goose thoo began to quek.
With how fox, how! With hey fox, hey!, etc.

The goodwife came out in her smok,
And at the fox she threw her rok.
With how fox, how! With hey fox, hey!, etc.

The goodman came out with his flail,
And smote the fox upon the tail.
With how fox, how! With hey fox, hey!, etc.

He threw a goose upon his back,
And furth he went thoo with his pack.
With how fox, how! With hey fox, hey!, etc.

The goodman swore if that he might
He would him slee or it were night.
With how fox, how! With hey fox, hey!, etc.

The false fox went into his den,
And there he was full merry then.
With how fox, how! With hey fox, hey!, etc.

He came ayene yet the next week,
And toke away both hen and cheke.
With how fox, how! With hey fox, hey!, etc.

The goodman said unto his wife,
This false fox liveth a merry life.
With how fox, how! With hey fox, hey!, etc.

The false fox came upon a day,
And with our geese he nade affray.
With how fox, how! With hey fox, hey!, etc.

He took a goose fast by the neck
And her to say wheccumquek.
With how fox, how! With hey fox, hey!, etc.

I pray thee, fox, said the goose thoo,
Take of my feders but not of my toe.

The Goose and the Gander

O the goose and the gander walk'd over the green,
O the goose she went barefoot for fear of being seen,
For fear of being seen, boys, for fear of being seen,
And the goose she went barefoot for fear of being seen.

I had a black hen and she had a white foot,
And she laid an egg in a willow tree root,
In a willow tree root, in a willow tree root,
And she laid a white egg in a willow tree root.

When the Rain Raineth

When the rain raineth
   And the Goose winketh,
Little wotteth the Gosling
   What the Goose thinketh.

The Old Gray Goose

Go tell Aunt Nancy,
Go tell Aunt Nancy,
Go tell Aunt Nancy
Her old gray goose is dead.

The one she'd been saving,
The one she'd been saving,
The one she'd been saving
To make a feather-bed.

She died last Friday,
She died last Friday,
She died last Friday
Behind the old barn shed.

Old gander's weeping,
Old gander's weeping,
Old gander's weeping
Because his wife is dead.

She's left five little goslings,
She's left five little goslings,
She's left five little goslings
To scratch for their own bread.

The Five Hens

There was an old man who liv'd in Middle Row,
He had five hens, and a name for them, oh!
Bill and Ned and Battock,
Cut-her-foot and Pattock.
Chuck, my lady Pattock,
Go to thy nest and lay.

Hen and Cock

Hen: Cock, cock, I have la-a-a-yd.
Cock: Hen, hen, that's well sa-a-a-yd.
Hen: Altho' I have to go barefooted every da-a-y.
Cock: Sell your eggs, and buy shoes.
Sell your eggs, and buy shoes.

Riddles

i

Four stiff standers,
Four lily landers,
Two lookers, two crookers,
And a wig-wag.

(*A cow*)

In marble halls as white as milk,
Lined with a skin as soft as silk,
Within a fountain crystal-clear,
A golden apple doth appear.
No doors there are to this stronghold,
Yet thieves break in and steal the gold.

(A hen's egg)

A long white barn,
Two roofs on it,
And no door at all, at all.

(A hen's egg)

The Bonny Grey

Come all you cockers, far and near,
I'll tell of a cock-fight, when and where.
At Tumbler's Hill, they all did say,
Between the black and the bonny grey.
　With a hip and a ha, and a loud hooray,
　The charcoal black and the bonny grey.

It's to the house to take a sup;
The cock-fight it was soon made up.
Ten guineas a side these cocks will play,
The charcoal black and the bonny grey.

Lord Derby he came swaggering down.
I'll lay ten guineas to half a crown,
If the charcoal black he gets fair play,
He'll rip the wings off the bonny grey.

These cocks hadn't struck past two or three blows,
When the Biggar lads cried, Now you'll lose,
Which made us all both wan and pale.
We wished we'd fought for a gallon of ale.

And the cocks they at it, one, two, three,
And the charcoal black got struck in the eye,
They picked him up to see fair play,
But the black wouldn't fight with the bonny grey.

With the silver breast and the silver wing,
Six brothers of his fought before the king.
With a hip and a ha, and a loud hooray,
And away we went with our bonny grey.

The Koocoo

In Aprill the koocoo can sing her song by rote,
In June of tune she cannot sing a note.
At first koo-coo, koo-coo, sing shrill can she do,
At last, kooke, kooke, kooke; six kookes to one koo.

The Cuckoo

O the cuckoo she's a pretty bird,
    She singeth as she flies,
She bringeth good tidings,
    She telleth no lies.

She sucketh white flowers
    For to keep her voice clear,
And the more she singeth cuckoo
    The summer draweth near.

The Lark

Liverockie, liverockie lee,
Don't herry me,
Or else y'ill be hangit on a high, high tree,
Or droont in a deep, deep sea.

The Lark

Malisons, malisons more than ten
That harries the Queen of Heaven's hen.

Crow's Ditty

Gowa! Gowa!
Wheea teea? Wheea teea?
Bagby Moor, Bagby Moor.
What ti dea there? What ti dea there?
Seek an au'd yeo, seek an au'd yeo.
Is she fat? Is she fat?
Gloor! Gloor! Gloor!

Against the Magpie

I cross'd pynot, an' t' pynot cross'd me.
T'devil tak t' pynot an' God save me.

The Dove

Clean birds by sevens,
Unclean by twos,
The dove in the heavens
Is the one I choose.

A Magpie Rhyme, Northumberland

Yen's sorry,
Twee's morry,
Three's a wedding,
Fower's deeth,
Five's hivin,
Six is hell,
And Sivin's the deel's aan sel.

Hop't She

A Pie sat on a pear tree,
A Pie sat on a pear tree,
A Pie sat on a pear tree,
   Heigho, heigho, heigho!

Then once so merrily hop't she,
Then once so merrily hop't she,
Then once so merrily hop't she,
   Heigho, heigho, heigho!

The Rooks

On the first of March
The craws begin to search.
By the first o April
They are sitting still.
By the first o May,
They're a flown away,
Croupin greedy back again
Wi October's wind and rain.

Blackbird's Song

Red head, red head,
Black apron, black apron,
Are you comin'? Are you comin'?
Tired waiting, tired waiting,
   Blackbird, blackbird.

The Sea-Gull

Sea-gull, sea-gull, sit on the sand.
It's never good weather when you're on the land.

Malison of the Stone-chat

Stane-chack!
Deevil tak!
They wha harry my nest
Will never rest,
Will meet the pest.
De'il brack their lang back
Wha my eggs wad tak, tak!

Robin, Wren, Martin, Swallow

The robin and the wren
Are God Almighty's cock and hen.
The martin and the swallow
Are God Almighty's bow and arrow.

The Cutty Wren

O where are you going? says Milder to Melder,
O where are you going? says the younger to the elder.
O I cannot tell, says Festel to Fose.
We're going to the woods, said John the Red Nose,
We're going to the woods, said John the Red Nose.

O what will you do there? says Milder to Melder,
O what will you do there? says the younger to the elder.
O I cannot tell, says Festel to Fose.
To shoot the cutty wren, said John the Red Nose,
To shoot the cutty wren, said John the Red Nose.

O what will you shoot her with? says Milder to Melder,
O what will you shoot her with? says the younger to the elder.
O I cannot tell, says Festel to Fose.
With bows and with arrows, said John the Red Nose,
With bows and with arrows, said John the Red Nose.

O that will not do, says Milder to Melder,
O that will not do, says the younger to the elder.
O what will do then? says Festel to Fose.
With great guns and cannons, said John the Red Nose,
With great guns and cannons, said John the Red Nose.

O what will you bring her home in? says Milder to Melder,
O what will you bring her home in? says the younger to the elder.
O I cannot tell, says Festel to Fose.
On four strong men's shoulders, said John the Red Nose,
On four strong men's shoulders, said John the Red Nose.

O that will not do, says Milder to Melder,
O that will not do, says the younger to the elder.
O what will do then? says Festel to Fose.
On big carts and waggons, said John the Red Nose,
On big carts and waggons, said John the Red Nose.

What will you cut her up with? says Milder to Melder,
What will you cut her up with? says the younger to the elder.
O I do not know, says Festel to Fose.
With knives and with forks, said John the Red Nose,
With knives and with forks, said John the Red Nose.

O that will not do, says Milder to Melder,
O that will not do, says the younger to the elder.
O what will do then? says Festel to Fose.
With hatchets and cleavers, said John the Red Nose,
With hatchets and cleavers, said John the Red Nose.

What will you boil her in? says Milder to Melder,
What will you boil her in? says the younger to the elder.
O I cannot tell, says Festel to Fose.
In pots and in kettles, said John the Red Nose,
In pots and in kettles, said John the Red Nose.

O that will not do, says Milder to Melder,
O that will not do, says the younger to the elder.
O what will do then? says Festel to Fose.
In brass pans and cauldrons, said John the Red Nose,
In brass pans and cauldrons, said John the Red Nose.

Bird Riddles

i

As I went out, so I came in,
And out of the dead I saw the living spring;
Seven there were and six there be,
Tell me the riddle and then hang me.

> (*A tit and its young from a nest
> between the jawbones of a
> gibbeted murderer*)

ii

I am called by name of man,
    Yet am as little as the mouse:
When winter comes, I love to be
    With my red gorget near the house.

> (*The Robin Redbreast*)

iii

What is it more eyes doth wear
    Than forty men within the land,
Which glister as the crystal clear
    Against the sun, when they do stand?

> (*A peacock's tail*)

iv

One day I went down in the golden harvest field,
I saw something neither fish, flesh, nor bone.
In three weeks it stood alone.

> (*A partridge's egg*)

Robin Redbreast's Testament

Guid day now, bonnie Robin.
    How lang have you been here?
Oh, I have been bird about this bush
    This mair than twenty year.

But now I am the sickest bird
    That ever sat on brier;
And I wad make my testament,
    Guidman, if ye wad hear.

Gar tak this bonnie neb o' mine,
    That picks upon the corn,
And gie't to the Duke o' Hamilton
    To be a hunting-horn.

Gar tak these bonnie feathers o' mine,
    The feathers o' my neb,
And gie to the Lady o' Hamilton
    To fill a feather-bed.

Gar tak this guid right leg o' mine,
    And mend the brig o'Tay,
It will be a post and pillar guid –
    It will neither bow nor gae.

And tak this other leg o' mine,
    And mend the brig o' Weir,
It will be a post and pillar guid –
    It'll neither bow nor steer.

Gar tak these bonnie feathers o' mine,
    The feathers o' my tail,
And gie to the lads o' Hamilton
    To be a barn flail.

And take these bonnie feathers o' mine,
    The feathers o' my breast,
And gie to ony bonnie lad
    That'll bring to me a priest.

Now in there came my Lady Wren,
    With mony a sigh and groan:
Oh what care I for a' the lads,
    If my wee lad be gone.

Then Robin turned him round about,
    E'en like a little king:
Go pack ye out at my chamber-door,
    Ye little cutty quean.

Robin made his testament
    Upon a coll of hay,
And by came a greedy gled,
    And snapt him a' away.

The Frog and the Crow

There was a jolly fat Frog that did in the river swim O,
And there was a comely black Crow that lived on the river
    brim O.
'Come ashore, come ashore,' said the Crow to the Frog, and
    then O
'No, you'll bite me, no, you'll bite me,' said the Frog to the
    Crow again O.

'But there is sweet music on yonder green hill O,
And you shall be a dancer, a dancer in yellow,
All in yellow, all in yellow,' said the Crow to the Frog, and
    then O
'Sir, I thank you, Sir, I thank you,' said the Frog to the Crow
    again O.

'Farewell, ye little fishes, that do in the river swim O,
For I am going to be a dancer, a dancer in yellow.'
'O beware, O beware,' said the fishes to the Frog again O
'All in yellow, all in yellow,' said the Frog to the fishes, and
    then O.

The Frog he came a-swimming, a-swimming to land O,
And the Crow he came a-hopping to lend him his hand O.
'Sir, I thank you, Sir, I thank you,' said the Frog to the Crow,
    and then O
'Sir, you're welcome, Sir you're welcome,' said the Crow to the
    Frog again O.

'But where is the music on yonder green, green hill O?
And where are the dancers, the dancers in yellow,
All in yellow, all in yellow?' said the Frog to the Crow, and
    then O
'Sir, they're here, Sir, they're here,' said the Crow to the
    Frog, and –
                                       Ate him all up O.

The Puddy and the Mouse

There lived a Puddy in a well,
   Cuddy alone, cuddy alone,
There lived a Puddy in a well,
   Cuddy alone and I.
There was a Puddy in a well,
And a mousie in a mill,
   Kickmaleerie, cowden down,
   Cuddy alone and I.

Puddy he'd a-wooin ride,
Sword and pistol by his side.

Puddy came to the mouse's wonne,
Mistress Mouse, are you within?

Yes, kind sir, I am within.
Saftly do I sit and spin.

Madam, I am come to woo.
Marriage I must have of you.

Marriage I will grant you nane
Till Uncle Rottan he comes hame.

Uncle Rottan's now come hame,
Fye, gar busk the bride alang.

Lord Rottan sat at the head o' the table,
Because he was baith stout and able.

What is't that sits next the wa,
But Lady Mouse, baith jimp and sma?

Wha ist that sits next the bride,
But the sola Puddy wi his yellow side?

Syne came the Dewk but and the Drake,
The Dewk took the Puddy, and gart him squaik.

Then in came the guid gray Cat
Wi a the kittlins at her back.

The Puddy he swam down the brook,
The Drake he catched him in his fluke.

The Cat he pu'd Lord Rottan down,
The kittlins they did claw his crown.

But Lady Mouse, baith jimp and sma,
Crept into a hole beneath the wa.
Squeak! quo she, I'm weel awa.

The Snail

Four and twenty tailors
    Went to kill a snail,
The best man among them
    Durst not touch her tail;
She put out her horns
    Like a little Kyloe cow,
Run, tailors, run,
    Or she'll kill you all e'en now.

The Ladybird

God Almighty's colly cow,
　Fly up to heaven,
　Carry up ten pounds,
　　And bring down eleven.

Insect Riddles

i

As I went owre the Hill o' Hoos,
I met a bonny flock o' doos.
They were a' nick nackit,
They were a' brown backit,
Sic a bonny flock o' doos,
Commin' owre the Hill o' Hoos.

(A swarm of bees)

ii

Wee man o' leather
Gaed through the heather,
Through a rock, through a reel,
Through an auld spinning-wheel,
Through a sheep-shank bane.
Sic a man was never seen.

(A beetle)

iii

I was round and small like a pearl,
Then long and slender, as brave as an earl.
Since like a hermit I lived in a cell,
And now like a rogue in the wide world I dwell.

(A butterfly)

The Persimmon Tree

Racoon up the 'simmon tree,
    Rabbit on the ground;
Rabbit says, You son-a-gun,
    Shake them 'simmons down.

Fruit, Flower and Tree Riddles

i

I am within as white as snow,
Without as green as herbs that grow.
I am higher than a house
And yet am lesser than a mouse.

(A walnut hanging on a tree)

ii

As soft as silk, as white as milk,
As bitter as gall. A thick wall
And a green coat covers me all.

(A walnut)

iii

Down by the waterside stand a house and a plat
And four and twenty maids dancing thereat,
Every one with a bell and a blue hat,
And what is that?

(A field of flax)

iv

Itum Paradisum all clothed in green,
The king could not read it, no more could the queen.
They sent for the wise men out of the East,
Who said it had horns, but was not a beast.

(A holly tree)

Stiff standing on the bed,
First it's white, and then it's red.
There's not a lady in the land
That would not take it in her hand.

(*A carrot*)

White as snow and snow it isn't,
Green as grass and grass it isn't,
Red as blood and blood it isn't,
Black as tar and tar it isn't.

(*A blackberry: white flower,
green fruit, changing to red,
then black*)

The Fishes

Oh, a ship she was rigged and ready for sea
And all of her sailors were fishes to be.
*Blow the winds westerly, westerly blow,
We're bound to the south'ard, now steady she goes.*

Oh first came the herring saying, I'm King of the Sea,
He jumped on the poop, Oh the captain I'll be.

Next came the shark with his two rows of teeth.
Cook, mind you the cabbage and I'll mind the beef.

Then came the porpoise with his little blue snout,
He went to the wheel shouting, Ready about.

Then came the mackerel with his pretty striped back,
He hauled aft each sheet, and he boarded each tack.

Next came the codfish with his chuckle head,
He jumped in the chains and began heaving the lead.

Then came the flounder that lies on the ground,
Saying, Damn your eyes, Chuckle Head, mind how you sound.

Next came the whale, the biggest in the sea,
Shouting, Haul in your head sheets, now hellums a lee.

Last came the sprat, he was smallest of all,
He jumped on the poop crying, Maintops'l haul.

Fish Riddles

i

Although it's cold no clothes I wear,
Frost and snow I do not fear,
I have no use for hose or shoes
Although I travel far and near.
All I eat comes free to me,
I need no cider, ale or sack,
I nothing buy or sell or lack.

(*A herring in the sea*)

ii

The robbers came to our house
    When we were a' in,
The house lap out at the windows
    And we were a' ta'en.

(*Fish caught in a net*)

73

The Animals in the Ark

Noe Have done, you men and women all!
Hie you lest this water fall,
That each beast were in his stall,
And into the ship brought.

Of clean beastes seven shall be,
Of unclean two, this God bade me;
This flood is nigh, well may we see,
Therefore tarry you nought.

Sem Sir, here are lions, libards in,
Horses, mares, oxen, and swine,
Geates, calves, sheep and kine
Here sitten thou may see.

Ham Camels, asses, men may find,
Buck, doe, hart, and hind,
And beastes of all manner kind
Here been, as thinkes me.

Japhet Take here cattes and dogs too,
Otter, fox, fulmart also,
Hares hopping gaylie can go
Have cowl here for to eat.

Noe's Wife And here are beares, wolfes sett,
Apes, owles, marmoset,
Weesells, squirrels, and firret;
Here they eaten their meat.

Sem's Wife Yet more beastes are in this house:
Here cattis maken it full crowse,
Here a rotten, here a mowse,
They stand nigh together.

Ham's Wife And here are fowles, less and more:
Hearnes, cranes and byttour,
Swans, peacocks, and them before
Meat for this wedder.

Japhet's Wife Here are cockes, kites, crows,
Rookes, ravens, many rows,
Ducks, curlews, who ever knows
Each one in his kind?

And here are doves, diggs, drakes,
Redshanks running through the lakes;
And each fowl that ledden makes
In this ship men may find.

In Come de Animuls Two by Two

In come de animuls two by two,
Hippopotamus and a kangaroo.
Dem bones gona rise agin.
Dem bones gona rise agin.
I knows it, indeed I knows it, brother.
I knows it, dem bones gona to rise agin.

In come de animuls three by three,
Two big cats and a bumble bee.
Dem bones gona rise agin.

In come de animuls fo' by fo',
Two thru de winder and two thru de do'.
Dem bones gona rise agin.

In come de animuls five by five,
Almost dead and hardly alive.
Dem bones gona rise again.

In come de animuls six by six,
Three wid clubs and three wid sticks.
Dem bones gona rise agin.

In come de animuls seben by seben,
Fo' from Hell and de others from Heaven.
Dem bones gona rise agin.

In come de animuls eight by eight,
Four on time and de others late.
Dem bones gona rise agin.

In come de animuls nine by nine,
Four in front and five behind.
Dem bones gona rise agin.

In come de animuls ten by ten,
Five big roosters and five big hens.
Dem bones gona rise again.
Dem bones gona rise agin.
I knows it, indeed I knows it, brother.
I knows it, dem bones gona rise agin.

The Kirk of the Birds, Beasts and Fishes

When I was a wee thing,
 'Bout six or seven year auld,
I had no worth a petticoat
 To keep me frae the cauld.

Then I went to Edinburgh,
 To bonnie burrows town,
And there I coft a petticoat,
 A kirtle, and a gown.

As I cam hame again,
 I thought I wad big a kirk,
And a' the fowls o' the air
 Wad help me to work.

The heron, wi' her lang neb,
    She moupit me the stanes,
The doo, wi' her rough legs,
    She led me them hame.

The gled he was a wily thief,
    He rackled up the wa',
The pyat was a curst thief,
    She dang down a'.

The hare came hirpling owre the knowe,
    To ring the morning bell,
The hurcheon she came after
    And said she wad do't hersel.

The herring was the high priest,
    The salmon was the clerk,
The howlet read the order,
    They held a bonnie work.

4 · Nonsense and Mystification

The Derby Ram

As I was going to Derby,
   'Twas on a market day,
I saw the finest ram, sir,
   That ever was fed on hay.
This ram was fat behind, sir,
   This ram was fat before,
This ram was ten yards high, sir,
   If he wasn't a little more.
      That's a lie, that's a lie,
      That's a tid i fa la lie.

Now the inside of this ram, sir,
   Would hold ten sacks of corn,
And you could turn a coach and six
   On the inside of his horn.
Now the wool upon his back, sir,
   It reached up to the sky,
And in it was a crow's nest,
   For I heard the young ones cry.
      That's a lie, that's a lie,
      That's a tid i fa la lie.

Now the wool upon his belly, sir,
   Went draggling on the ground,
And that was took to Derby, sir,
   And sold for ten thousand pound.
Now the wool upon his tail, sir,
   Was ten inches and an ell,
And that was took to Derby, sir,
   To toll the old market-bell.
      That's a lie, that's a lie,
      That's a tid i fa la lie.

Now the man that fed this ram, sir,
   He fed him twice a day,
And each time that he fed him, sir,
   He ate a rick of hay.

Now the man that watered this ram, sir,
    He watered him twice a day,
And each time that he watered him
    He drank the river dry.
        That's a lie, that's a lie,
        That's a tid i fa la lie.

Now the butcher that killed the ram, sir,
    Was up to his knees in blood,
And the boy that held the bowl, sir,
    Got washed away in the flood.
Now all the boys in Derby, sir,
    Went begging for his eyes,
They kicked them up and down the street,
    For they were a good football size.
        That's a lie, that's a lie,
        That's a tid i fa la lie.

Now all the women of Derby, sir,
    Went begging for his ears,
To make their leather aprons of
    That lasted them forty years.
And the man that fatted the ram, sir,
    He must be very rich,
And the man that sung this song, sir,
    Is a lying son of a bitch.
        That's the truth, that's the truth,
        That's the tid i fa la truth.

The One-Horned Ewe

There was an owd yowe wi' only one horn,
    Fifty naw me nonny,
And she picked up her living among the green corn,
    So turn the wheel round so bonny.

One day said the pindar to his man,
    Fifty naw me nonny,
I prithee go pen that owd yowe if tha can,
    So turn the wheel round so bonny.

So off went the man to pen this owd yowe,
    Fifty naw me nonny,
 She knocked him three times among the green corn,
    So turn the wheel round so bonny.

Then the butcher was sent for to take this yowe's life,
    Fifty naw me nonny,
And along come the butcher a-whetting his knife,
    So turn the wheel round so bonny.

The owd yowe she started a-whetting her pegs,
    Fifty naw me nonny,
She run at the butcher and broke both his legs,
    So turn the wheel round so bonny.

This owd yowe was sent to fight for the king,
    Fifty naw me nonny,
She killed horsemen and footmen just as they came in,
    So turn the wheel round so bonny.

A Man in the Wilderness

A man in the wilderness asked of me,
How many red strawberries grow'd in the sea?
I answered him again as well as I could,
So many red herrings as swim'd in the wood.

Hey-ho Knave: A Catch

Hey-ho knave canst thou
Knit a knot in the cup in the cup knit a knot,
Knot knit in the cup canst thou.

The Tokens of Love: 1

I have a yong suster
   Fer beyondyn the sea,
Many be the drowries
   That she sente me.

She sente me the cherry
   With-outen ony stone,
And so she ded the dove
   With-outen ony bone.

She sente me the brer
   With-outen ony rind,
She bad me love my lemman
   With-oute longing.

How shuld ony cherry
   Be with-oute stone?
And how shuld ony dove
   Ben with-oute bone?

How shuld ony brer
   Ben with-oute rind?
How shuld I love mine lemman
   With-oute longing?

Whan the cherry was a flowr
   Than hadde it non stone,
Whan the dove was an ey
   Than hadde it non bone.

Whan the brer was onbred
   Than hadde it non rind,
Whan the maiden hath that she lovit,
   She is with-out longing.

I had four brothers over the sea,
Perrie, merrie, dixi, domine.
And they each sent a present unto me,
Petrum, partrum, paradisi tempore,
Perrie, merrie, dixi, domine.

The first sent a goose without a bone,
Perrie, merrie, dixi, domine.
The second sent a cherry without a stone,
Petrum, partrum, paradisi tempore,
Perrie, merrie, dixi, domine.

The third sent a blanket without a thread,
Perrie, merrie, dixi, domine.
The fourth sent a book that no man could read,
Petrum, partrum, paradisi tempore,
Perrie, merrie, dixi, domine.

How can there be a goose without a bone?
Perrie, merrie, dixi, domine.
How can there be a cherry without a stone?
Petrum, partrum, paradisi tempore,
Perrie, merrie, dixi, domine.

How can there be a blanket without a thread?
Perrie, merrie, dixi, domine.
How can there be a book that no man can read?
Petrum, partrum, paradisi tempore,
Perrie, merrie, dixi, domine.

When the goose is in the egg-shell, there is no bone,
Perrie, merrie, dixi, domine.
When the cherry's in the blossom, there is no stone,
Petrum, partrum, paradisi tempore,
Perrie, merrie, dixi, domine.

When the wool's on the sheep's back, there is no thread.
Perrie, merrie, dixi, domine.
When the book's in the press, no man can it read,
Petrum, partrum, paradisi tempore,
Perrie, merrie, dixi, domine.

There Were Three Jovial Welshman

There were three jovial Welshmen,
  As I have heard men say,
And they would go a-hunting
  Upon St. David's Day.

All the day they hunted
  And nothing could they find,
But a ship a-sailing,
  A-sailing with the wind.

One said it was a ship,
  The other he said, Nay.
The third said it was a house,
  With the chimney blown away.

And all the night they hunted
  And nothing could they find
But the moon a-gliding,
  A-gliding with the wind.

One said it was the moon,
  The other he said, Nay.
The third said it was a cheese,
  And half of it cut away.

And all the day they hunted
  And nothing could they find,
But a hedgehog in a bramble bush,
  And that they left behind.

The first said it was a hedgehog,
   The second he said, Nay.
The third said it was a pincushion,
   And the pins stuck in wrong way.

And all the night they hunted
   And nothing could they find,
But a hare in a turnip field,
   And that they left behind.

The first said it was a hare,
   The second he said, Nay.
The third said it was a calf,
   And the cow had run away.

And all the day they hunted
   And nothing could they find,
But an owl in a holly tree,
   And that they left behind.

One said it was an owl,
   The other he said, Nay.
The third said 'twas an old man,
   And his beard growing grey.

I will have the Whetstone

Hey, hey, hey, hey,
I will have the whetstone and I may.

I saw a dog seething souse
And an ape thatching an house
And a pudding eating a mouse.
   I will have the whetstone and I may.

I saw an urchin shape and sewe
And anoder bake and brew,
Scour the pots as they were new.
   I will have the whetstone and I may.

I saw a codfish corn sow,
And a worm a whistle blow
And a pye treading a crow.
  I will have the whetstone and I may.

I saw a stockfish drawing a harrow
And anoder driving a barrow
And a saltfish shooting an arrow.
  I will have the whetstone and I may.

I saw a boar burdens bind
And a frog clewens wind
And a toad mustard grind.
  I will have the whetstone and I may.

I saw a sow bear kyrchers to wash,
The second sow had an hedge to plash,
The third sow went to the barn to thrash.
  I will have the whetstone and I may.

I saw an egg eating a pie,
Geve me drink, my mouth is dry,
It is not long sith I made a lie.
  I will have the whetstone and I may.

The Cow Ate the Piper

In the year ninety-eight, when our troubles were great,
It was treason to be a Milesian.
I can never forget the big black whiskered set
That history tells us were Hessians.
In them heart breaking times we had all sorts of crimes,
As murder never was rifer.
On the hill of Glencree not an acre from me,
Lived bould Denny Byrne, the piper.

Neither wedding nor wake was worth an old shake,
If Denny was not first invited,
For at emptying kegs or squeezing the bags
He astonished as well as delighted.

88

In such times poor Denny could not earn a penny,
Martial law had a sting like a viper –
It kept Denny within till his bones and his skin
Were a-grin through the rags of the piper.

'Twas one heavenly night, with the moon shining bright,
Coming home from the fair of Rathangan,
He happened to see, from the branch of a tree,
The corpse of a Hessian there hanging;
Says Denny, 'These rogues have fine boots, I've no brogues,'
He laid on the heels such a griper,
They were so gallus tight, and he pulled with such might,
Legs and boots came away with the piper.

So he tucked up the legs and he took to his pegs,
Till he came to Tim Kavanagh's cabin,
'By the powers,' says Tim, 'I can't let you in,
You'll be shot if you stop out there rappin'.'
He went round to the shed, where the cow was in bed,
With a wisp he began for to wipe her –
They lay down together on the seven foot feather,
And the cow fell a-hugging the piper.

The daylight soon dawned, Denny got up and yawned,
Then he dragged on the boots of the Hessian:
The legs, by the law! he threw them on the straw,
And he gave them leg-bail on his mission.
When Tim's breakfast was done he sent out his son
To make Denny lep like a lamp-lighter –
When two legs there he saw, he roared like a daw
'Oh! daddy, de cow eat de piper.'

'Sweet bad luck to the baste, she'd a musical taste,'
Says Tim, 'to go eat such a chanter,
Here Pádraic, avic, take this lump of a stick,
Drive her up to Glenealy, I'll cant her.'
Mrs. Kavanagh bawled – the neighbours were called,
They began for to humbug and jibe her,
To the churchyard she walks with the legs in a box,
Crying out, 'We'll be hanged for the piper.'

The cow then was drove just a mile or two off,
To a fair by the side of Glenealy,
And the crathur was sold for four guineas in gold
To the clerk of the parish, Tim Daly.
They went into a tent, and the luck-penny spent,
(For the clerk was a woeful old swiper),
Who the divil was there, playing the Rakes of Kildare,
But their friend, Denny Byrne, the piper.

Then Tim gave a bolt like a half-broken colt,
At the piper he gazed like a gommach;
Says he, 'By the powers, I thought these eight hours,
You were playing in Dhrimindhu's stomach.'
But Denny observed how the Hessian was served,
So they all wished Nick's cure to the viper,
And for grá that they met, their whistles they wet,
And like devils they danced round the piper.

I saw a Peacock with a Fiery Tail

I saw a Peacock with a fiery tail,
I saw a blazing Comet drop down hail,
I saw a Cloud with ivy circled round,
I saw a sturdy Oak creep on the ground,
I saw a Pismire swallow up a whale,
I saw a raging Sea brim full of ale,
I saw a Venice Glass sixteen foot deep,
I saw a Well full of men's tears that weep,
I saw their Eyes all in a flame of fire,
I saw a House as big as the moon and higher,
I saw the Sun even in the midst of night,
I saw the Man that saw this wondrous sight.

(*In each line move the comma
back to follow the first noun*)

I Saw a Fishpond

I saw a fishpond all on fire,
I saw a house bow to a squire,
I saw a parson twelve feet high,
I saw a cottage near the sky
I saw a balloon made of lead,
I saw a coffin drop down dead,
I saw two sparrows run a race,
I saw two horses making lace,
I saw a girl just like a cat,
I saw a kitten wear a hat,
I saw a man who saw these too,
And said though strange they all were true.

(*Again move the comma back to
the first noun in each line*)

Riddle

I saw five birds all in a cage,
Each bird had but a single wing,
They were an hundred years of age,
And yet did fly and sweetly sing.
The wonder did my mind possess,
When I beheld their age and strength.
Besides as near as I can guess,
Their tails were thirty feet in length.

(*A peal of bells in a steeple*)

If All the World were Paper

If all the world were paper,
    And all the sea were ink,
If all the trees were bread and cheese,
    How should we do for drink?

91

If all the world were sand O,
   Oh then what should we lack O,
If as they say there were no clay,
   How should we take tobacco?

If all our vessels ran-a,
   If none but had a crack-a,
If Spanish apes ate all the grapes,
   How should we do for sack-a?

If friars had no bald pates,
   Nor nuns had no dark cloisters,
If all the seas were beans and peas,
   How should we do for oysters?

If there had been no projects,
   Nor none that did great wrongs,
If fiddlers shall turn players all,
   How should we do for songs?

If all things were eternal,
   And nothing their end bringing,
If this should be, then how should we
   Here make an end of singing?

Rats, Ducks, Dogs, Cats, Pigs

Three young rats with black felt hats,
Three young ducks with white straw flats,
Three young dogs with curling tails,
Three young cats with demi-veils
Went out to walk with two young pigs
In satin vests and sorrel wigs.
   But suddenly it chanced to rain
   And so they all went home again.

We're All in the Dumps

We're all in the dumps,
For diamonds are trumps,
The kittens are gone to St. Paul's,
The babies are bit,
The moon's in a fit
And the houses are built without walls.

There was a Man of Double Deed

There was a man of double deed
Who sowed his garden full of seed.
When the seed began to grow,
It was like a garden full of snow.
When the snow began to melt,
It was like a ship without a bell.
When the ship began to sail,
It was like a bird without a tail.
When the bird began to fly,
It was like an eagle in the sky.
When the sky began to roar,
It was like a lion at the door.
When the door began to crack,
It was like a stick across my back.
When my back began to smart,
It was like a penknife in my heart.
When my heart began to bleed,
It was death, and death indeed.

There was a Man and he was Mad

There was a man and he was mad
And he ran up the steeple,
And there he cut his nose off
And flung it at the people.

5 · Love

There Gowans are Gay

There gowans are gay, my joy,
   There gowans are gay;
They gar me wake when I shou'd sleep,
   The first morning of May.

About the fields as I did pass,
   There gowans are gay;
I chanc'd to meet a proper lass,
   The first morning of May.

Right busy was that bonny maid,
   There gowans are gay;
I halst her, syne to her I said,
   The first morning of May:

O mistress fair, what do you here?
   There gowans are gay;
Gathering the dew, what neid ye speir?
   The first morning of May.

The dew, quoth I, what can that mean?
   There gowans are gay;
Quoth she, To wash my mistress clean,
   The first morning of May.

I asked farder at hir syne,
   There gowans are gay,
Gif to my will she wad incline?
   The first morning of May.

She said, her errand was not there,
   Where gowans are gay;
Her maidenhood on me to ware,
   The first morning of May.

Then like an arrow frae a bow,
   There gowans are gay;
She skift away out o'er the know,
   The first morning of May.

And left me in the garth my lane,
  There gowans are gay;
And in my heart a twang of pain,
  The first morning of May.

The little birds they sang full sweet,
  There gowans are gay;
Unto my comfort was right meet,
  The first morning of May.

And thereabout I past my time,
  There gowans are gay;
Until it was the hour of prime,
  The first morning of May.

And then returned hame bedeen,
  There gowans are gay;
Pansand what maiden that had been,
  The first morning of May.

The Hawthorn

Of everykune tree,
Of everykune tree,
The hawthorn bloweth sweetest
Of everykune tree.

My leman she shall be,
My leman she shall be,
The fairest of earthkin
My leman she shall be.

Whistle o'er the Lave o't

My mither sent me to the well,
She had better gane hersell,
I got the thing I dare nae tell,
  Whistle o'er the lave o't.

98

My mither sent me to the sea,
For to gather mussles three,
A sailor lad fell in wi me,
   Whistle o'er the lave o't.

Tom, he was a piper's son

Tom, he was a piper's son,
He learnt to play when he was young,
And all the tune that he could play
Was, Over the hills and far away,
Over the hills and a great way off,
The wind shall blow my topknot off.

Tom with his pipe made such a noise
That he pleased both the girls and boys,
And they all stopped to hear him play
Over the hills and far away,
Over the hills and a great way off,
The wind shall blow my topknot off.

Johnie cam to our Toun

Johnie cam to our toun,
To our toun, to our toun,
Johnie cam to our toun,
   The body wi' the tye.
And O as he kittled me,
Kittled me, kittled me,
And O as he kittled me –
   But I forgot to cry.

He gaed through the fields wi' me,
The fields wi' me, the fields wi' me,
He gaed through the fields wi' me,
   And doun among the rye.
Then O as he kittled me,
Kittled me, kittled me,
Then O as he kittled me –
   But I forgot to cry.

Cockerel

I have a gentle cock, croweth me day.
He doth me risen early my matins for to say.

I have a gentle cock, comen he is of gret,
His comb is of red coral, his tail is of jet.

I have a gentle cock, comen he is of kinde,
His comb is of red coral, his tail is of Inde.

His legges ben of asor, so gentle and so smale,
His spores arn of silver white into the wortewale.

His eynen arn of crystal loken all in aumber,
And every night he percheth him in mine lady's chaumber.

Came you not from Newcastle

Came you not from Newcastle?
    Came ye not there away?
Met ye not my true love
    Riding on a bonny bay?
Why should not I love my love?
    Why should not my love love me?
Why should not I love my love,
    Gallant hound sedelee?

And I have land at Newcastle
    Will buy both hose and shoon,
And I have land at Durham
    Will fetch my heart to boon.
And why should not I love my love?
    Why should not my love love me?
Why should not I love my love,
    Gallant hound sedelee?

The Yellow-haired Laddie

The yellow-hair'd laddie sat doun on yon brae,
Cried, Milk the yowes, lassie, let nane o' them gae;
And aye as she milkit, she merrily sang,
The yellow-hair'd laddie shall be my gudeman.
    And aye as she milkit, she merrily sang,
    The yellow-hair'd laddie shall be my gudeman.

The weather is cauld, and my cleadin is thin,
The yowes are new clipt, ai d they winna bucht in,
They winna bucht in, although I should dee.
Oh, yellow-hair'd laddie, be kind unto me.

The gudewife cries butt the house, Jennie, come ben,
The cheese is to mak, and the butter's to kirn.
Though butter, and cheese, and a' should gang sour,
I'll crack and I'll kiss wi' my love ae half hour.
    It's ae lang half hour, and we'll e'en mak it three,
    For the yellow-hair'd laddie my gudeman shall be.

Kiss'd Yestreen

Kiss'd yestreen, and kiss'd yestreen,
Up the Gallowgate, down the Green.
I've woo'd wi' lords, and woo'd wi' lairds,
I've mool'd wi' carles and mell'd wi' cairds,
I've kiss'd wi' priests — 'twas done i' the dark,
Twice in my gown and thrice in my sark.
But priest nor lord nor loon can gie
Sic kindly kisses as he gae me.

Green grows the Rashes

Green grows the rashes O,
    Green grows the rashes O:
The feather-bed is na sae saft
    As a bed amang the rashes O.

We're a dry wi drinking o' t,
   We're a dry wi drinking o 't;
The parson kist the fidler's wife,
   And he coud na preach for thinking o 't.

Green grows the rashes O,
   Green grows the rashes O:
The feather-bed is na sae saft
   As a bed amang the rashes O.

The down-bed, the feather-bed,
   The bed amang the rashes O;
Yet a the beds is na sae saft
   As the bellies o the lasses O.

Green Sleeves

Green sleeves and tartan ties
Mark my true love whare she lies:
I'll be at her or she rise,
   My fiddle and I thegither.

Be it by the chrystal burn,
Be it by the milk-white thorn,
I shall rouse her in the morn,
   My fiddle and I thegither.

May no Man Sleep in Your Hall

May no man sleep in your hall
   For dogs, madam, for dogs, madam,
But if he have a tent of fifteen inch
   With twey clogs,
To drive away the dogs, madam.
   I – blessed be such clogs,
   That giveth such bogs,
   Between my lady legs,
To drive away the dogs, madam.

May no man sleep in your hall,
    For rats, madam, for rats, madam,
But if he have a tent of fifteen inch
    With leatheren knaps,
To drive away the rats, madam,
    I – blessed be such knaps,
    That giveth such swaps,
    Under my lady laps,
To drive away the rats, madam.

May no man sleep in your hall
    For flies, madam, for flies, madam,
But if he have a tent of fifteen inch
    With twey byes,
To drive away the flies, madam.
    I – blessed be such byes,
    That maketh such swyes,
    Between my lady thighs,
To drive away the flies, madam.

O my bonny, bonny May

O my bonny, bonny May,
    Will ye not rue upon me;
A sound, sound sleep I'll never get,
    Until I lye ayont thee.

I'll gie ye four-and-twenty gude milk kye,
    Were a cast in ae year, May;
And a bonnie bull to gang them by,
    That blude-red is his hair, May.

I hae nae houses, I hae nae land,
    I hae nae gowd or fee, Sir;
I am o'er low to be your bryde,
    Your lown I'll never be, Sir.

Bobby Shaftoe

Bobby Shaftoe's gone to sea,
With silver buckles on his knee,
He'll come back and marry me,
   Bonny Bobby Shaftoe.

Bobby Shaftoe's bright and fair,
Combing down his yellow hair,
He's my ain for ever mair,
   Bonny Bobby Shaftoe.

Bobby Shaftoe's gettin' a bairn,
For to dandle on his airm,
On his airm and on his knee,
   Bobby Shaftoe loves me.

Bobby Shaftoe's gone to sea,
With silver buckles on his knee,
He'll come back and marry me,
   Bonny Bobby Shaftoe.

Merry may the Keel Row

As I came down the Cano'gate,
The Cano'gate, the Cano'gate,
As I came down the Cano'gate
   I heard a lassie sing:
O merry may the keel row,
The keel row, the keel row,
Merry may the keel row,
   The ship that my love's in.

My love has breath o roses,
O roses, o roses,
Wi arms o lily posies
   To fauld a lassie in.

O merry may the keel row,
The keel row, the keel row,
Merry may the keel row,
    The ship that my love's in.

My love he wears a bonnet,
A bonnet, a bonnet,
A snawy rose upon it,
    A dimple on his chin.
O merry may the keel row,
The keel row, the keel row,
Merry may the keel row,
    The ship that my love's in.

Cam Ye by the Salmon Fishers

Cam ye by the salmon fishers?
Cam ye by the roperee?
Saw ye a sailor laddie
Waiting on the coast for me?

I ken fahr I'm gyain,
I ken fahs gyain wi me,
I hae a lad o my ain,
Ye daurna tack 'im fae me.

Stockings of blue silk,
Shoes of patent leather,
Kid to tie them up,
And gold rings on his finger.

Oh for six o'clock!
Oh for seven I weary!
Oh for eight o'clock,
And then I'll see my dearie!

The Friar and the Nun

Inducas, inducas,
In temptationibus.

The nun walked on her prayer,
Inducas, inducas,
Ther cam a frere and met with her
In temptationibus.

This nun began to fall asleep,
Inducas, inducas,
The frere kneeled down at her feet
In temptationibus.

This frere began the nun to grope,
Inducas, inducas,
It was a morsel for the Pope,
In temptationibus.

The frere and the nun, whan they had done,
Inducas, inducas,
Each to their cloister did they gone
Sine temptationibus.

A Maid of Brenten Arse

Sing dyllum, dyllum, dyllum, dyllum,
I can tell you, and I will,
Of my lady's water-mill.

It was a maid of brenten arse,
She rode to mill upon a horse,
Yet was she maiden never the worse.

Laid she was upon a sack,
Strike soft, she said, hurt not my back,
And spare not, let the mill clack.

Iwis, the miller was full nice,
His millstones hanged by a vice
And would be walking at a trice.

This maid to mill oft did resort
And of her game made no report,
But to her it was full great comfort.

There was a Maid went to the Mill

There was a maid went to the mill,
   Sing trolly, lolly, lolly, lolly lo,
The mill turn'd round, but the maid stood still,
    Oh, Oh, ho! Oh, Oh, ho! Oh, Oh, ho! did she so?

The miller he kiss'd her; away she went,
   Sing trolly, lolly, lolly, lolly lo.
The maid was well pleas'd, and the miller content,
    Oh ho! Oh ho! Oh ho! was it so?

He danc'd and he sung, while the mill went clack.
   Sing trolly, lolly, lolly, lolly lo,
And he cherish'd his heart with a cup of old sack,
    Oh ho! Oh ho! Oh ho! did he so?

The Lady's Song in Leap Year

Roses are red, diddle diddle, lavender's blue,
If you will have me, diddle diddle, I will have you.
Lillies are white, diddle diddle, rosemary's green,
When you are king, diddle diddle, I will be queen.
Call up your men, diddle diddle, set them to work,
Some to the plough, diddle diddle, some to the cart,
Some to make hay, diddle diddle, some to cut corn,
While you and I, diddle diddle, keep the bed warm.

Hogyn

Hogyn came to bower's door,
Hogyn came to bower's door,
He tirled upon the pin for love,
 Hum, ha, trill go bell,
He tirled upon the pin for love,
 Hum, ha, trill go bell.

Up she rose and let him in,
Up she rose and let him in,
She had awent she had worshipped all her kin,
 Hum, ha, trill go bell,
She had awent she had worshipped all her kin,
 Hum, ha, trill go bell.

When they were to bed brought,
When they were to bed brought,
The old churl he could do nought,
 Hum, ha, trill go bell.
The old churl he could do nought,
 Hum, ha, trill go bell.

Go ye forth to yonder window,
Go ye forth to yonder window
And I will come to you within a throw,
 Hum, ha, trill go bell,
And I will come to you within a throw,
 Hum, ha, trill go bell.

When she him at the window wist,
When she him at the window wist
She turned out her arse and that he kissed,
 Hum, ha, trill go bell,
She turned out her arse and that he kissed,
 Hum, ha, trill go bell.

Iwis, leman, ye do me wrong,
Iwis, leman, ye do me wrong,
Or else your breath is wonder strong,
  Hum, ha, trill go bell,
Or else your breath is wonder strong,
  Hum, ha, trill go bell.

Kate Dalrymple

In a wee cot hoose far across the muir,
  Where peeseweeps, plovers, and whaups cry dreary,
There lived an auld maid for many a lang year,
  Wha ne'er a wooer did e'er ca' dearie.
A lanely lass was Kate Dalrymple,
A thrufty quean was Kate Dalrymple,
Nae music exceptin' the clear burnie's wimple
Was heard rovin' the dwellin' o' Kate Dalrymple.

Her face had a smack o' the gruesome an' grim,
  That did frae the fash o' a' wooers defend her,
Her lang Roman nose nearly met wi' her chin,
  And brang folk in mind o' the auld witch o' Endor.
A wiggle in her walk had Kate Dalrymple,
A snivel in her talk had Kate Dalrymple,
An' mony a cornelian an' cairngorm pimple
Did blaze on the dun face o' Kate Dalrymple.

But mony are the ups an' the douns in life,
  When the dice-box o' fate's jumbled tapsalteerie.
Sae Kate fell heiress to a rich frien's estate,
  An' nae longer for wooers had she cause to weary.
The squire cam' a wooin' syne o' Kate Dalrymple,
The lawyer, scrapin', bowin', fan' out Kate Dalrymple,
On ilk wooer's face was seen love's smiling dimple,
For noo she's nae mair Kate, but Miss Dalrymple.

She'd aften times thocht, when she dwelt by hersel',
    She could wed Willie Speedyspool, the surkin' weaver,
An' noo unto Will she the secret did tell,
    Wha for love or for int'rest did kindly receive her,
He flang by his treadles sune for Kate Dalrymple,
He brunt a' his treadles doun for Kate Dalrymple,
Tho' his richt e'e doth skellie, an' his left leg doth limp ill,
He's won the heart and got the hand o' Kate Dalrymple.

Apples be Ripe

Apples be ripe
And nuts be brown,
Petticoats up
And trousers down.

Blow the Winds, I-Ho

There was a shepherd's son,
    He kept sheep on yonder hill;
He laid his pipe and his crook aside,
    And there he slept his fill.
        And blow the winds, I-ho!
        Sing, blow the winds, I-ho!
        Clear away the morning dew,
        And blow the winds, I-ho!

He looked east, and he looked west,
    He took another look,
And there he spied a lady gay,
    Was dipping in a brook.

She said, 'Sir, don't touch my mantle,
    Come, let my clothes alone;
I will give you as much money
    As you can carry home.'

'I will not touch your mantle,
    I'll let your clothes alone;
I'll take you out of the water clear,
    My dear, to be my own.'

He did not touch her mantle,
    He let her clothes alone;
But he took her from the clear water,
    And all to be his own.

He set her on a milk-white steed,
    Himself upon another;
And there they rode, along the road,
    Like sister and like brother.

And as they rode along the road,
    He spied some cocks of hay;
'Yonder,' he says, 'is a lovely place
    For men and maids to play!'

And when they came to her father's gate,
    She pulled at a ring;
And ready was the proud porter
    For to let the lady in.

And when the gates were open,
    This lady jumped in;
She says, 'You are a fool without,
    And I'm a maid within.

'Good morrow to you, modest boy,
    I thank you for your care;
If you had been what you should have been,
    I would not have left you there.

'There is a horse in my father's stable,
    He stands beyond the thorn;
He shakes his head above the trough,
    But dares not prie the corn.

'There is a bird in my father's flock,
    A double comb he wears;
He flaps his wings, and crows full loud,
    But a capon's crest he bears.

'There is a flower in my father's garden,
    They call it marygold;
The fool that will not when he may,
    He shall not when he wold.'

Said the shepherd's son, as he doft his shoon,
    'My feet they shall run bare.
And if ever I meet another maid,
    I rede that maid beware.'

If you don't like my Apples

    If you don't like my apples,
        Don't shake my tree.
    I'm not after your boy friend,
        He's after me.

The Gardener

All ye young men, I pray draw near,
    I'll let you hear my mind
Concerning those who fickle are,
    And inconstant as the wind.

A pretty maid who late livd here,
    And sweethearts many had,
The gardener-lad he viewd them all,
    Just as they came and gaed.

The gardener-lad he viewd them all,
    But swore he had no skill.
If I were to go as oft to her,
    Ye surely would me kill.

112

I'm sure she's not a proper maid,
   I'm sure she is not tall.
Another young man standing by,
   He said, Slight none at all.

For we're all come of woman, he said,
   If ye woud call to mind,
And to all women for her sake
   Ye surely should be kind.

The summer hours and warm showers
   Make the trees yield in the ground,
And kindly words will woman win,
   And this maid I'll surround.

The maid then stood in her bower-door,
   As straight as ony wand,
When by it came the gardener-lad,
   With his hat in his hand.

Will ye live on fruit, he said?
   Or will ye marry me?
And amongst the flowers in my garden
   I'll shape a weed for thee.

I will live on fruit, she says,
   But I'll never marry thee,
For I can live without mankind,
   And without mankind I'll die.

Ye shall not live without mankind,
   If ye'll accept of me,
For among the flowers in my garden
   I'll shape a weed for thee.

The lily white to be your smock
   Becomes your body best
And the jelly-flower to be your quill,
   And the red rose in your breast.

Your gown shall be o the pingo white,
    Your petticoat cammovine,
Your apron o the seel o downs,
    Come smile, sweet heart o mine.

Your shoes shall be o the gude rue red –
    Never did I garden ill –
Your stockings o the mary mild,
    Come smile, sweet heart, your fill.

Your gloves shall be o the green clover,
    Comes lockerin to your hand,
Well dropped oer wi blue blavers,
    That grow among white land.

  Young man, ye've shap'd a weed for me,
    In summer among your flowers,
Now I will shape another for you,
    Among the winter showers.

The snow so white shall be your shirt.
    It becomes your body best.
The cold bleak wind to be your coat,
    And the cold wind in your breast.

The steed that you shall ride upon
    Shall be o the weather snell,
Well bridled wi the northern wind,
    And cold sharp showers o hail.

The hat you on your head shall wear
    Shall be o the weather gray,
And aye when you come into my sight
    I'll wish you were away.

The Broken-Hearted Gardener

I'm a broken-hearted Gardener, and don't know what to do,
My love she is inconstant, and a fickle jade, too,
One smile from her lips will never be forgot,
It refreshes, like a shower from a watering pot.
  Oh, Oh! she's a fickle wild rose,
  A damask, a cabbage, a young China Rose.

She's my myrtle, my geranium,
My Sun flower, my sweet marjorum.
My honey suckle, my tulip, my violet,
My holy hock, my dahlia, my mignonette.

We grew up together like two apple trees,
And clung to each other like double sweet peas,
Now they're going to trim her, and plant her in a pot,
And I'm left to wither, neglected and forgot.

She's my snowdrop, my ranunculus,
My hyacinth, my gilliflower, my polyanthus,
My heart's ease, my pink water lily,
My buttercup, my daisy, my daffydown dilly.

I'm like a scarlet runner that has lost its stick,
Or a cherry that's left for the dickey to pick,
Like a waterpot I weep, like a paviour I sigh,
Like a mushroom I'll wither, like a cucumber, die.

I'm like a humble bee that doesn't know where to settle,
And she's a dandelion, and a stinging nettle,
My heart's like a beet root choked with chickweed,
And my head's like a pumpkin running to seed.

I'm a great mind to make myself a felo-de-se,
And finish all my woes on the branch of a tree:
But I won't, for I know at my kicking you'd roar,
And honour my death with a double encore.

The Drynaun Dhun

My love he is fairer than a summer day,
His breath it is sweeter than the newly mown hay,
His hair shines like gold when exposed to the sun,
And they gave him his name from the Drynaun Dhun.

My love he is gone from me over the main,
May God send him safe to his true love again.
I am mourning each day till the dark night comes on,
And I sleep beneath the blossoms of the Drynaun Dhun.

I am waiting impatient for my love's return,
And for his long absence I'll never cease to mourn.
I will join with the small birds when spring time comes on,
And welcome home the blossom of the Drynaun Dhun.

Blackbirds and Thrushes

O if all the young maidens was blackbirds and thrushes,
    Fol de dol, ol de dol, ol de dol lay,
'Tis then the young men would go beatin' the bushes,
    Fol de dol, ol de dol, ol de dol lay.
If the maidens was all just like green rushes growing,
    Fol de dol, ol de dol, ol de dol lay,
'Tis then the young men would take scythes and go mowing,
    Fol de dol, ol de dol, ol de dol lay.

O if all the young maidens was hares on the mountain,
The lads and their hounds would be out without countin',
If the maidens was all just like grouse in the heather,
The boys would be out and be damn'd to the weather.

O if all the young maidens was ducks on the water,
'Tis then the young men would jump in and swim after.
If the maidens was all trout and salmon so lively,
The divil a man would eat fish of a Friday.

116

O gin my Love were yon red Rose

O gin my love were yon red rose,
That grows upon the castle wa'!
And I mysell a drap of dew
Into her bonny breast to fa'!

Oh, there beyond expression blest
I'd feast on beauty a' the night;
Seal'd on her silk-saft falds to rest,
Till fleyed awa by Phoebus light.

I Know Where I'm Going

I know where I'm going,
I know who's going with me,
I know who I love,
But the dear knows who I'll marry.

I'll have stockings of silk,
Shoes of fine green leather,
Combs to buckle my hair
And a ring for every finger.

Feather beds are soft,
Painted rooms are bonny;
But I'd leave them all
To go with my love Johnny.

Some say he's dark,
I say he's bonny,
He's the flower of them all
My handsome, coaxing Johnny.

I know where I'm going,
I know who's going with me,
I know who I love,
But the dear knows who I'll marry.

Black is the Colour

But black is the colour of my true love's hair,
Her cheeks are like some rosy fair,
The prettiest eyes and the neatest hands,
I love the ground whereon she stands.

I love my love and well she knows,
I love the ground whereon she goes,
If you no more on earth I see
I won't serve you as you have me.

The winter's passed and the leaves are green,
The time is passed that we have seen,
But still I hope the time will come
When you and I shall be as one.

I go to the Clyde for to mourn and weep,
But satisfied I never could sleep,
I'll write you a letter in a few short lines,
I'll suffer death ten thousand times.

So fare you well, my own true love,
The time has passed, but I wish you well,
But still I hope the time will come
When you and I will be as one.

I love my love and well she knows,
I love the ground whereon she goes,
The prettiest face and the neatest hands,
I love the ground whereon she stands.

Western Wind

Westron wind, when will thou blow,
The small rain down can rain?
Christ if my love were in my arms,
And I in my bed again.

Shackley-Hay

Young Palmus was a ferryman
   Whom Sheldra fair did love,
At Shackley where her sheep did graze,
   She there his thoughts did prove:
But he unkindly stole away,
And left his love at Shackley-hay.
So loud at Shackley did she cry
The words resound at Shackley-hay.

But all in vain she did complain,
   For nothing could him move.
The wind did turn him back again,
   And brought him to his love.
When she saw him thus turn'd by fate,
She turn'd her love to mortal hate;
Then weeping, to her he did say,
I'll live with thee at Shackley-hay.

No, no, quoth she, I thee deny,
   My love thou once did scorn,
And my prayers wouldst not hear,
   But left me here forlorn.
And now, being turn'd by fate of wind,
Thou thinkst to win me to thy mind;
Go, go, farewell! I thee deny,
Thou shalt not live at Shackley-hay.

The Valiant Seaman's Happy Return to his Love, after a Long Seven Years' Absence

When Sol did cast no light,
   being darken'd over,
And the dark time of night
   did the skies cover,
Running a river by
   There were ships sailing,
A maid most fair I spy'd,
   crying and wailing.

Unto this maid I stept,
   asking what griev'd her,
She answer'd me and wept,
   fates had deceiv'd her:
My love is prest, quoth she,
   to cross the ocean,
Proud waves to make the ship
   ever in motion.

We lov'd seven years and more,
   both being sure,
But I am left on shore,
   grief to endure.
He promis'd back to turn,
   if life was spar'd him,
With grief I dayly mourn,
   death hath debar'd him.

Straight a brisk lad she spy'd,
   made her admire,
A present she receiv'd,
   pleas'd her desire.
Is my love safe, quoth she,
   will he come near me,
The young man answer made,
   Virgin pray hear me.

Under one banner bright,
   for England's glory,
Your love and I did fight,
   mark well my story;
By an unhappy shot,
   we two were parted,
His deaths wound then he got,
   though valiant-hearted.

All this I witness can,
   for I stood by him,
For courage I must say,
   none did out-vye him;
He still would foremost be,
   striving for honour;
But fortune is a whore,
   vengeance upon her.

But e're he was quite dead,
   or his heart broken,
To me these words he said,
   pray give this token
To my love, for there is
   then she none fairer,
Tell her she must be kind
   and love the bearer.

Intomb'd he now doth lye,
   in stately manner,
'Cause he fought valiantly,
   for love and honour:
That right he had in you,
   to me he gave it:
Now since it is my due,
   pray let me have it.

She raging flung away,
   like one distracted,
Not knowing what to say,
   nor what she acted:
To last she curst her fate,
   and shew'd her anger,
Saying, friend you come too late,
   I'le have no stranger.

To your own house return,
    I am best pleased,
Here for my love to mourn,
    since he's deceased:
In sable weeds I'le go,
    let who will jear me;
Since death has serv'd me so,
    none shall come near me.

The chast Penelope
    mourn'd for Ulisses,
I have more grief then she,
    rob'd of my blisses:
I'le ne'er love man again,
    therefore pray hear me;
I'le slight you with disdain,
    if you come near me.

I know he lov'd me well
    for when we parted,
None did in grief excell,
    both were true-hearted.
Those promises we made,
    ne'r shall be broken;
Those words that then he said,
    ne'r shall be spoken.

He hearing what she said,
    made his love stronger,
Off his disguise he laid,
    and staid no longer:
When her dear love she knew,
    in wanton fashion,
Into his arms she flew,
    such is loves passion.

He ask'd her how she lik'd
    his counterfeiting,
Whether she was well pleas'd
    with such like greeting:
You are well vers'd, quoth she,
    in several speeches,
Could you coyn money so,
    you might get riches.

O happy gale of wind,
    that waft thee over,
May Heaven preserve that ship,
    that brought my lover;
Come kiss me now my sweet,
    true love's no slander;
Thou shalt my Hero be,
    I thy Leander.

Dido of Carthage Queen
    lov'd stout Aeneas,
But my true love is found
    more true then he was:
Venus ne'r fonder was
    of young Adonis,
Then I will be of thee,
    since thy love known is.

Then hand in hand they walk,
    with mirth and pleasure,
They laugh, they kiss, they talk,
    love knows no measure;
Now both do sit and sing,
    but she sings clearest;
Like nightingale in spring,
    welcome my dearest.

The Waters of Tyne

I cannot get to my love if I should dee,
The waters of Tyne run between him and me;
And here I must stand with the tear in my e'e
Both sighing and sickly my sweetheart to see.

O where is the boatman, my bonny honey?
O where is the boatman? – bring him to me –
To ferry me over the Tyne to my honey,
And I will remember the boatman and thee.

O bring me a boatman – I'll give any money,
(And you for your trouble rewarded shall be)
To ferry me over the Tyne to my honey,
Or scull him across that rough river to me!

Sourwood Mountain

Chickens a-crowin' on Sourwood Mountain,
　Ho-dee-ing-dong-doodle allay day,
So many pretty girls I can't count 'em,
　Ho-dee-ing-dong-doodle allay day.

My true love, she's a blue-eyed dandy,
　Ho-dee-ing-dong-doodle allay day,
A kiss from her is sweeter than candy,
　Ho-dee-ing-dong-doodle allay day.

My true love lives over the river,
　Ho-dee-ing-dong-doodle allay day,
A hop and a skip and I'll be with her,
　Ho-dee-ing-dong-doodle allay day.

My true love is a blue-eyed daisy,
　Ho-dee-ing-dong-doodle allay day,
If she don't marry me I'll go crazy,
　Ho-dee-ing-dong-doodle allay day.

124

Back my jenny up the Sourwood Mountain,
   Ho-dee-ing-dong-doodle allay day,
So many pretty girls I can't count 'em,
   Ho-dee-ing-dong-doodle allay day.

My true love is a sunburnt daisy,
   Ho-dee-ing-dong-doodle allay day,
She won't work and I'm too lazy,
   Ho-dee-ing-dong-doodle allay day.

Sucking Cider Through a Straw

The prettiest girl
That ever I saw,
Was sucking cider
Through a straw.

I told that girl
I didn't see how
She sucked the cider
Through a straw.

And cheek by cheek
And jaw by jaw
We sucked that cider
Through that straw.

And all at once
That straw did slip;
I sucked some cider
From her lip.

And now I've got
Me a mother-in-law
From sucking cider
Through a straw.

A Kiss in the Morning Early

'Twas early one morning a fair maid arose,
　　All alone in the lo li lo lin,
And off to the shoemaker's shop sure she goes,
　　For her kiss in the morning early.

The cobbler he rose and he soon let her in,
　　All alone in the lo li lo lin,
And he had the will for to greet her so slim
　　With a kiss in the morning early.

Saying 'Cobbler, O Cobbler, 'tis soon we'll be wed,
　　All alone in the lo li lo lin,
So give me two shoes with two buckles o' red
　　For my kiss in the morning early.'

The maid hid the shoes at the back of her waist,
　　All alone in the lo li lo lin,
And home to her father she mournfully faced,
　　For it was in the morning early.

The maid kept the shoes in the heel of her hand,
　　All alone in the lo li lo lin
She met with her father and he walking the land,
　　Oh it was in the morning early.

Saying 'Father, O father, I've got me a man,
　　All alone in the lo li lo lin,
As handsome as ever in leather did stand
　　For my kiss in the morning early.'

The father was thinking and thinking again,
　　All alone in the lo li lo lin,
Who knows that it might be a prince or a king
　　That she met in the morning early?

Who knows but it might be a jobber from town,
　　All alone in the lo li lo lin,
A man with some thousands and thousands of pounds
　　That she met in the morning early?

So the father was smiling and pacing the land,
    All alone in the lo li lo lin,
Till he spied the red shoes in the heel of her hand,
    Oh it was in the morning early.

'Oh, daughter, Oh, daughter,' he started to shout,
    All alone in the lo li lo lin,
'God knows but 'twas none but that cobbling old clout
    That you met in the morning early.'

6 · Fatalities and Fruits of Love

The Unquiet Grave

The wind doth blow today, my love,
    And a few small drops of rain.
I never had but one true-love,
    In cold grave she was lain.

I'll do as much for my true-love
    As any young man may,
I'll sit and mourn all at her grave
    For a twelvemonth and a day.

The twelvemonth and a day being up,
    The dead began to speak:
Oh who sits weeping on my grave,
    And will not let me sleep?

'Tis I, my love, sits on your grave,
    And will not let you sleep,
For I crave one kiss of your clay-cold lips.
    And that is all I seek.

You crave one kiss of my clay-cold lips,
    But my breath smells earthy strong.
If you have one kiss of my clay-cold lips,
    Your time will not be long.

'Tis down in yonder garden green,
    Love, where we used to walk,
The finest flower that ere was seen
    Is withered to a stalk.

The stalk is withered dry, my love,
    So will our hearts decay.
So make yourself content, my love,
    Till God calls you away.

Lowlands Away

Lowlands, Lowlands, away, my John,
Lowlands away I heard them say,
My Lowlands away.

I dreamed a dream the other night,
  Lowlands, Lowlands, away, my John,
My love she came dressed all in white,
  My Lowlands away.

I dreamed my love came in my sleep,
  Lowlands, Lowlands, away, my John,
Her cheeks were wet, her eyes did weep,
  My Lowlands away.

She came to me as my best bride,
  Lowlands, Lowlands, away, my John,
All dressed in white like some fair bride,
  My Lowlands away.

And bravely in her bosom fair,
  Lowlands, Lowlands, away, my John,
A red, red rose did my love wear,
  My Lowlands away.

She made no sound, no word she said,
  Lowlands, Lowlands, away, my John,
And then I knew my love was dead,
  My Lowlands away.

I bound the weeper round my head,
  Lowlands, Lowlands, away, my John,
For now I knew my love was dead,
  My Lowlands away.

She waved her hand, she said goodbye,
  Lowlands, Lowlands, away, my John,
I wiped the tear from out my eye,
  My Lowlands away.

And then awoke to hear the cry,
    Lowlands, Lowlands, away, my John,
Oh, watch on deck, oh, watch ahoy,
    My Lowlands away.

Rare Willie Drowned in Yarrow

Willy's rare, and Willy's fair,
    And Willy's wondrous bony,
And Willy heght to marry me,
    Gin eer he marryd ony.

Yestreen I made my bed fu brade,
    The night I'll make it narrow,
For a' the live-long winter's night
    I lie twin'd of my marrow.

O came you by yon water-side?
    Pu'd you the rose or lilly?
Or came you by yon meadow green?
    Or saw you my sweet Willy?

She sought him east, she sought him west,
    She sought him brade and narrow
Sine in the clifting of a craig
    She found him drownd in Yarrow.

Maw Bonnie Lad

Hev ye seen owt o' maw bonnie lad,
    An' are ye sure he's weel O?
He's gyen ower land, wiv a stick in his hand,
    He's gyen te moor the keel O.

Yes, aw've seen yor bonnie lad,
    Upon the sea aw spied him,
His grave is green, but not wi' grass
    And thou'lt never lie aside him.

133

A Miner Coming Home One Night

A miner coming home one night
Found his house without a light,
So he went upstairs to bed
And then a thought entered his head.

He went into his daughter's room
And found her hanging from a beam,
He took a knife and cut her down
And in her hand this note he found.

'My love is for a bold marine,
I always, always think of him,
And though he's far across the sea,
He never, never thinks of me.

'So all you maidens bear in mind
A good man's love is hard to find.
Dig my grave both wide and deep
And rest my weary bones in sleep.'

They dug her grave both wide and deep
And laid white lilies at her feet,
On her breast a turtle dove
To signify she died of love.

The Ratcatcher's Daughter

In Westminster not long ago,
There lived a Ratcatcher's Daughter.
She was not born at Westminster,
But on the t'other side of the water.
Her father killed rats and she sold sprats
All round and over the water,
And the gentlefolks, they all bought sprats
Of the pretty Ratcatcher's daughter.

She wore no hat upon her head,
Nor cap nor dandy bonnet,
Her hair of her head it hung down her neck
Like a bunch of carrots upon it.
When she cried sprats in Westminster,
She had such a sweet loud voice, Sir,
You could hear her all down Parliament Street,
And as far as Charing Cross, Sir.

The rich and poor both far and near
In matrimony sought her,
But at friends and foes she cocked her nose,
Did this pretty little Ratcatcher's daughter.
For there was a man cried 'Lily white Sand,'
Who in Cupid's net had caught her,
And over head and ears in love,
Was the pretty little Ratcatcher's daughter.

Now 'Lily white Sand' so ran in her head,
When coming down the Strand, oh,
She forgot that she'd got sprats on her head,
And cried, 'buy my Lily white Sand, oh!'
The folks, amazed, all thought her crazed
All along the Strand, oh,
To hear a girl with sprats on her head,
Cry, 'buy my Lily white Sand, oh!'

The Ratcatcher's Daughter so ran in his head,
He didn't know what he was arter,
Instead of crying 'Lily white Sand,'
He cried 'Do you want any Ratcatcher's daughter.'
His donkey cocked his ears and brayed,
Folks couldn't tell what he was arter,
To hear a lily white sand man cry,
'Do you want any Ratcatcher's daughter?'

Now they both agreed to married be
Upon next Easter Sunday,
But the Ratcatcher's daughter had a dream
That she shouldn't be alive next Monday,
To buy some sprats once more she went,
And tumbled into the water,
Went down to the bottom all covered with mud,
Did the pretty little Ratcatcher's daughter.

When Lily white Sand he heard the news,
His eyes ran down with water,
Says he in love I'll constant prove,
And, blow me if I live long arter,
So he cut his throat with a piece of glass,
And stabbed his donkey arter,
So there was an end of Lily white Sand,
His ass, and the Ratcatcher's daughter!

Neddy Nibble'm and Biddy Finn

'Twas in Rosemary Lane, sirs,
Where first my heart felt pain, sirs,
    I loved a maid in the public trade,
A pot-girl, to be plain, sirs.

                              Ah! that I did.

Her name was Biddy Finn, sirs,
She'd a pretty nose and chin, sirs,
    She'd one fault – if so you'll call't,
She was devilish fond of gin, sirs,

                              Ah! that she was.

Now 'twas at the Crown and Shears, sirs,
Where she had passed her years, sirs,
    And this charming fair would ax me there,
With eyes quite full of tears, sirs.

                              Ah! so she did.

Now I thought she had grown steady,
For she said, 'I'll have you, Neddy;'
   So 'Good night' I said – and went home to bed,
For to wed her I was ready.
                              Ah! so I was.

Now my blood was in a fever,
In case I should deceive her;
   So away I sped – but she was in bed,
And so was a coal-heaver.
                         Indeed, he was.

This coaley boasted science,
So he bid me defiance;
   He broke my snout – and kick'd me out,
Without my own compliance.
                   'Pon my soul! he did.

Folks said, 'What do you cry at?'
And I was holloed fie at,
   When two queer chaps – they call'em traps,
They seize me for a riot.
         Says they, You'll go to Brixton Mill.

Then I look'd devilish blue, sirs,
For I was mill'd and tread-mill'd too, sirs,
   And then I swore – not to love no more!
And I'm dash'd if ever I do, sirs,
                  O! no I won't.

The Seeds of Love

I sowed the seeds of love,
   It was all in the spring,
In April, May, and June, likewise,
   When small birds they do sing.

My garden's well planted
   With flowers everywhere,
Yet I had not the liberty to choose for myself
   The flower that I loved so dear.

137

My gardener he stood by,
   I asked him to choose for me,
He chose me the violet, the lily and pink,
   But those I refused all three.

The violet I forsook,
   Because it fades so soon,
The lily and pink I did o'erlook,
   And I vowed I'd stay till June.

In June there's a red rose-bud,
   And that's the flower for me!
But often have I plucked at the red rose-bud
   Till I gained the willow-tree.

The willow-tree will twist,
   And the willow-tree will twine –
O I wish I was in the dear youth's arms
   That once had the heart of mine.

My gardener he stood by,
   He told me to take great care,
For in the middle of a red rose-bud
   There grows a sharp thorn there.

I told him I'd take no care
   Till I did feel the smart,
And oft I plucked at the red rose-bud
   Till I pierced it to the heart.

I'll make me a posy of hyssop,
   No other can I touch,
That all the world may plainly see
   I love one flower too much.

My garden is run wild!
   Where shall I plant anew –
For my bed, that once was covered with thyme,
   Is all overrun with rue?

False luve, and hae ye played me this?

False luve, and hae ye played me this,
    In the simmer, mid the flowers?
I sall repay ye back agen,
    In the winter mid the showers.

But again, dear luve, and again, dear luve,
    Will ye not turn again?
As ye look to ither women,
    Sall I to ither men.

Whittingham Fair

Are you going to Whittingham Fair?
    Parsley, sage, rosemary, and thyme;
Remember me to one who lives there,
    For once she was a true love of mine.

Tell her to make me a cambric shirt,
    Parsley, sage, rosemary, and thyme;
Without any seam or needlework,
    For once she was a true love of mine.

Tell her to wash it in yonder well,
    Parsley, sage, rosemary, and thyme;
Where never spring water or rain ever fell,
    For once she was a true love of mine.

Tell her to dry it on yonder thorn,
    Parsley, sage, rosemary, and thyme;
Which never bore blossom since Adam was born,
    For once she was a true love of mine.

Now he has asked me questions three,
    Parsley, sage, rosemary, and thyme;
I hope he will answer as many for me,
    For once he was a true love of mine.

Tell him to find me an acre of land,
    Parsley, sage, rosemary, and thyme,
Betwixt the salt water and the sea-sand,
    For once he was a true love of mine.

Tell him to plough it with a ram's horn,
    Parsley, sage, rosemary, and thyme,
And sow it all over with one pepper corn,
    For once he was a true love of mine.

Tell him to reap it with a sickle of leather,
    Parsley, sage, rosemary, and thyme,
And bind it up with a peacock's feather,
    For once he was a true love of mine.

When he has done and finished his work,
    Parsley, sage, rosemary, and thyme.
O tell him to come and he'll have his shirt,
    For once he was a true love of mine.

The Pear-Tree

I have a new garden, and new is begun,
Such another garden know I not under sun.

In the middis of my garden is a peryr set,
And it wele none pear bern but a pear Jennet.

The fairest maid of this town preyid me
For to griffin her a grif of mine pery tree.

When I had hem griffid all at her will,
The wine and the ale she did in fill.

And I griffid her right up in her home
And by that day twenty wowkes it was quick in her womb.

That day twelfus month that maid I met,
She said it was pear Robert, but non pear Jennet.

Jolly Jankin

Kyrie, so kyrie,
Jankin singit merry,
With Aleyson.

As I went on Yol Day
In our prosession,
Knew I joly Jankin
By his merry ton,
Kyrieleyson.

Jankin began the office
On the Yol Day,
And yit me thinkit it does me good
So merry gan he say
Kyrieleyson.

Jankin read the Pistle
Full fair and full well,
And yit me thinkit it does me good
As ever have I sel.
Kyrieleyson.

Jankin at the Sanctus
Crackit a merry note,
And yit me thinkit it does me good
I payid for his coat.
Kyrieleyson.

Jankin crackit notes
An hunderid on a knot,
And yit he hackit hem smaller
Than wortes to the pot.
Kyrieleyson.

Jankin at the Agnus
Beryt the pax-bread.
He twinkelid but said nowt,
And on mine foot he tread.
Kyrieleyson.

Benedicamus Domino,
Christ from shame me shield.
Deo gracias, therto —
Alas, I go with child.
Kyrieleyson.

The Wake at the Well

I have forsworn it while I life,
To wake the well-ey.

The last time I the well woke
Sir John caught me with a croke,
He made me swear by bell and boke
    I should not tell-ey.

Yet he did me a well worse turn,
He laid my head again the burn,
He gafe my maidenhead a spurn
    And rofe my bell-y.

Sir John came to our house to play
Fro evensong time til light of the day,
We made as merry as flowers in May.
    I was beguiled-ey.

Sir John he came to our house,
He made it wonder copious.
He said that I was gracious
    To bear a child-ey.

I go with child, well I wot.
I shrew the fader that it gat,
Withouten he find it milk and pap
    A long while-ey.

Bird in a Cage

As I went out one May morning
    To hear the birds so sweet,
I hid myself in a green shady dell
    And watched two lovers meet.

You courted me, was what she said,
    Till you got me to comply.
You courted me with a merry mood,
    All night with you I lie.

And when your heart was mine, false love,
    And your head lay on my breast,
You could make me believe by the fall of your arm
    That the sun rose in the west.

I wish your breast was made of glass
    That all in it might behold,
I'd write our secret in your breast
    In letters made of gold.

There's many a girl can go about
    And hear the birds so sweet,
While I, poor girl, must stay alone
    And rock my cradle and weep.

There's many a star shall dwindle in the west,
    There's many a leaf below,
There's many a curse shall light on a man
    For treating a poor girl so.

Oh I can sing as lonely a song
    As any little bird in a cage,
Who twelve long months astray have been gone,
    And scarce fifteen of age.

O Waly, Waly up the Bank

O waly, waly up the bank,
   And waly, waly down the brae,
And waly, waly yon burn-side,
   Where I and my love wont to gae.

I lean'd my back unto an aik,
   I thought it was a trusty tree,
But first it bow'd, and syne it brak,
   Sae my true-love did lightly me.

O waly, waly, but love be bonny
   A little time, while it is new,
But when 'tis auld it waxeth cauld,
   And fades away like morning dew.

O wherefore should I busk my head?
   Or wherefore should I kame my hair?
For my true-love has me forsook,
   And says he will never love me mair.

Now Arthur-Seat shall be my bed,
   The sheets shall neer be fyl'd by me;
Saint Anton's well shall be my drink,
   Since my true-love has forsaken me.

Martinmas wind, when wilt thou blaw,
   And shake the green leaves off the tree?
O gentle death, when wilt thou come?
   For of my life I am weary.

'Tis not the frost that freezes fell,
   Nor blawing snaw's inclemency;
'Tis not sic cauld that makes me cry,
   But my love's heart grown cauld to me.

When we came in by Glasgow town,
We were a comely sight to see;
My love was cled in the black velvet,
    And I my sell in cramasie.

But had I wist, before I kiss'd,
    That love had been sae ill to win,
I'd locked my heart in a case of gold,
    And pin'd it with a silver pin.

Oh, oh, if my young babes were born,
    And set upon the nurse's knee,
And I my sell were dead and gane!
    For a maid again I'll never be.

Up I arose in Verno Tempore

Up I arose *in verno tempore*,
And found a maiden *sub quadam arbore*,
That did complain *in suo pectore*,
Saying, I feel *puerum movere*.

Adieu, pleasures *antique tempore*.
Full oft with you *solebam ludere*,
But for my miss *mihi deridere;*
With right good cause *incipeo flere*.

Now what shall I say *meis parentibus*?
Because I lay with *quidam clericus*,
They will me beat *cum virgis ac fustibus*,
And me sore chast *coram omnibus*.

With the said child *quid faciam*?
Shall I it keep *vel interficiam*?
If I slay it, *quo loco fugiam*?
I shall lose God *et vitam eternam*.

145

O My Belly

O my belly, my belly, John Trench!
What's the matter with your belly, my wench?
Som'at in my belly goes niddity-nod,
What can it be, good God, good God.

Now Jentil Belly Down

With all the heart in my body,
Now jentil belly down.
And she was sore afraid,
And grievously dismayed,
    With putting on her gown.
Her belly was so grete,
Her gown was not fete,
Her gown was not fete,
For sorrow did she swete,
    And sang
        Down, belly, down.

This game go'th all amiss;
I loved so well to kiss,
I thought it joy and bliss
    To daunce in every town;
But alas and well away
That ever I used such play,
For now with sorrow may
    I say
        Down, belly, down.

Every morning early
My stomach is all quasie;
It hurteth me
Full grievously
    With sickness am I bound:

God and our blessed Lady
And also good king Henry
Send me some remedy
   To keep
      My belly down.
      Down, down,
      Now jentil belly down.

The Foggy, Foggy Dew

When I was a bachelor I lived all alone
   And I worked at the weaver's trade,
And the only, only thing that I ever did wrong
   Was to woo a fair young maid.

I wooed her in the winter time,
   And in the summer too,
And the only only thing that I ever did wrong
   Was to keep her from the foggy foggy dew.

One night she came to my bedside
   When I was fast asleep,
She flung her arms around my neck
   And she began to weep.

She wept, she cried, she damn near died,
   She said, What can I do?
So I rolled her into bed and I covered up her head,
   Just to keep her from the foggy foggy dew.

O I am a bachelor, I live with my son
   And we work at the weaver's trade,
And every single time that I look into his eyes
   He reminds me of that fair young maid.

He reminds me of the winter time
   And of the summer too,
And of the many, many times I held her in my arms
   Just to keep her from the foggy foggy dew.

To Know Whom One Shall Marry

You must lie in another county, and knit the left garter about the right legged stocking (let the other garter and stocking alone) and as you rehearse these following verses, at every comma, knit a knot.

> This knot I knit,
> To know the thing, I know not yet,
> That I may see,
> The man that shall my husband be,
> How he goes, and what he wears,
> And what he does, all days, and years.

7 · Marriage

Marriage

Put your hand in the creel,
And draw an adder or an eel.

I Have Been a Foster

I have been a foster long and many day,
 My locks ben hoar.
I shall hang up my horn by the greenwood spray.
 Foster will I be no more.

All the whiles that I may my bow bend
 Shall I wed no wife.
I shall bigg me a bower at the wood's end,
 There to lead my life.

There was a Lady Loved a Swine

There was a lady loved a swine.
Honey, said she,
Pig-hog, wilt thou be mine?
Hunc, said he.

I'll build for thee a silver sty,
Honey, said she,
And in it softly thou shalt lie.
Hunc, said he.

Pinned with a silver pin,
Honey, said she,
That you may go both out and in.
Hunc, said he.

When shall we two be wed,
Honey? said she.
Hunc, hunc, hunc, he said.
And away went he.

Harry Parry

O rare Harry Parry,
    When will you marry?
When apples and pears are ripe.
    I'll come to your wedding
    Without any bidding,
And lie with your bride all night.

Supper is na Ready

Roseberry to his lady says,
    My hinnie and my succour,
O shall we do the thing you ken
    Or shall we take our supper?
        Fal, lal, etc.

Wi' modest face, sae fu' o' grace,
    Replied the bonny lady,
My noble lord, do as you please
    But supper is na ready.
        Fal, lal, etc.

Blythsome Bridal

Fy let us a to the bridal,
    For there will be lilting there,
For Jock's to be married to Maggie,
    The lass wi the gowden hair.
And there will be langkail and porridge,
    And bannocks of barley-meal,
And there will be good sawt herring,
    To relish a cogue of good ale.
        Fy let us, etc.

And there will be Sawney the soutar,
   And Will wi the meikle mou:
And there will be Tam the blutter,
   With Andrew the tinkler I trow;
And there will be bow'd-legged Robie,
   With thumbless Katie's goodman;
And there will be blue-cheeked Dowbie,
   And Lawrie the laird of the land.
     Fy let us, etc.

And there will be sowlibber Patie,
   And plucky-fac'd Wat i th' mill,
Capper-nos'd Francie, and Gibbie
   That wons in the how o the hill;
And there will be Alaster Sibbie,
   Wha in wi black Bessie did mool,
With snivling Lilly, and Tibby,
   The lass that stands oft on the stool.
     Fy let us, etc.

And Madge that was buckled to Stennie,
   And coft him grey breeks to his arse,
Wha after was hangit for stealing,
   Great mercy it happen'd nae warse:
And there will be gleed Georgy Janners,
   And Kirsh wi the lily-white leg,
Who gade to the south for manners,
   And bang'd up her wame in Mons Meg.
     Fy let us, etc.

And there will be Juden Maclourie,
   And blinkin daft Barbara Macleg,
Wi flea-lugged sharney-fac'd Lawrie,
   And shangy-mou'd halucket Meg,
And there will be happer-arsed Nansy,
   And fairy-fac'd Flowrie by name,
Muck Madie, and fat-hippet Grisy,
   The lass wi the gowden wame.
     Fy let us, etc.

And there will be girn-again Gibby,
  Wi his glaiket wife Jenny Bell,
And measly-shin'd Mungo Macapie,
  The lad that was skipper himsel:
There lads, and lasses in pearlings,
  Will feast i the heart of the ha,
On sybows, and risarts, and carlings,
  That are baith sodden and raw.
    Fy let us, etc.

And there will be fadges and brochen,
  With fouth of good gabbocks of skate,
Powsowdie, and drammock, and crowdie,
  And caller nowtfeet in a plate.
And there will be partens and buckies,
  And whytens and spaldings enew,
And singit sheepheads, and a haggies,
  And scadlips to sup till ye spue.
    Fy let us, etc.

And there will be lapper'd-milk kebbucks,
  And sowens, and farles, and baps,
With swats, and well-scraped paunches,
  And brandy in stoups and in caps:
And there will be mealkail and castocks,
  And skink to sup till ye rive;
And roasts to roast on a brander
  Of flowks that were taken alive.
    Fy let us, etc.

Scrapt haddocks, wilks, dulse and tangles,
  And a mill of good snishing to prie;
When weary with eating, and drinking,
  We'll rise up and dance till we die.
    Then fy let us a to the bridal,
      For there will be lilting there,
    For Jock's to be married to Maggie,
      The lass wi the gowden hair.

Ma Canny Hinny

Where hast 'te been, ma' canny hinny?
An' where hast 'te been, ma' bonny bairn?
Aw was up and down seekin ma' hinny,
Aw was thro' the town, seekin for my bairn;
Aw went up the Butcher Bank and down Grundin Chare,
Call'd at the Dun Cow, but aw cuddent find thee there.
      Where hast 'te been, etc.

Then aw went t' th' Cassel Garth, and caw'd on Johnny Fife.
The beer drawer tell'd me she ne'er saw thee in her life.
      Where hast 'te been, etc.

Then aw went into the Three Bulls Heads, and down the Lang
   Stairs,
And a' the way alang the Close, as far as Mr. Mayor's.
      Where hast 'te been, etc.

Fra there aw went alang the brig, an up t' Jackson's Chare,
Then back again t' the Cross Keys, but cuddent find thee there.
      Where hast 'te been, etc.

Then comin out o' Pipergate, aw met wi' Willy Rigg,
Whe tell'd me that he saw thee stannin pissin on the brig.
      Where hast 'te been, etc.

Comin alang the brig again, aw met wi' Cristy Gee,
He tell'd me et he saw thee gannin down Humeses entery.
      Where hast 'te been, etc.

Where hev aw been! aw sune can tell ye that:
Comin up the Key, aw met wi' Peter Pratt,
Meeting Peter Pratt, we met wi' Tommy Wear,
and went t' Humeses t' get a gill o' beer.

That's where a've been, ma' canny hinny,
That's where a've been, ma' bonny lamb!
Wast 'tu up and down seekin for yur hinny?
Wast 'tu up an down seekin for yur lamb?

Then aw met yur Ben, an we were like to fight;
An when we cam to Sandgate it was pick night;
Crossin the road, aw met wi' Bobby Swinny:
Hing on the girdle, let's hev a singin hinny.

Aw my sorrow's ower now, a've fund my hinny,
Aw my sorrow's ower now, a've fund my bairn;
Lang may aw shout, ma' canny hinny!
Lang may aw shout, ma' canny bairn!

Robertin Tush

Robertin Tush, he married a wife,
  Hoppity boppity bibo,
   She turned out the plague of his life,
     With a hi jig jiggity, hi jig jiggity
     Hoppity boppity bibo.

She swept her house but once a year,
And that was because the brooms were dear.

Whenever she churned, she churned in a boot,
Instead of a staff she used her foot.

She made a cheese which she laid on the shelf,
She never turned it till it turned of itself.

It turned and it turned till it came to the floor,
Then it got up and it ran to the door.

It rolled and it rolled to Banbury Cross,
And she gallopped after it on a white horse.

Kissing of My Dame

Sing jigmijole the pudding-bowl,
   The table and the frame,
My master he did cudgel me
   For kissing of my dame.

The Hunt is up

The hunt is up,
The hunt is up,
And now it is almost day;
And he that's in bed with another man's wife,
It's time to get him away.

Little Billy

Now Little Billy is gone to the kirk,
    And so merrily he doth sing:
I catch'd the parson in bed with my mother,
    But I wouldn't tell it for any thing.

Thou art a liar, says Mess John,
    I never did thy mother no harm,
I never was in her house in my life,
    But once or twice for a penn'orth of barm.

Thou art a liar, says Little Billy,
    As sure as thou'rt on thy knees at prayer:
Didn't I catch thee in bed with my mother,
    And didn't I tumble thee down the stairs.

Thou art a liar, says Mess John,
    Thou shalt be whipp'd with a rod of birk;
And shalt be set in the stocks to-morn,
    For telling such lies o' the kirk.

Oh Lucky Jim

Jim and I as children played together,
Best of friends for many years were we
I, alas! had no luck, was a Jonah,
Jim, my chum, was lucky as could be.
    Oh lucky Jim, how I envy him!

Years passed by, still Jim and I were comrades
He and I both loved the same sweet maid.
She loved Jim, and married him one evening.
Jim was lucky, I unlucky stayed.
    Oh lucky Jim, how I envy him!

Years rolled on, and death took Jim away, boys,
Left his widow, and she married me.
Now we're married, oft I think of Jim, boys,
Sleeping in the churchyard peacefully.
    Oh lucky Jim, how I envy him!

The Old Farmer and his Young Wife

I went into the stable to see what I could see,
And there I saw three horses standing by one, two, and three.
I called unto my loving wife – I'm coming, sir, said she.
Pray, what do these three horses here without the leave of me?
Why, you old fool! blind fool! Can't you very well see?
They are three milking cows my granny sent to me.
    Ods bobs! What fun! Milking cows with saddles on!
            The like was never seen!
    If ever I go out from home a cuckold I come in.

I went into the kitchen to see what I could see,
And there I saw three hats hang by one, two, and three.
I called unto my loving wife – I'm coming, sir, said she.
Pray, what do these three hats here without the leave of me?
Why, you old fool! blind fool! Can't you very well see?
They are three milking pails my granny sent to me.
    Ods bobs! What fun! Milking pails with brims on!
            The like was never seen!
    If ever I go out from home a cuckold I come in.

I went into the kitchen to see what I could see,
And there I saw three whips hang by one, two, and three.
I called unto my loving wife – I'm coming, sir, said she.
Pray, what do these three whips here without the leave of me?

Why, you old fool! blind fool! Can't you very well see?
They are three pokers my granny sent to me.
  Ods bobs! What fun! Pokers all with lashes on!
      The like was never seen!
  If ever I go out from home a cuckold I come in.

I went into the kitchen to see what I could see,
And there I saw three coats hang by one, two, and three.
I called unto my loving wife – I'm coming, sir, said she.
Pray, what do these three coats here without the leave of me?
Why, you old fool! blind fool! Can't you very well see?
They are three butter cloths my granny sent to me.
  Ods bobs! What fun! Butter cloths with buttons on!
      The like was never seen!
  If ever I go out from home a cuckold I come in.

I looked beneath the table to see what I could see,
And there I saw three pairs of boots by one, two, and three.
I called unto my loving wife – I'm coming, sir, said she.
Pray, what do these three pairs of boots without the leave of
    me?
Why, you old fool! blind fool! Can't you very well see?
They are three flower-pots my granny sent to me.
  Ods bobs! What fun! Flower-pots with spurs on!
      The like was never seen!
  If ever I go out from home a cuckold I come in.

I went into the chamber to see what I could see,
And there I saw three strange men lie by one, two, and three.
I called unto my loving wife – I'm coming, sir, said she.
Pray, what do these three men here without the leave of me?
Why, you old fool! blind fool! Can't you very well see?
They are three dairymaids my granny sent to me.
  Ods bobs! What fun! Dairymaids with beards on!
      The like was never seen!
  If ever I go out from home a cuckold I come in.

My Auld Wife

O fare ye weel, my auld wife!
    Sing bum, biberry bum.
O fare ye weel, my auld wife!
    Sing bum.
O fare ye weel, my auld wife,
Thou steerer up o' sturt and strife!
The maut's aboon the meal the nicht
    Wi' some.

And fare ye weel, my pike-staff!
    Sing bum, biberry bum.
And fare ye weel, my pike-staff!
    Sing bum.
And fare ye weel, my pike-staff,
Nae mair with thee my wife I'll baff!
The maut's aboon the meal the nicht
    Wi' some.

Fu' white white was her winding sheet!
    Sing bum, biberry bum.
Fu' white white was her winding sheet!
    Sing bum.
I was ower gladsome far to greet,
I danced my lane, and sang to see' t.
The maut's aboon the meal the nicht
    Wi' some.

8 · The Others: Different People, Different Countries, Different Places

The English

Long beardes heartles,
Paynted hoodes witles,
Gay cotes graceles,
Maketh Englande thriftles.

A Scot, a Welsh and an Irish Man

To Arthur's court, when men began
    To wear long flowing sleeves,
A Scot, a Welsh and an Irish man came,
    And all of them were thieves.

The Irishman he loved usquebaugh,
    The Scot loved ale called Blue Cap,
The Welshman he loved toasted cheese
    And made of his mouth a mouse-trap.

Usquebaugh burned the Irishman,
    The Scot was drowned in ale,
And the Welshman was like to be choked by a mouse,
    But he pulled it out by the tail.

Shon a Morgan

Little Shon a Morgan, shentleman of Wales
Came riding on a nanny goat, selling of pigstails.

Taffy was a Welshman

Taffy was a Welshman, Taffy was a thief,
Taffy came to my house and stole a piece of beef,
I went to Taffy's house, Taffy wasn't in,
I jumped upon his Sunday hat, and poked it with a pin.

Taffy was a Welshman, Taffy was a sham,
Taffy came to my house and stole a leg of lamb,
I went to Taffy's house, Taffy was away,
I stuffed his socks with sawdust and filled his shoes with clay.

Taffy was a Welshman, Taffy was a cheat,
Taffy came to my house and stole a piece of meat,
I went to Taffy's house, Taffy wasn't there,
I hung his coat and trousers to roast before a fire.

I am of Ireland

Ich am of Irlaunde
Ant of the holy londe
    Of Irlande.

Gode sire, pray ich thee,
For of saynte charite
Come ant daunce wyt me
    In Irlaunde.

Bryan O'Lynn

Bryan O'Lynn was a gentleman born,
He lived at a time when no clothes they were worn.
As fashions were out of course Bryan walked in –
I'll soon head the fashions, says Bryan O'Lynn.
  It'll do, it'll do, says Bryan O'Lynn,
  Says Bryan O'Lynn, says Bryan O'Lynn, it'll do.

Bryan O'Lynn had no breeches to wear,
So he cut up a sheepskin to make him a pair,
With the fleshy side out, and the woolly side in –
They are pleasant and cool, says Bryan O'Lynn.

Bryan O'Lynn had no shirt to his back,
So he went to his neighbours to borrow a sack.
He puckered the meal bag up under his chin –
Oh, they'll take it for ruffles, says Bryan O'Lynn.

Bryan O'Lynn was hard up for a coat,
So he borrowed a skin from a neighbouring goat,
With the horns sticking out from the shoulders within –
They'll take them for pistols, says Bryan O'Lynn.

Bryan O'Lynn had no watch to put on,
So he scooped out a turnip to make himself one,
Then he planted a cricket right under his skin –
Oh, they'll think it's a-ticking, says Bryan O'Lynn.

Bryan O'Lynn went courting one night,
And he set both his mother and sister to fight.
To fight for his hand they both stripped to the skin –
Oh, I'll marry you both, says Bryan O'Lynn.

Bryan, his wife, and his wife's mother,
Were all coming over the bridge together,
But the bridge broke down and let them all in –
Oh, we'll go home by boat, says Bryan O'Lynn.

Ho, Brother Teig

Ho, brother Teig, what is your story?
I went to the wood and shot a Tory.
I went to the wood and shot another,
Was it the same, or was it his brother?

I hunted him in, I hunted him out,
Three times through the bog, out and about,
Till out through the bush I spied his head,
So I levelled my gun and I shot him dead.

Yankee Doodle

Yankee Doodle went to town,
He rode a little pony,
He stuck a feather in his hat
And called it macaroni.
    Yankee Doodle fa, so, la,
    Yankee Doodle dandy.
    Yankee Doodle fa, so, la,
    Buttermilk and brandy.

Yankee Doodle went to town
To buy a pair of trousers,
He swore he could not see the town
For so many houses.

    Yankee Doodle fa, so, la,
    Yankee Doodle dandy.
    Yankee Doodle fa, so, la,
    Buttermilk and brandy.

The Isle of Man

Do as they do in the Isle of Man.
How's that? They do as they can.

How the First Hielandman of God was made of ane Horse Turd in Argyll as is said

God and Sanct Peter
    Was gangand be the way
Heich up in Argyll
    Where their gait lay.

Sanct Peter said to God
    In a sport word,
Can ye not mak a Hielandman
    Of this horse turd?

God turn'd owre the horse turd
    With his pykit staff
And up start a Hielandman
    Blak as ony draff.

Quod God to the Hielandman,
    Where wilt thow now?
I will doun in the Lawland, Lord,
    And there steill a cow.

And thou steill a cow, cairle,
    Than they will hang thee.
What rack, Lord, of that,
    For anis mon I die.

God then he leuch
    And owre the dyke lap,
And out of his sheath
    His gully outgat.

Sanct Peter socht this gully
    Fast up and doun,
Yet could not find it
    In all that braid roun.

Now, quod God, here a marvel,
    How can this be,
That I suld want my gully,
    And we here bot three?

Humff, quod the Hielandman,
    And turn'd him about,
And at his plaid neuk
    The gully fell out.

Fy, quod Sanct Peter,
    Thou will never do weill,
And thou bot new made
    And sa soon gais to steill.

Umff, quod the Hielandman,
   And sware be yon kirk,
Sa lang as I may gear get to steill
   Will I never work.

John Hielandman

Whaur are ye gaun, my wee Johnnie Hielanman?
   I'm gaun awa to steal a wee coo.
You'll be hanged, my fine Johnnie Hielanman.
   What do a care if my belly be fu'?

The Properties of the Shires of England

The properte of every shire
I shall you tell, and ye will hear.
   Herefordshire shield and spear:
   Worsetshire wring pear.
   Gloucetershire shoe and nail:
   Bristowe ship and sail.
   Oxenfordshire gird the mare:
   Warwykshire bind bere.
   London resortere:
   Sowtherey great bragere.
   Esex full of good hoswifes:
   Middlesex full of strives.
   Kentshire hot as fire:
   Sowseke full of dirt and mire.
   Hertfordshire full of wood:
   Huntingdonshire corn full good.
   Bedfordshire is nought to lack:
   Bokinghamshire is his make.
   Northamptonshire full of love
   Beneath the girdle and not above.
   Lancastreshire fair archere:
   Chestreshire thwakkere.
   Northumbreland hasty and hot:

Westmorland [tot for sote!]
Yorkshire full of knights:
Lincolnshire men full of mightes.
Cambridgeshire full of pikes:
Holond full of great dykes.
Norfolk full of wiles:
Southfolk full of stiles.
I am of *Shropshire* my shins be sharp:
Lay wood to the fire, and dress me my harp.
Notinghamshire full of hogs:
Derbyshire full of dogs.
Leicetershire full of beans:
Staffordshire full of queans.
Wiltshire fair and plain:
Barkshire fill the wain.
Hampshire dry and wete.
Somersetshire good for wheat.
Devenshire mighty and strong:
Dorseteshire will have no wrong.
Pinnokshire is not to praise:
A man may go it in two days.
Cornewaile full of tin:
Walis full of goote and kene.
That Lord that for us all did die
Save all these shires. *Amen* say I.

Buckinghamshire

Buckinghamshire, bread and beef.
If you beat a bush, you'll start a thief.

Lancashire Born

Little boy, little boy, where wast thou born?
Far away in Lancashire under a thorn,
Where they sup sour milk in a ram's horn.

The Merchants of London

Hey diddle dinketty, poppetty pet,
The merchants of London they wear scarlet,
Silk at the collar and gold at the hem:
So merrily march the merchantmen.

A, U, Hinny Burd

It's O! but aw ken well
   A, U, hinny burd,
The bonny lass o' Benwell,
   A, U, A.

She's lang-legg'd and mother-like,
   A, U, hinny burd;
See, she's ragin' up the dyke.
   A, U, A.

The quayside for sailors,
   A, U, hinny burd,
The Castle garth for tailors,
   A, U, A.

The Gateshead Hills for millers,
   A, U, hinny burd,
The North Shore for keelers,
   A, U, A.

There's Sandgate for auld rags,
   A, U, hinny burd,
And Gallowgate for trolly bags,
   A, U, A.

Ther's Denton and Kenton,
   A, U, hinny burd,
And canny Lang Benton,
   A, U, A.

There's Tynemouth and Cullercoats,
 A, U, hinny burd,
And North Shields for sculler boats,
 A, U, A.

There's Westoe lies in a neuk,
 A, U, hinny burd,
And South Shields the place for seut,
 A, U, A.

There's Harton and Holywell,
 A, U, hinny burd,
And bonny Seaton Delaval,
 A, U, A.

Hartley pans for sailors,
 A, U, hinny burd,
And Bedlington for nailers,
 A, U, A.

Strand on the Green

Strand on the Green,
Thirteen houses, fourteen cuckolds,
And never a house between.

Winwick, Lancashire

The church at little Winwick,
 It stands upon a sod,
And when a maid is married there,
 The steeple gives a nod.

Erith, on the Thames

There are men in the village of Erith
Whom nobody seeth or heareth,
 And there looms, on the marge
 Of the river a barge
That nobody roweth or steereth.

At Brill on the Hill

At Brill on the Hill the wind blows shrill,
    The cook no meat can dress;
At Stow on the Wold the wind blows cold,
    I know no more than this.

I Went to Noke

I went to Noke,
But nobody spoke.
I went to Thame,
It was just the same.
Burford and Brill
Were silent and still.
But I went to Beckley
And they spoke directly.

The River Dart

Dart, here's a man
To chill
Or to kill.
Now let me over
To go where I will.

The Dart

River of Dart, O river of Dart,
Every year thou claimest a heart.

Horsey Gap

When the sea comes in at Horsey Gap
    Without any previous warning,
A swan shall build its rushy nest
    On the roof of the Swan at Horning.

And a bald headed crow, contented and merry,
Shall feast on the corpses that float by the ferry.

The Powte's Complaint

(on the undertaking or draining of the Fens)

Come, brethren of the water,
    and let us all assemble
To treat upon this matter,
    which makes us quake and tremble,
For we shall rue it, if 't be true,
    that the Fens be undertaken,
And where we feed in fen and reed,
    they'll feed both beef and bacon.

They'll sow both beans and oats,
    where never man yet thought it,
Where men did row in boats,
    ere undertakers bought it:
But Ceres, thou behold us now,
    let wild-oats be their venture.
Oh let the frogs and miry bogs
    destroy where they do enter.

Away with boats and rudders;
    farewell both boots and skatches,
No need of one nor th'other,
    men now make better matches;
Stilt-makers all and tanners shall
    complain of this disaster;
For they will make each muddy lake
    for Essex calves a pasture.

Wherefore let us entreat
    our ancient winter nurses,
To shew their power so great
    as t' help to drain their purses;
And send us good old Captain Flood
    to lead us out to battle,
Then Twopenny Jack, with scales on's back,
    will drive out all the cattle.

This noble captain yet
   was never known to fail us,
But did the conquest get
   of all that did assail us;
His furious rage who could assuage?
   but, to the world's great wonder,
He bears down banks, and breaks their cranks
   and whirligigs asunder.

Great Neptune (god of seas),
   this work must needs provoke thee,
They mean thee to disease,
   and with fen water choke thee:
But with thy mace do thou deface
   and quite confound this matter,
And send thy sands to make dry lands,
   when they shall want fresh water.

Boston, Lincolnshire

Oh, Boston, Boston, thou hast nought to boast on
But a grand sluice and a high steeple
And a coast as souls are lost on.

Legsby, Lincolnshire

A thack church and a wooden steeple,
A drunken parson and wicked people.

Acton Beauchamp, Herefordshire

Acton Beauchamp, the poorest place in all the nation,
A lousy parson, a nitty clerk, and a shabby congregation.

Hoo, Suffolk

You must do as they do at Hoo,
What you can't do in one day,
You must do in two.

The People of Blakeney

The Blakeney people
Stand on the steeple,
And crack hazel-nuts
With a five-farthing beetle.

The River Don

The shelving slimy river Don,
Each year a daughter or a son.

Preston

Proud Preston, poor people,
Eight bells in a cracked steeple.

The Pentland Hills

Behold the house of Sir William Forbes,
Surrounded with trees which are covered with corbies,
From which the Pentland Hills are seen,
Pastured with sheep, forever green.

Durham Old Women

As aw was gannin to Durham
    Aw met wi' three jolly brisk women,
Aw ask'd what news at Durham?
    They said joyful news is coming:
There's three sheep's heads i' the pot,
    A peck o' peasemeal in the pudding.
They jump'd, laugh'd, and skipp'd at that,
    For the joyful days are coming.
                                    Fal la la.

Pigs o' Pelton

The swine com jingling doun Pelton lonin,
The swine com jingling doun Pelton lonin,
The swine com jingling doun Pelton lonin,
There's five black swine and never an odd one:

Three's i' the dyke and two i' the lonin,
Three's i' the dyke and two i' the lonin,
Three's i' the dyke and two i' the lonin,
There's five black swine and never an odd one.

The Wives of Spittal

The Spittal wives are no' very nice,
They bake their bread wi' bugs and lice;
And after that they skin the cat
And put it in their kail pot
That makes their broo' baith thick and fat.

Tweed and Till

Says Tweed to Till,
What gars ye rin sae still?
Says Till to Tweed,
Though ye rin wi' speed
And I rin slaw,
For ae man that ye droun
I droun twa.

Pont and Blyth

Says the Pont to the Blyth,
    Where thou drowns yan, I drown five.
Says the Blyth to the Pont,
    The mair shame on't.

Cauld Cornwood

Cauld Cornwood, where the Devil wadn't bring his mother,
But carried her up to High Crossfell
Where the snow ligs baith winter and summer.

Tintock

On Tintock-Tap there is a mist,
And in that mist there is a kist,
And in the kist there is a caup,
And in the caup there is a drap.
Tak up the caup, drink off the drap,
And set the caup on Tintock-Tap.

Gin I were a Doo

Oh gin I were a doo
I'd flee awa the noo
Wi' my neb to the Lomonds
And my wings beatin' steady,

And I'd never rest a fit
Till at gloamin' I wad sit
Wi' ilka neebor doo
On the lums of Balgedie.

Little Dunkeld

Was there ere sic a parish, a parish, a parish,
    Was there ere sic a parish as Little Dunkeld?
They've stickit the minister, hanged the precentor,
    Dung doun the steeple, and brucken the bell.

Johnshaven

Said the trout to the fluke,
When did your mou crook?
My mou was never even
Since I cam by Johnshaven.

Buchlyvie

Baron of Buchlyvie,
May the foul fiend drive ye
And a' tae pieces rive ye
    For buildin' sic a toun,
Where there's neither horse meat nor man's meat,
    Nor a chair to sit doon.

Manor Water

There stand three mills on Manor Water,
    A fourth at Posso Cleugh.
Gin heather bells were corn and bere
    They wad get grist eneugh.

Idaho

They say there is a land
    Where crystal waters flow,
Where veins of purest gold are found
    Way out in Idaho.

We'll need no pick or spade,
    No shovel, pan or hoe,
The largest chunks are on the ground
    Way out in Idaho.

The Codfish Shanty

Cape Cod girls they've got no combs,
 Heave away, heave away,
They comb their hair with codfish bones,
 And we're bound for South Australia.
  Heave away, my bully-bully boys,
  Heave away, heave away.
  Heave away, why don't you make some noise?
  And we're bound for South Australia.

Cape Cod boys they have no sleds,
 Heave away, heave away,
They slide down hills on codfish heads,
 And we're bound for South Australia.

Cape Cod cats they've got no tails,
 Heave away, heave away,
They blew away in heavy gales,
 And we're bound for South Australia.

9 · Affairs of State, War, Freedom and Faction

The Wars of the Roses

Huff the talbot and our cat Tib
  They took up sword and shield,
Tib for the red rose, Huff for the white,
  To fight upon Bosworth Field.

Oh, it was dreary that night to bury
  Those doughty warriors dead,
Under a white rose brave dog Huff,
  And fierce Tib under a red.

Low lay Huff and long may he lie!
  But our Tib took little harm:
He was up and away at dawn of day
  With the rose-bush under his arm.

The Norfolk Rebellion

The Rebels' Rhyme

Mr. Pratt, your sheep are very fat,
And we thank you for that.
We have left you the skins
To pay for your wife's pins
And you must thank us for that.

The Slaughter of the Rebels

The country gnoffes Hob, Dick, and Hick,
  With clubbes and clouted shoon,
Shall fill the vale of Dussindale
  With slaughtered bodies soon.

A Lament for the Priory of Walsingham

In the wracks of Walsingham
    Whom should I chuse,
But the Queen of Walsingham,
    To be guide to my muse.

Then, thou Prince of Walsingham,
    Graunt me to frame
Bitter plaints to rue thy wrong,
    Bitter woe for thy name.

Bitter was it oh to see
    The seely sheep
Murdered by the ravening wolves
    While the shepherds did sleep.

Bitter was it oh to view
    The sacred vine,
Whiles the gardeners played all close,
    Rooted up by the swine.

Bitter, bitter oh to behold
    The grass to grow,
Where the walls of Walsingham
    So stately did show.

Such were the works of Walsingham
    Whiles she did stand,
Such are the wracks as now do show
    Of that holy land.

Level, level with the ground
    The towers do lie,
Which with their golden glittering tops
    Pierced once to the sky.

Where were gates no gates are now,
    The ways unknowen
Where the press of peers did pass
    While her fame far was blowen.

Owls do scrike where the sweetest hymns
    Lately were song,
Toads and serpents hold their dens
    Where the palmers did throng.

Weep, weep, O Walsingham,
    Whose days are nights,
Blessing turned to blasphemies,
    Holy deeds to despites.

Sin is where our Lady sat,
    Heaven turned is to hell,
Sathan sits where our Lord did sway,
    Walsingham, Oh farewell!

Sir Francis Drake; or Eighty-Eight

Some years of late, in 'Eighty-Eight, as I do well remember-a,
It was, some say, the nineteenth of May, and some say of
    September-a,

The Spanish train launch'd forth amain, with many a fine
    bravado,
Their (as they thought, but it prov'd nought) invincible
    Armado.

There was a little man, that dwelt in Spain, that shot well in a
    gun-a,
Sir Pedro hight, as black a wight as the Knight of the Sun-a.

King Philip made him Admiral, and bade him not to stay-a,
But to destroy both man and boy, and so to come away-a.

Their navy was well victualled, with bisket, pease, and bacon;
They brought two ships well fraught with whips; but I think
    they were mistaken.

Their men were young, munition strong, and to do us more
    harm-a,
They thought it meet, to join their fleet all with the Prince of
    Parma.

They coasted round about our land, and so came in by Dover,
But we had men set on 'em then, and threw the rascals over.

The Queen was then at Tilbury: what could we more desire-a?
Sir Francis Drake, for her sweet sake, did set 'em all on fire-a.

Away they ran, by sea and land, so that one man slew three
   score-a;
And had not they all run away, o' my soul! we had kill'd
   more-a.

Then let them neither brag nor boast, for if they come again-a,
Let 'em take heed, they do not speed as they did they know
   when-a!

Bad Bishop Jegon

Our short fat, lord bishop
   of Norfolk 'twas he
That caused that great fire
   At Luddom to be.
There burnt were the goods
   that came by his devine
That might have relieved
   poor subjects of thine.

He could not abide, King,
   the poor at his gate,
No nor yet for to see them,
   neither early nor late.
He made strop and waste, King,
   most plain we may see,
Both of wood and timber
   in every degree.

He bought many lordships,
    as goes the report,
Was not such a bishop, King,
    fit for a rope?
He dwelt since at Alsome,
    as we did hear tell,
He died and was buried
    without ring of bell.

For even as he lived,
    even so he did die,
And like a swine buried,
    and so he do lie.
That Lord's secretary,
    as we did hear say,
Fell drunk and was drowned
    upon the high way.

Good King, look upon us
    and put our sins away from us,
For they overwhelm us,
    what shall become on us?
Such drinking and glossing,
    such swearing and lying,
Such dicing and carding,
    such [whoring] and thieving.

Such cursing and banning,
    such brawling and scolding,
Such wrangling and jangling,
    such suing and lawing.
Such pride and progality
    as now a days show,
The like here in England
    we never did know.

Such need and such poverty
    as now a days be,
The like, King, in England
    we never did see.

Such covetousness, King,
    and such oserie,
Such great oppressions
    we never did spie.

For the rich men oppress, King,
    the poor men with might,
And keep them from that is
    their due and their right.
They will set us a work, King,
    and then will not pay,
But give us some part
    and send us away.

Some keep back a quarter,
    some more and some less.
'Tis thou, thine own self, King,
    this gear must redress.
For those men of authority
    that should take it in hand,
They join house to house, King,
    and land unto land.

They join house to house, King,
    and land unto land,
Contrary to God's word,
    good King understand.
For they buy up the houses
    and the land, King, away,
And bring thy poor
    commonwealth into decay.

King Charles the First

As I was going by Charing Cross
I saw a black man upon a black horse.
They told me it was King Charles the First –
Oh dear, my heart was ready to burst.

The Parliament Soldiers

High ding a ding, and ho ding a ding,
The Parliament soldiers are gone to the king,
Some with new beavers, some with new bands,
The Parliament soldiers are all to be hang'd.

The Battle of Sole Bay

One day as I was sitting still
Upon the side of Dunwich hill,
   And looking on the ocean,
By chance I saw De Ruyter's fleet
With royal James's squadron meet;
In sooth, it was a noble treat
   To see that brave commotion.

I cannot stay to name the names
Of all the ships that fought with James,
   Their number or their tonnage;
But this I say, the noble host
Right gallantly did take its post,
And covered all the hollow coast
   From Walberswyck to Dunwich.

The French, who should have joined the Duke,
Full far astern did lag and look,
   Although their hulls were lighter;
But nobly faced the Duke of York,
(Though some may wink and some may talk)
Right stoutly did his vessel stalk
   To buffet with De Ruyter.

Well might you hear their guns, I guess
From Sizewell Gap to Easton Ness,
   The show was rare and sightly;
They battled without let or stay
Until the evening of that day,
'Twas then the Dutchmen ran away,
   The Duke had beat them tightly.

Of all the battles gained at sea
This was the rarest victory
    Since Philip's grand armada;
I will not name the rebel Blake,
He fought for whoreson Cromwell's sake,
And yet was forced three days to take
    To quell the Dutch bravado.

So now we've seen them take to flight,
This way and that, where'er they might,
    To windward or to lew'ard;
Here's to King Charles and here's to James,
And here's to all the captains' names,
And here's to all the Suffolk dames;
    And here's the house of Stuart.

O What's the Rhyme to Porringer

O what's the rhyme to porringer?
Ken ye the rhyme to porringer?
King James the Seventh had ae dochter
    And he gae her to an Oranger.

Ken ye how he requited him?
Ken ye how he requited him?
The lad has into England come,
    And taen the crown in spite o him.

The dog he sanna keep it lang,
    To flinch we'll make him fain again,
We'll hing him hie upon a tree,
    And James shall hae his ain again.

Ken ye the rhyme to grasshopper?
Ken ye the rhyme to grasshopper?
A hempen rein, a horse o tree,
    A psalm-book, and a Presbyter.

The Bonny Moorhen

My bonny moorhen, my bonny moorhen,
Up in the gray hill, down in the glen;
It's when ye gang but the house, when ye gang ben,
Aye drink a health to my bonny moorhen.

My bonny moorhen's gane over the main,
And it will be simmer or she come again;
But when she comes back again, some folk will ken:
Joy be wi' thee, my bonny moorhen!

My bonny moorhen has feathers enew,
She's a' fine colours, but nane o' them blue;
She's red, and she's white, and she's green, and she's gray,
My bonny moorhen, come hither away.

Come up by Glenduich, and down by Glendee,
And round by Kinclaven, and hither to me;
For Ronald and Donald are out on the fen,
To break the wing o' my bonny moorhen.

The Orange Lily

Oh, did you go to see the show,
    Each rose and pink and lily O,
To feast your eyes upon the prize
    Won by the Orange Lily O?

The Viceroy there so debonair,
    Just like a daffydilly O,
And Lady Clarke, blithe as a lark,
    Approached the Orange Lily O.

Then heigh-ho the Lily O,
    The royal loyal Lily O,
Beneath the sky what flow'r can vie
    With Ireland's Orange Lily O.

The elated muse, to hear the news,
　　Jumped like a Connacht filly O,
As gossip fame did loud proclaim
　　The triumph of the Lily O.

The lowland field may roses yield,
　　Gay heaths the highlands hilly O,
But high or low, no flower can show
　　Like the glorious Orange Lily O.

Then heigh-ho the Lily O,
　　The royal, loyal Lily O,
There's not a flower in Erin's bower,
　　Can match the Orange Lily O.

Old Orange Flute

In the County Tyrone, in the town of Dungannon,
Where many a ruction myself had a han' in,
Bob Williamson lived, a weaver by trade,
And all of us thought him a stout Orange blade.
On the Twelfth of July as around it would come,
Bob played on the flute to the sound of the drum.
You may talk of your harp, your piano or lute
But there's nothing compared with the ould Orange flute.

But Bob the deceiver he took us all in,
For he married a Papish called Brigid McGinn,
Turned Papish himself, and forsook the old cause,
That gave us our freedom, religion, and laws.
Now the boys of the place made some comment upon it,
And Bob had to fly to the Province of Connacht.
He fled with his wife and his fixings to boot,
And along with the latter his old Orange flute.

At the chapel on Sundays, to atone for past deeds,
He said Paters and Aves and counted his beads,
Till after some time, at the priest's own desire,
He went with his old flute to play in the choir.
He went with his old flute to play for the Mass,
And the instrument shivered, and sighed: 'Oh, alas!'
And blow as he would, though it made a great noise,
The flute would play only 'The Protestant Boys.'

Bob jumped, and he started, and got in a flutter,
And threw his old flute in the blest Holy Water;
He thought that this charm would bring some other sound,
When he blew it again, it played 'Croppies lie down';
And for all he could whistle, and finger, and blow,
To play Papish music he found it no go;
'Kick the Pope,' 'The Boyne Water,' it freely would sound,
But one Papish squeak in it couldn't be found.

At a council of priests that was held the next day,
They decided to banish the old flute away,
For they couldn't knock heresy out of its head
And they bought Bob a new one to play in its stead.
So the old flute was doomed and its fate was pathetic,
'Twas fastened and burned at the stake as heretic,
While the flames roared around it they heard a strange noise –
'Twas the old flute still whistling 'The Protestant Boys.'

The Wearing of the Green

O Paddy dear, and did you hear the news that's going round?
The shamrock is forbid by law to grow on Irish ground;
St. Patrick's day no more we'll keep, his colours can't be seen,
For there's a bloody law again the wearing of the green.
I met with Napper Tandy, and he took me by the hand,
And he said, 'How's poor old Ireland, and how does she stand?'
She's the most distressful country that ever yet was seen,
They're hanging men and women for the wearing of the green.

Then since the colour we must wear is England's cruel red,
Sure Ireland's sons will ne'er forget the blood that they have
    shed.
You may take the shamrock from your hat and cast it on the
    sod,
But 'twill take root and flourish there, though underfoot 'tis
    trod.
When law can stop the blades of grass from growing as they
    grow,
And when the leaves in summer time their verdure dare not
    show,
Then I will change the colour that I wear in my caubeen,
But 'till that day, please God, I'll stick to wearing of the green.

But if at last our colour should be torn from Ireland's heart,
Her sons with shame and sorrow from the dear old isle will part.
I've heard a whisper of a country that lies beyond the sea,
Where rich and poor stand equal in the light of freedom's day.
O Erin, must we leave you, driven by a tyrant's hand?
Must we ask a mother's blessing from a strange and distant
    land,
Where the cruel cross of England shall nevermore be seen,
And where, please God, we'll live and die still wearing of the
    green?

The Shan Van Vocht

O the French are on the sea,
    Says the Shan Van Vocht,
The French are on the sea,
    Says the Shan Van Vocht.
O the French are in the bay,
They'll be here without delay,
And the Orange will decay,
    Says the Shan Van Vocht.
        O the French are in the bay,
        They'll be here by break of day,
        And the Orange will decay,
            Says the Shan Van Vocht.

And their camp it shall be where?
  Says the Shan Van Vocht,
Their camp it shall be where?
  Says the Shan Van Vocht.
On the Currach of Kildare,
The boys they will be there,
With their pikes in good repair,
  Says the Shan Van Vocht.
     To the Currach of Kildare
     The boys they will repair,
     And Lord Edward will be there,
     Says the Shan Van Vocht.

Then what will the yeomen do?
  Says the Shan Van Vocht,
What will the yeomen do?
  Says the Shan Van Vocht.
What should the yeomen do
But throw off the red and blue
And swear that they'll be true
  To the Shan Van Vocht.
     What should the yeomen do
     But throw off the red and blue,
     And swear that they'll be true
     To the Shan Van Vocht?

And what colour will they wear?
  Says the Shan Van Vocht,
What colour will they wear?
  Says the Shan Van Vocht.
What colour should be seen
Where our fathers' homes have been,
But our own immortal green?
  Says the Shan Van Vocht.
     What colour should be seen
     Where our fathers' homes have been,
     But our own immortal green?
     Says the Shan Van Vocht.

And will Ireland then be free?
   Says the Shan Van Vocht,
Will Ireland then be free?
   Says the Shan Van Vocht.
Yes, Ireland shall be free,
From the centre to the sea.
Then hurrah for liberty!
   Says the Shan Van Vocht.
      Yes, Ireland shall be free,
      From the centre to the sea.
      Then hurrah for liberty,
         Says the Shan Van Vocht.

Lord Waterford

Lord Waterford is dead, says the Shan Van Vocht,
Lord Waterford is dead, says the Shan Van Vocht,
Lord Waterford is dead, and the devil's at his head,
And hell shall be his bed, says the Shan Van Vocht.

When he went down below, says the Shan Van Vocht,
Where the landlords all do go, says the Shan Van Vocht,
Queen Bess she did appear, and says she, you're wanted here
For this five and fifty year, says the Shan Van Vocht.

Then the divil he came on, says the Shan Van Vocht,
And says he to Bess, Begone! says the Shan Van Vocht,
Says Lord George, How are you all, I think I've made an
   awkward call,
Says the divil, Not at all! says the Shan Van Vocht.

Then the next one he did see, says the Shan Van Vocht,
Was his bailiff, Black Magee, says the Shan Van Vocht,
He was sitting on the shelf, washing up the divil's delf,
Och, says George, is that yourself? says the Shan Van Vocht.

We'll not put him in the pit, says the Shan Van Vocht,
Where the common sinners sit, says the Shan Van Vocht,
But we'll build a brand-new grate, where his fathers bake in
state,
With a nice resarvèd sate, says the Shan Van Vocht.

What will we do for Linen?

Och! what will we do for linen?
  Says the Shan Van Vocht.
Och! what will we do for linen?
  Says the Shan Van Vocht.
Och! we'll go to Enniskillen
And we'll flay an Orange villin,
And we'll wear his skin for linen,
  Says the Shan Van Vocht.

I am the Duke of Norfolk

I am the Duke of Norfolk,
Newly come to Suffolk,
Say shall I be attended,
  Or no, no, no?

Good duke, be not offended,
And you shall be attended,
You shall be attended,
  Now, now, now.

The Grand Old Duke of York

O the grand old Duke of York,
  He had ten thousand men,
He marched them up to the top of the hill,
  And he marched them down again.

And when they were up, they were up,
  And when they were down, they were down,
And when they were only half-way up,
  They were neither up nor down.

The Vicar of Bray

In good King Charles's golden days,
   When loyalty no harm meant,
A zealous High-Churchman I was,
   And so I got preferment;
To teach my flock I never missed –
   Kings are by God appointed,
And damned are those who do resist
   Or touch the Lord's anointed.
     And this is law, I will maintain,
      Until my dying day, Sir,
     That whatsoever king shall reign,
      I'll be the Vicar of Bray, Sir.

When royal James obtained the crown,
   And Popery came in fashion,
The penal laws I hooted down,
   And read the declaration:
The Church of Rome I found would fit
   Full well my constitution,
And had become a Jesuit –
   But for the Revolution.
     And this is law, I will maintain,
      Until my dying day, Sir,
     That whatsoever king shall reign,
      I'll be the Vicar of Bray, Sir.

When William was our king declared
   To ease the nation's grievance,
With this new wind about I steered,
   And swore to him allegiance;
Old principles I did revoke,
   Set conscience at a distance;
Passive obedience was a joke,
   A jest was non-resistance.
     And this is law, I will maintain,
      Until my dying day, Sir,
     That whatsoever king shall reign,
      I'll be the Vicar of Bray, Sir.

When gracious Anne became our queen,
　　The Church of England's glory,
Another face of things was seen –
　　And I became a Tory:
Occasional Conformists base,
　　I scorned their moderation,
And thought the church in danger was
　　By such prevarication.
　　　　And this is law, I will maintain,
　　　　　　Until my dying day, Sir,
　　　　That whatsoever king shall reign,
　　　　　　I'll be the Vicar of Bray, Sir.

When George in pudding-time came o'er,
　　And moderate men looked big, Sir,
I turned a cat-in-pan once more –
　　And so became a Whig, Sir:
And this preferment I procured
　　From our new faith's defender,
And almost every day abjured
　　The Pope and the Pretender.
　　　　And this is law, I will maintain,
　　　　　　Until my dying day, Sir,
　　　　That whatsoever king shall reign,
　　　　　　I'll be the Vicar of Bray, Sir.

The illustrious house of Hanover,
　　And Protestant succession,
To these I do allegiance swear –
　　While they can keep possession:
For in my faith and loyalty
　　I never more will falter,
And George my lawful King shall be –
　　Until the times do alter.
　　　　And this is law, I will maintain,
　　　　　　Until my dying day, Sir,
　　　　That whatsoever king shall reign,
　　　　　　I'll be the Vicar of Bray, Sir.

Old England Forever and Do it no More

As the Queen and Prince Albert, so buxom and all pert,
  Were jovially conversing together one day,
Old Bull heard them talking as they were awalking,
  And V. unto A. so boldly did say
The State seems bewildering about little children,
  And we are increasing every day, you know we have four,
We kindly do treat them and seldom do beat them,
  So Albert, dear Albert, we'll do it no more.

Said A., my dearest, there's nothing thou fearest,
  Thou art loved and respected in every degree,
If Old Bull don't like it why then he may pipe it,
  And kiss our royal twins, twee diddle dee,
So do not degrade me and try to persuade me
  All pleasure and pastime to freely give o'er,
If you do I'll be jolting and off I'll be bolting,
  Right over the seas singing do it no more.

An old anti-reformer lives near Hyde Park Corner,
  A regular old swaddy who wears scarlet clothes,
There is no one bolder than this rum old soldier,
  Let him go where he will he is known by his nose,
He cried shoulder arms boys and banish alarm boys,
  The 18th of June will now shortly be o'er,
He once strong and hearty whopped old Buonaparte,
  But pipe-clay and powder will do it no more.

Now let me approach then ye cooks and ye coachmen,
  You footmen and servants of every degree,
If out in the stable or under the table
  You have danced to a hornpipe called twee diddle dee,
By noon night and morning from me take a warning,
  Such vile naughty tricks strive to quickly give o'er,
For fear of time telling the tide may be swelling,
  And you may get nicked so do it no more.

All you that are single in harmony mingle,
　And say that you'll never be left in the lurch,
Moping single don't tarry, but strive for to marry,
　Look out for a partner and toddle to church,
And when you have hurried to church and got married
　Live and be happy, each other adore,
Then you'll not be forsaken, sing fried eggs and bacon,
　The Queen and Prince Albert, and do it no more.

The Dodger

Yes, the candidate's a dodger, yes, a well-known dodger,
Yes, the candidate's a dodger, yes, and I'm a dodger too.
He'll meet you and treat you and ask you for your vote,
But look out, boys, he's a dodging for a vote.
　Yes, we're all dodging, a-dodging, dodging, dodging,
　Yes, we're all dodging out a way through the world.

Yes, the lawyer he's a dodger, yes, a well-known dodger,
Yes, the lawyer he's a dodger, and I'm a dodger too.
He'll plead you a case and claim you as a friend,
And look out, boys, he's easy for to bend.

Yes, the doctor he's a dodger, yes, a well-known dodger,
Yes, the doctor he's a dodger, and I'm a dodger too.
He'll doctor you and cure you for half you possess,
But look out, boys, he's a-dodging for the rest.

Yes, the preacher he's a dodger, yes, a well-known dodger,
Yes, the preacher he's a dodger, and I'm a dodger too.
He'll preach you a gospel and tell you of your crimes,
But look out, boys, he's a-dodging for your dimes.

Yes, the merchant he's a dodger, yes, a well-known dodger,
Yes, the merchant he's a dodger, and I'm a dodger too.
He'll sell you the goods at double the price,
But when you go to pay him, you'll have to pay him twice.

Yes, the farmer he's a dodger, yes, a well-known dodger,
Yes, the farmer he's a dodger, and I'm a dodger too.
He'll plow his cotton, he'll blow his corn,
He'll make a living just as sure as you're born.

Yes, the lover he's a dodger, yes, a well-known dodger,
Yes, the lover he's a dodger, and I'm a dodger too.
He'll hug you and kiss you and call you his bride,
But look out, girls, he's telling you a lie.

10 · The Round of Life and Work

Labours of the Months

January	By this fire I warm my hands.
February	And with my spade I delfe my lands.
March	Here I set my thynge to spring.
April	And here I hear the fowlis sing.
May	I am as light as bird in bough.
June	And I weed my corn well inow.
July	With my scythe my mead I mawe.
August	And here I shear my corn full low.
September	With my flail I earn my bread.
October	And here I sawe my wheat so red.
November	At Martinsmass I kill my swine.
December	And at Christesmass I drink red wine.

Jog on, Jog on, the Footpath Way

Jog on, jog on, the footpath way,
    And merrily hent the stile-a;
A merry heart goes all the day,
    And your sad heart tires in a mile-a.

Your paltry money-bags of gold
    What need have we to stare for?
When little or nothing soon is told,
    And we have the less to care for.

Cast away care, let sorrow cease,
    A fig for melancholy;
Let's laugh and sing, or, if you please,
    We'll frolic with sweet Dolly.

John Grumlie

John Grumlie swore by the light o' the moon
    And the green leaf on the tree
That he could dae more wark in a day
    Than his wife could dae in three.

His wife rose up in the morning
        Wi' cares and troubles enow:
John Grumlie, bide at hame, John,
    And I'll gae haud the plow.
        Singing fal de lal lal de ral fal
            Fal lal lal lal lal la
        John Grumlie, bide at hame, John,
            And I'll gae haud the plow.

First ye maun dress your children fair,
        And put them a' in their gear,
And ye maun turn the maut, John,
    Or else ye'll spoil the beer.
And ye maun reel the tweel, John,
    That I span yesterday,
And ye maun ca' in the hens, John,
    Else they'll a' lay away.

Oh, he did dress his children fair,
    And he put them a' in their gear,
But he forgot to turn the maut
    And so he spoiled the beer.
And he sang aloud as he ruled the tweel
    That his wife span yesterday,
But he forgot to put up the hens,
    And the hens a' laid away.

The hawkit crummie loot down nae milk,
    He kirned, nor butter gat,
And a' gaed wrang and nocht gaed richt,
    He danced wi' rage and grat.
Then up he ran to the heid o' the knowe
    Wi' mony a wave and shout –
She heard him as she heard him not,
    And steered the stots about.

John Grumlie's wife cam' hame at e'en
    And laughed as she'd been mad,
When she saw the house in siccan a plight
    And John sae glum and sad.
Quo' he, I gie up my housewife's kep,
    I'll be nae mair guidwife.
Indeed, quo she, I'm weel content,
    Ye may keep it the rest o' your life.

The deil be in that, quo' surly John,
    I'll do as I've done before.
Wi' that the gudewife took up a stoot rung,
    And John made aff to the door.
Stop, stop, gude wife, I'll haud my tongue,
    I ken I'm sair to blame,
But henceforth I maun mind the plow,
    And ye maun bide at hame.

A Woman is a Worthy Thing

    I am as light as any roe
    To praise women where that I go.

To unpraise women it were a shame,
For a woman was thy dame.
Our Blessed Lady bereth the name
    Of all women wher that they go.

A woman is a worthy thing,
They do thee wash and do thee wring,
Lullay, lullay, she doth thee sing,
    And yet she hath but care and woe.

A woman is a worthy wight,
She serveth a man both day and night,
Thereto she putteth all her might,
    And yet she hath but care and woe.

Chamber-pot Rhyme

Keep me clean,
    And serve me well,
And what I see
    I'll never tell.

The Blacksmith's Song

Here's a health to the blacksmith, the best of all fellows,
He works at the anvil while the boy blows the bellows,
Which makes my bright hammer to rise and to fall.
Here's to old Cole, and to young Cole, and the old Cole of all.
  Twanky dillo, twanky dillo, twanky dillo, dillo, dillo, dillo,
  A roaring pair of bagpipes made of the green willow,
  Willow, willow, willow, willow. Willow, willow, willow,
    willow.
  A roaring pair of bagpipes made of the green willow.

If a gentleman brings his horse for to shoe,
He makes no denial of one pot or two,
Which makes my bright hammer to rise and to fall,
Here's to old Cole, and to young Cole, and the old Cole of all.

Here's a health to King George and likewise his Queen,
And to all the royal little ones wherever they are seen,
Which makes my bright hammer to rise and to fall.
Here's to old Cole, and to young Cole, and the old Cole of all.

Here's a health to the pretty maid with the lily-white frock,
Who's a heart that is true, and as firm as a rock,
Which makes my bright hammer to rise and to fall.
Here's to old Cole, and to young Cole, and the old Cole of all.

Turkey in the Straw

As I was a-gwine down the road,
Tired team and a heavy load,
Crack my whip and the leader sprung;
I says day-day to the wagon tongue.

Turkey in the straw, turkey in the hay,
Roll 'em up and twist 'em up a high tuckahaw,
And hit 'em up a tune called Turkey in the Straw.

Went out to milk and I didn't know how,
I milked the goat instead of the cow.
A monkey sittin' on a pile of straw
A-winkin' at his mother-in-law.

Met Mr. Catfish comin' down stream,
Says Mr. Catfish, 'What does you mean?'
Caught Mr. Catfish by the snout
And turned Mr. Catfish wrong side out.

Came to the river and I couldn't get across,
Paid five dollars for an old blind hoss,
Wouldn't go ahead, nor he wouldn't stand still
So he went up and down like an old saw mill.

As I came down the new cut road
Met Mr. Bullfrog, met Miss Toad,
And every time Miss Toad would sing
Ole Bullfrog cut a pigeon wing.

O I jumped in the seat, and I gave a little yell,
The horses run away, broke the wagon all to hell;
Sugar in the gourd and honey in the horn,
I never was so happy since the hour I was born.

Riddle

He went to the wood and caught it,
He sate him down and sought it.
Because he could not find it,
Home with him he brought it.

(*A thorn in his foot*)

Drumdelgie

There's a fairmer up in Cairnie,
   Wha's kent baith far and wide
To be the great Drumdelgie
   Upon sweet Deveron side.
The fairmer o' yon muckle toon
   He is baith hard and sair,
And the cauldest day that ever blaws
   His servants get their share.

At five o'clock we quickly rise
   And hurry doon the stair,
It's there to corn our horses,
   Likewise to straik their hair.
Syne after working half an hour
   Each to the kitchen goes,
It's there to get our breakfast,
   Which generally is brose.

When daylicht does begin to peep,
   And the sky begins to clear,
The foreman he cries out, My lads,
   Ye'll stay nae langer here.
There's sax o' you'll gae to the ploo,
   And twa will drive the neeps,
And the owsen they'll be after you
   Wi' strae raips roun' their queets.

But when that we were gyaun furth,
    And turnin' out to yoke,
The snaw dang on sae thick and fast
    That we were like to choke.
The frost had been sae very hard,
    The ploo she wadna go,
And sae our cairting days commenced
    Amang the frost and snow.

Our horses being but young and sma'
    The shafts they didna fill,
And they aft required the saiddler
    To pull them up the hill.
But we will sing our horses' praise,
    Though they be young and sma',
They far outshine the Broadland anes
    That gang sae full and braw.

Sae fare ye well, Drumdelgie,
    For I maun gang awa,
Sae fare ye well, Drumdelgie,
    Your weety weather and a'.
Sae fareweel, Drumdelgie,
    I bid ye a' adieu.
I leave ye as I got ye –
    A maist unceevil crew.

The Ploughman

The ploughman he comes home at night,
    When he is wet and weary,
Put off the wet, put on the dry,
    And go to bed, my deary.

I will wash the ploughman's clothes,
    I will wash them clean, O;
I will wash the ploughman's clothes,
    And dry them on the green, O.

The ploughman he comes home fu' late,
    When he wi' wark is weary;
Dights off his shirt that is se wet;
    And supper makes him cheery.

I will wash the ploughman's clothes,
    I will wash them white, O;
I will wash the ploughman's clothes,
    And dry them on the dyke, O.

The Banks of the Condamine

Oh, hark the dogs are barking, love,
I can no longer stay.
The men are all gone mustering
And it is nearly day,
And I must be off by the morning light
Before the sun doth shine
To meet the Sydney shearers
On the banks of the Condamine.

Oh, Willie, dearest Willie,
I'll go along with you,
I'll cut off all my auburn fringe
And be a shearer, too,
I'll cook and count your tally, love,
While ringer-o you shine,
And I'll wash your greasy moleskins
On the banks of the Condamine.

Oh, Nancy, dearest Nancy,
With me you cannot go,
The squatters have given orders, love,
No woman should do so;
Your delicate constitution
Is not equal unto mine
To stand the constant tigering
On the banks of the Condamine.

Oh, Willie, dearest Willie,
Then stay back home with me,
We'll take up a selection
And a farmer's wife I'll be.
I'll help you husk the corn, love,
And cook your meals so fine
You'll forget the ram-stag mutton
On the banks of the Condamine.

Oh, Nancy, dearest Nancy,
Please do not hold me back,
Down there the boys are waiting,
And I must be on the track;
So here's a good-bye kiss, love,
Back home here I'll incline
When we've shore the last of the jumbucks
On the banks of the Condamine.

The Waggoner

Saw ye owt o' ma' lad
    Gang the waggon way,
His pocket full of money,
    And his poke full of hay?

Aye but he's a bonny lad,
    As ever ye did see,
Tho' he's sair pock brocken,
    And he's blind of an e'e.

There's ne'er a lad like ma' lad
    Drives to a staithe on Tyne;
Tho' coal black on work days,
    On holidays he's fine.

Aye but he's a bonny lad,
    As ever ye did see,
Tho' he's sair pock brocken,
    And he's blind of an e'e.

Ma' lad's a bonny lad,
    The bonniest I see,
Wiv his fine posey waistcoat,
    And buckles at his knee.

Aye but he's a bonny lad,
    As ever ye did see,
Tho' he's sair pock brocken,
    And he's blind of an e'e.

The Miller of Dee

There dwelt a miller hale and bold
    Down by the River Dee,
He worked and sang from morn till night,
    No lark more blithe than he,
And this the burden of his song
    For ever used to be —
I envy nobody, no, not I,
    Nor nobody envies me.

Thou'rt wrong, my friend, cried old King Hal
    Thou'rt wrong as wrong can be,
For had I half such health as thine
    I would gladly change with thee.
Then tell me now what makes thee sing,
    With heart so light and free,
While I am sad although I am king,
    Down by the River Dee?

The miller smiled and doffed his cap —
    I love my wife, said he,
I love my friends, I love my mill,
    I love my children three.
I owe no penny I cannot pay,
    I thank the River Dee,
That turns the mill to grind the corn,
    That feeds my babes and me.

Farewell, my friend! cried old King Hal,
  And happy may you be!
And had I half such health as thine
  I would gladly change with thee.
Thy mealy cap is worth my crown,
  Thy mill my kingdoms three,
Such men as thou are England's boast,
  Oh, miller of the Dee.

The Bonny Keel Laddie

My bonny keel laddie, my canny keel laddie,
  My bonny keel laddie for me O!
He sits in his keel as black as the diel,
  And he brings the white money to me O.

Ha' ye seen owt o' my canny man,
  An' are ye shure he's weel O?
He's geane oer land wiv a stick in his hand
  T'help to moor the keel O.

The canny keel laddie, the bonny keel laddie,
  The canny keel laddie for me O;
He sits in his huddock, and claws his bare buttock,
  And brings the white money to me O.

We'll go to Sea No More

Oh blythely shines the bonnie sun
  Upon the isle of May,
And blytheley comes the morning tide
  Into St. Andrew's Bay.
Then up, gude-man, the breeze is fair,
  And up, my braw bairns three;
There's gold in yonder bonnie boat
  That sails so well the sea!

I've seen the waves as blue as air,
    I've seen them green as grass;
But I never feared their heaving yet,
    From Grangemouth to the Bass.
I've seen the sea as black as pitch,
    I've seen it white as snow:
But I never feared its foaming yet,
    Though the winds blew high or low.

I never like the landsman's life,
    The earth is aye the same;
Give me the ocean for my dower,
    My vessel for my hame.
Give me the fields that no man ploughs,
    The farm that pays no fee:
Give me the bonnie fish, that glance
    So gladly through the sea.

The sun is up, and round Inchkeith
    The breezes softly blaw;
The gude-man has his lines aboard –
    Awa', my bairns, awa'.
An' ye'll be back by gloaming grey,
    An' bright the fire will low,
An' in your tales and songs we'll tell
    How weel the boat ye row.

The Fisher's Life

What joys attend the fisher's life!
        Blow, winds, blow!
The fisher and his faithful wife!
        Row, boys, row!
He drives no plough on stubborn land,
His fields are ready to his hand;
No nipping frosts his orchards fear,
He has his autumn all the year!

The husbandman has rent to pay,
    Blow, winds, blow
And seed to purchase every day,
    Row, boys, row!
But he who farms the rolling deeps,
Though never sowing, always reaps;
The ocean's fields are fair and free,
There are no rent days on the sea!

Rhyme of the Fishermen's Children

Souther, wind, souther!
An' blaw my father heame to my moother.

The Greenland Whale

'Twas in the year of forty-nine,
    On March, the twentieth day,
Our gallant ship her anchor weigh'd,
    And to the sea she bore away,
      Brave boys,
And to the sea she bore away.
      With a fa la la la la la la
      Fa la la la la la la
      Fa la la fa la la
      Fa la la la la.

Old Blowhard was our captain's name,
    Our ship the *Lion* bold,
And we were bound to the North Country
    To face the frost and the cold.

And when we came to that cold country
    Where the ice and the snow do lie,
Where there's ice and snow, and the great whales blow,
    And the daylight does not die,

Our mate went up to the topmast head
    With a spyglass in his hand.
A whale, a whale, a whale, he cries,
    And she spouts at every span,

Up jumped old Blowhard on the deck,
    And a clever little man was he —
Overhaul, overhaul, let your main-tackle fall,
    And launch your boat to sea.

We struck that fish and away she flew
    With a flourish of her tail,
But oh! and alas! we lost one man
    And we did not catch that whale.

Now when the news to our captain came
    He called up all his crew,
And for the losing of that man
    He down his colours drew,

Says he, My men, be not dismayed
    At the losing of one man,
For Providence will have his will,
    Let man do what he can.

Now the losing of that prentice boy
    It grieved our captain sore,
But the losing of that great big whale
    It grieved him a damned sight more,
        Brave boys,
    It grieved him a damned sight more.
        With a fa la la la la la la
        Fa la la la la la la
        Fa la la fa la la
        Fa la la la la.

The Banks of Newfoundland

My bully boys of Liverpool, I'd have you to beware,
When you sail in a packet ship no dungaree jumpers wear,
But have a good monkey-jacket all ready to your hand,
For there blows some cold nor'-westers on the Banks of
Newfoundland.

> *So we'll scrape her and we'll scrub her with holystone and*
> *sand,*
> *And we'll think of them cold nor'-westers on the Banks of*
> *Newfoundland.*

There was Jack Lynch from Ballinhinch, Jim Murphy and Sam
Moore,
It was in the year of sixty-two those poor boys suffered sore,
For they'd pawned their clothes in Liverpool, and they sailed as
they did stand,
And there blows some cold nor'-westers on the Banks of
Newfoundland.

The mate came up on the foc'sle head and loudly he did roar,
Come rattle her in, my lively lads, we're bound for America's
shore.
Then lay aloft and shake her out and give her all she can
stand,
And there blows some cold nor'-westers on the Banks of
Newfoundland.

And now it's reef and reef, my boys, with the canvas frozen
hard,
And it's mount and pass, you son of a gun, on a ninety-foot
top'sl yard.
Never mind your boots and oilskins, but haul to beat the
band,
For there blows some cold nor'-westers on the Banks of
Newfoundland.

And now we're off the Hook, my boys, and the land's all
    covered in snow,
With the tug-boat due ahead of us into New York we will tow,
And as we tie up at the dock them pretty girls will stand,
Crying, It's snugger with me than it is at sea on the Banks of
    Newfoundland.
       So we'll scrape her and we'll scrub her with holystone and
          sand,
        And we'll bid farewell to the Virgin Rocks and the Banks of
          Newfoundland.

The Buffalo Skinners

Come all you jolly cowboys and listen to my song,
There are not many verses, it will not detain you long;
It's concerning some young fellows who did agree to go
And spend one summer pleasantly on the range of the buffalo.

It happened in Jacksboro in the spring of seventy-three,
A man by the name of Crego came stepping up to me,
Saying, 'How do you do, young fellow, and how would you like
    to go
And spend one summer pleasantly on the range of the buffalo?'

'It's me being out of employment,' this to Crego I did say,
'This going out on the buffalo range depends upon the pay.
But if you will pay good wages and transportation too,
I think, sir, I will go with you to the range of the buffalo.'

'Yes, I will pay good wages, give transportation too,
Provided you will go with me and stay the summer through;
But if you should grow homesick, come back to Jacksboro,
I won't pay transportation from the range of the buffalo.'

It's now our outfit was complete – seven able-bodied men,
With navy six and needle gun – our troubles did begin;
Our way it was a pleasant one, the route we had to go,
Until we crossed Pease River on the range of the buffalo.

It's now we've crossed Pease River, our troubles have begun.
The first damned tail I went to rip, Christ! how I cut my
thumb!
While skinning the damned old stinkers our lives wasn't a
show,
For the Indians watched to pick us off while skinning the
buffalo.

He fed us on such sorry chuck I wished myself most dead,
It was old jerked beef, croton coffee, and sour bread.
Pease River's as salty as hell fire, the water I could never go –
Oh, God! I wished I had never come to the range of the buffalo.

Our meat it was buffalo rump and iron wedge bread,
And all we had to sleep on was a buffalo robe for a bed;
The fleas and graybacks worked on us, O boys, it was not slow,
I'll tell you there's no worse hell on earth than the range of the
buffalo.

Our hearts were cased with buffalo hocks, our souls were cased
with steel,
And the hardships of that summer would nearly make us reel.
While skinning the damned old stinkers our lives they had no
show,
For the Indians waited to pick us off on the hills of Mexico.

The season being near over, old Crego he did say
The crowd had been extravagant, was in debt to him that day,
We coaxed him and we begged him and still it was no go –
We left old Crego's bones to bleach on the range of the buffalo.

Oh, it's now we've crossed Pease River and homeward we are
bound,
No more in that hell-fired country shall ever we be found.
Go home to our wives and sweethearts, tell others not to go,
For God's forsaken the buffalo range and the damned old
buffalo.

Driving the Mule

My sweetheart's the mule in the mines,
I drive her without reins or lines,
   On the bumper I sit,
   I chew and I spit
All over my sweetheart's behind.

The Grinders, or The Saddle on the Right Horse

The Sheffield grinder's a terrible blade.
   Tally hi-o, the grinder!
He sets his little 'uns down to trade.
   Tally hi-o, the grinder!
He turns his baby to grind in the hull,
Till his body is stinted and his eyes are dull,
And the brains are dizzy and dazed in his skull.
   Tally hi-o, the grinder!

He shortens his life and he hastens his death.
   Tally hi-o, the grinder!
Will drink steel dust in every breath.
   Tally hi-o, the grinder!
Won't use a fan as he turns his wheel,
Won't wash his hands ere he eats his meal,
But dies as he lives, as hard as steel.
   Tally hi-o, the grinder!

These Sheffield grinders of whom we speak,
   Tally hi-o, the grinder!
Are men who earn a pound a week.
   Tally hi-o, the grinder!
But of Sheffield grinders another sort
Methinks ought to be called in court,
And that is the grinding Government Board.
   Tally hi-o, the grinder!

At whose door lies the blacker blame?
  Tally hi-o, the grinder!
Where rests the heavier weight of shame?
  Tally hi-o, the grinder!
On the famine-price contractor's head,
Or the workman's, under-taught and fed,
Who grinds his own bones and his child's for bread?
  Tally hi-o, the grinder!

The Blackleg Miners

Oh, early in the evenin', just after dark,
The blackleg miners creep te wark,
Wi' their moleskin trousers an' dorty short,
There go the blackleg miners!

They take their picks an' doon they go
To dig the coal that lies belaw,
An' there's not a woman in this toon-raw
Will look at a blackleg miner.

Oh, Delaval is a terrible place,
They rub wet clay in a blackleg's face,
An' roond the pit-heaps they run a foot-race
Wi' the dorty blackleg miners.

Now, don't go near the Seghill mine,
Across the way they stretch a line,
Te catch the throat an' break the spine
O' the dorty blackleg miners.

They'll take your tools an' duds as well,
An' hoy them doon the pit o' hell,
It's doon ye go, an' fare ye well,
Ye dorty blackleg miners!

Se join the union while ye may,
Don't wait till your dyin' day,
For that may not be far away,
Ye dorty blackleg miners!

De Black Girl

Oh, de white gal ride in a automobile,
Oh, de yaller gal try to do de same,
Oh, de black gal ride in a slow oxcart,
But she git dar jes' de same.

Oh, de white gal have a silk petticoat,
Oh, de yaller gal have de same,
Oh, de black gal have no petticoat a-tall,
But she git dar jes' de same.

Oh, de white gal ride in a parlor car,
Oh, de yaller gal try to do de same,
Oh, de black gal ride in de Jim Crow car,
But she git dar jes' de same.

Oh, de white gal have a high-heel shoe,
Oh, de yaller gal try to have de same,
Oh, de black gal have no shoe a-tall,
But she git dar jes' de same.

Oh, de white gal have a nice long ha'r,
Oh, de yaller gal try to have de same,
Oh, de black gal have a one-cent wig,
But he her ha'r jes' de same.

Oh, a white gal eats de cake an' pie,
Oh, de yaller gal try to do de same,
Oh, de black gal eats de ashy cake,
But she's eatin' jes' de same.

Oh, a white gal sleeps in a bed,
Oh, a yaller gal try to do de same,
Oh, a black gal sleeps on de flo',
But she's sleepin' jes' de same.

Oh, de white gal smell like sweet perfume,
Oh, de yaller gal try to smell de same,
Oh, de black gal smell like a billy goat,
But he her smell jes' de same.

The Gresford Disaster

You've heard of the Gresford disaster,
The terrible price that was paid,
Two hundred and forty-two colliers were lost
And three men of a rescue brigade.

It occurred in the month of September,
At three in the morning, that pit
Was racked by a violent explosion
In the Dennis where gas lay so thick.

The gas in the Dennis deep section
Was packed there like snow in a drift,
And many a man had to leave the coal-face
Before he had worked out his shift.

A fortnight before the explosion,
To the shot-firer Tomlinson cried
'If you fire that shot we'll be all blown to hell!'
And no one can say that he lied.

The fireman's reports they are missing,
The records of forty-two days;
The colliery manager had them destroyed
To cover his criminal ways.

Down there in the dark they are lying,
They died for nine shillings a day.
They have worked out their shift and now they must lie
In the darkness until Judgement Day.

The Lord Mayor of London's collecting
To help both our children and wives,
The owners have sent some white lilies
To pay for the poor colliers' lives.

Farewell, our dear wives and our children,
Farewell, our old comrades as well.
Don't send your sons down the dark dreary pit,
They'll be damned like the sinners in hell.

An Invitation to Lubberland

There's all sorts of fowl and fish,
  With wine and store of brandy,
Ye have there what your hearts can wish,
  The hills are sugar candy.

There is a ship we understand
  Now riding in the river,
'Tis newly come from Lubberland,
  The like I think was never;
You that a lazy life do love,
  I'd have you now go over,
They say land is not above
  Two thousand leagues from Dover.

The Captain and the Master too
  Do's give us this relation,
And so do's all the whole ship's crew,
  Concerning this strange nation.
The streets are pav'd with pudding-pies,
  Nay powder'd beef and bacon,
They say they scorn to tell you lies,
  Who think it is mistaken.

The king of knaves and queen of sluts
  Reign there in peace and quiet;
You need not fear to starve your guts,
  There is such store of diet:
There you may live free from all care,
  Like hogs set up a fatning,
The garments which the people wear
  Is silver, silk and sattin.

The lofty buildings of this place
  For many years have lasted,
With nutmegs, pepper, cloves and mace
  The walls are roughly casted,

226

In curious hasty-pudding boil'd,
    And most ingenious carving.
Likewise they are with pancakes ty'd,
    Sure, here's no fear of starving.

The Captain says, in every town
    Hot roasted pigs will meet ye,
They in the streets run up and down,
    Still crying out, come eat me:
Likewise he says, at every feast
    The very fowls and fishes,
Nay, from the biggest to the least,
    Comes tumbling to the dishes.

The rivers run with claret fine,
    The brooks with rich Canary,
The ponds with other sorts of wine,
    To make your hearts full merry:
Nay, more than this, you may behold
    The fountains flow with brandy,
The rocks are like refined gold,
    The hills are sugar candy.

Rosewater is the rain they have
    Which comes in pleasant showers,
All places are adorned brave
    With sweet and fragrant flowers;
Hot custards grow on ev'ry tree,
    Each ditch affords rich jellies.
Now, if you will be rul'd by me,
    Go there, and fill your bellies.

There's nothing there but holy-days,
    With musick out of measure;
Who can forbear to speak the praise
    Of such a land of pleasure?
There you may lead a lazy life,
    Free from all kinds of labour,
And he that is without a wife,
    May borrow of his neighbour.

There is no law, nor lawyers fees,
    All men are free from fury,
For ev'ry one do's what he please,
    Without a judge or jury:
The summer-time is warm they say,
    The winter's ne'er the colder,
They have no landlord's rent to pay,
    Each man is a free-holder.

You that are free to cross the seas,
    Make no more disputation,
At Lubberland you'll live at ease,
    With pleasant recreation:
The captain waits but for a gale,
    Of prosperous wind and weather,
And that they soon will hoist up sail,
    Make haste away together.

The Beggars are coming to Town

    Hark, hark,
    The dogs do bark,
  The beggars are coming to town,
    Some in rags
    And some in jags
  And one in a velvet gown.

The Big Rock Candy Mountains

One evening when the sun was low
And the jungle fires were burning
Down the track came a hobo hamming
And he said, Boys, I'm not turning;
I'm headed for a land that's far away
Beside the crystal fountains.
So come with me, we'll go and see
The Big Rock Candy Mountains.

In the Big Rock Candy Mountains
There's a land that's fair and bright,
Where the handouts grow on bushes
And you sleep out every night.
Where the box-cars all are empty
And the sun shines everyday
On the birds and the bees
And the cigarette trees
The rock-and-rye springs
Where the whangdoodle sings,
In the Big Rock Candy Mountains.

In the Big Rock Candy Mountains
All the cops have wooden legs
And the bulldogs all have rubber teeth
And the hens lay hard-boiled eggs;
The farmers' trees are full of fruit
And the barns are full of hay:
O I'm bound to go
Where there ain't no snow,
And the rain don't fall,
The wind don't blow,
In the Big Rock Candy Mountains.

In the Big Rock Candy Mountains
You never change your socks
And the little streams of alkyhol
Come a-trickling down the rocks;
The shacks all have to top their hats
And the railroad bulls are blind;
There's a lake of stew,
And of whisky too,
You can paddle all around
In a big canoe,
In the Big Rock Candy Mountains.

In the Big Rock Candy Mountains
The jails are made of tin
And you can bust right out again
As soon as they put you in;
There ain't no short-handled shovels,
No axes, saw or picks:
O I'm going to stay
Where you sleep all day,
Where they hung the Turk
That invented work,
In the Big Rock Candy Mountains.
I'll see you all
This coming fall
In the Big Rock Candy Mountains.

Craigbilly Fair

As I went up to Craigbilly Fair,
Who did I meet but a jolly beggar,
And the name of this beggar they callèd him Rover,
And the name of his wife it was Kitty-lie-over.
There was Rover and Rover and Kitty-lie-over,
There was Rooney and Mooney,
And Nancy and Francey,
and Lily and Billy,
And Jamie and Joe,
And away went the beggar-men all in a row.

Again I went up to Craigbilly Fair,
And who should I meet but another beggar,
And this beggar's name they callèd him Rallax,
And the name of his wife it was Ould Madam Ball-o'-Wax.
There was Rallax and Rallax and Ould Madam Ball-o'-Wax,
There was Rover and Rover and Kitty-lie-over,
There was Rooney and Mooney,
And Nancy and Francey,
and Lily and Billy,
And Jamie and Joe,
And away went the beggar-men all in a row.

Again I went up to Craigbilly Fair,
And who should I meet but another beggar,
And the name of this beggar they callèd him Dick,
And the name of his wife it was Ould Lady Splooterstick.
There was Dick and Dick and Ould Lady Splooterstick,
There was Rallax and Rallax and Ould Madam Ball-o'-Wax,
There was Rover and Rover and Kitty-lie-over,
There was Rooney and Mooney,
And Nancy and Francey,
And Lily and Billy,
And Jamie and Joe,
And away went the beggar-men all in a row.

Hallelujah, Bum Again

Oh, why don't I work like other men do?
How the hell can I work when the skies are so blue?
Hallelujah, I'm a bum!
Hallelujah, bum again,
Hallelujah, give us a hand-out,
Revive us again.

If I was to work and save all I earn,
I could buy me a bar and have money to burn.

Oh, the winter is over and we're all out of jail;
We are tired of walking and hungry as hell.

Oh, I ride box cars and I ride fast mails,
When it's cold in the winter I sleep in the jails.

I passed by a saloon and I hear someone snore,
And I found the bartender asleep on the floor.

I stayed there and drank till a fly-mug came in,
And he put me to sleep with a sap on the chin.

Next morning in court I was still in a haze,
When the judge looked at me, he said 'Thirty days.'

Some day a long train will run over my head,
And the sawbones will say 'Old One-Finger's dead.'

Shovelling Iron Ore

Something happened the other day that never happened before,
A man tried to get me to shovel iron ore.
Says I, 'Old man now what will you pay?' Says he, 'Two bits a
    ton.'
Says I, 'Old man, go diddle yourself, I'd rather bum.'

Reason I stay on job so long

Reason I stay on job so long,
Lawd, dey gimme flamdonies
An' coffee strong.

Reason I love my captain so,
'Cause I ast him for a dollar,
Lawd, he give me fo'.

Reason why I love Boleen,
She keeps my house
An' shanty clean.

Why I like Roberta so,
She rolls her jelly
Like she rolls her dough.

11 · Soldiers and Sailors

We be Soldiers Three

We be soldiers three,
Pardona moy, je vous an pree,
Lately come forth of the Low Country,
With never a penny of money.
Fa la la la lantido dilly.

Here, good fellow, I drink to thee,
Pardona moy, je vous an pree,
To all good fellows where ever they be,
With never a penny of money.

And he that will not pledge me this,
Pardona moy, je vous an pree,
Pays the shot for whatever it is,
With never a penny of money.

Charge it again, boy, charge it again,
Pardona moy, je vous an pree,
As long as there is any ink in thy pen,
With never a penny of money.

The Forty-Second

Fa saw the Forty-Second,
Fa saw them gang awa?
Fa saw the Forty-Second
Gaein' to the Waupinschaw?

Some o' them gat chappit tatties,
Some o' them gat nane ava,
Some o' them get barley bannocks,
Gaein' to the Waupinschaw.

Fa saw the Forty-Second,
Fa saw them gang awa?
Fa saw the Forty-Second
Marchin' doun the Broomie-Law?

Some o' them had tartan troosers,
Some o' them had nane ava,
Some o' them had green umbrellas,
Marchin' doun the Broomie-Law.

Do Li A

Fresh I'm cum fra Sandgate Street,
    Do li, do li,
My best friends here to meet,
    Do li a.
    Do li th' dil len dol,
    Do li, do li,
    Do li th' dil len dol,
    Do li a.

The Black Cuffs is gawn away,
    Do li, do li,
And that will be a crying day,
    Do li a, etc.

Dolly Coxon's pawned her sark,
    Do li, do li,
To ride upon the baggage cart,
    Do li a, etc.

The Green Cuffs is cummin in,
    Do li, do li,
An' that 'ill make the lasses sing,
    Do li a, etc.

Arthur McBride

I once knew a fellow named Arthur McBride,
And he and I rambled down by the sea-side,
A-looking for pleasure or what might betide,
And the weather was pleasant and charming.

So gaily and gallant we went on our tramp,
And we met Sergeant Harper and Corporal Cramp,
And the little wee fellow who roused up the camp
With his row-de-dow-dow in the morning.

Good morning, young fellows, the sergeant he cried.
And the same to you, sergeant, was all our reply.
There was nothing more spoken, we made to pass by,
And continue our walk in the morning.

Well now, my fine fellows, if you will enlist,
A guinea in gold I will slap in your fist,
And a crown in the bargain to kick up the dust
And drink the Queen's health in the morning.

Oh no, mister sergeant, we aren't for sale,
We'll make no such bargain, and your bribe won't avail.
We're not tired of our country, and don't care to sail,
Though your offer is pleasant and charming.

If we were such fools as to take your advance,
It's right bloody slender would be our poor chance,
For the Queen wouldn't scruple to send us to France
And get us all shot in the morning.

Ha now, you young blackguards, if you say one more word,
I swear by the herrins, I'll draw out my sword
And run through your bodies as my strength may afford.
So now, you young buggers, take warning.

Well, we beat that bold drummer as flat as a shoe,
And we make a football of his row-de-dow-do,
And as for the others we knocked out the two.
Oh, we were the boys in that morning.

We took the old weapons that hung by their side
And flung them as far as we could in the tide.
May the devil go with you, says Arthur McBride,
For delaying our walk this fine morning.

The Grenadier

Who comes here?
   A grenadier.
What do you want?
   A pot of beer.
Where is your money?
   I've forgot.
Get you gone,
   You drunken lot.

Captain Bover

Where has ti been, maw canny hinny?
Where has ti been, maw winsome man?
Aw've been ti the norrard, cruising back and forrard,
Aw've been ti the norrard, cruising sair and lang.
Aw've been ti the norrard, cruising back and forrard,
But daurna come ashore for Bover and his gang.

Here's the Tender Coming

Here's the tender coming, pressing all the men.
O dear, hinny, what shall we do then?
Here's the tender coming, off at Shields Bar.
Here's the tender coming, full of men o' war.

Here's the tender coming, stealing of my dear.
O dear, hinny, they'll ship you out of here.
They will ship you foreign, that is what it means.
Here's the tender coming, full of red marines.

Oh Cruel was the Press-gang

Oh cruel was the press-gang
   That took my love from me.
Oh cruel was the little ship
   That took him out to sea.

And cruel was the splinter-board
  That took away his leg.
Now he is forced to fiddle-scrape,
  And I am forced to beg.

The Death of Admiral Benbow

Come all you sailors bold,
  Lend an ear,
Come all you sailors bold,
  Lend an ear:
'Tis of our Admiral's fame,
Brave Benbow called by name,
How he fought on the main
  You shall hear.

Brave Benbow he set sail
  For to fight,
Brave Benbow he set sail
  For to fight:
Brave Benbow he set sail,
With a fine and pleasant gale,
But his captains they turned tail
  In a fight.

Says Kirkby unto Wade,
  I will run,
Says Kirkby unto Wade,
  I will run:
I value not disgrace,
Nor the losing of my place,
My foes I will not face
  With a gun.

'Twas the *Ruby* and *Noah's Ark*
  Fought the French,
'Twas the *Ruby* and *Noah's Ark*
  Fought the French:
And there was ten in all,
Poor souls they fought them all,
They recked them not at all
  Nor their noise.

It was our Admiral's lot,
  With a chain-shot,
It was our Admiral's lot,
  With a chain-shot:
Our Admiral lost his legs,
And to his men he begs,
Fight on, my boys, he says,
  'Tis my lot.

While the surgeon dressed his wounds,
  Thus he said,
While the surgeon dressed his wounds,
  Thus he said,
Let my cradle now in haste
On the quarter-deck be placed,
That the Frenchmen I may face,
  Till I'm dead.

And there bold Benbow lay,
  Crying out,
And there bold Benbow lay,
  Crying out,
O let us tack once more,
We'll drive them to the shore,
As our fathers did before
  Long ago.

Johnny, I hardly knew Ye

While going the road to sweet Athy,
 Hurroo! Hurroo!
While going the road to sweet Athy,
 Hurroo! Hurroo!
While going the road to sweet Athy,
A stick in my hand and a drop in my eye,
A doleful damsel I heard cry:
 Och, Johnny, I hardly knew ye!
  With drums and guns and guns and drums,
   The enemy nearly slew ye!
   My darling dear, you look so queer,
  Och, Johnny, I hardly knew ye!

'Where are your eyes that looked so mild?
 Hurroo! Hurroo!
Where are your eyes that looked so mild?
 Hurroo! Hurroo!
Where are your eyes that looked so mild
When my poor heart you first beguiled?
Why did you run from me and the child?
 Och, Johnny, I hardly knew ye!

'Where are the legs with which you run?
 Hurroo! Hurroo!
Where are the legs with which you run?
 Hurroo! Hurroo!
Where are the legs with which you run,
When you went to carry a gun? –
Indeed your dancing days are done!
 Och, Johnny, I hardly knew ye!

'It grieved my heart to see you sail,
 Hurroo! Hurroo!
It grieved my heart to see you sail,
 Hurroo! Hurroo!
It grieved my heart to see you sail,
Though from my heart you took leg bail, –
Like a cod you're doubled up head and tail,
 Och, Johnny, I hardly knew ye!

'You haven't an arm and you haven't a leg,
      Hurroo! Hurroo!
You haven't an arm and you haven't a leg,
      Hurroo! Hurroo!
You haven't an arm and you haven't a leg,
You're an eyeless, noseless, chickenless egg:
You'll have to be put in a bowl to beg,
    Och, Johnny, I hardly knew ye!

'I'm happy for to see you home,
      Hurroo! Hurroo!
I'm happy for to see you home,
      Hurroo! Hurroo!
I'm happy for to see you home,
All from the island of Sulloon,
So low in flesh, so high in bone,
    Och, Johnny, I hardly knew ye!

'But sad as it is to see you so,
      Hurroo! Hurroo!
But sad as it is to see you so,
      Hurroo! Hurroo!
But sad as it is to see you so,
And to think of you now as an object of woe,
Your Peggy'll still keep ye on as her beau.
    Och, Johnny, I hardly knew ye!
        With drums and guns and guns and drums,
          The enemy nearly slew ye,
          My darling dear, you look so queer,
      Och, Johnny, I hardly knew ye!

Soldiers

Soldiers who wish to be a hero
Are practically zero,
But those who wish to be civilians,
Jesus, they run into millions.

12 · Outside the Law: Trouble, Violence and Crime

The Three Ravens

There were three ravens sat on a tree,
  Downe a downe, hay down, hay downe,
There were three ravens sat on a tree,
  With a downe,
There were three ravens sat on a tree,
They were as black as they might be,
  With a downe derrie, derrie, derrie, downe, downe.

The one of them said to his mate,
Where shall we our breakfast take?

Down in yonder greene field,
There lies a knight slain under his shield.

His hounds they lie down at his feete,
So well they can their master keepe.

His haukes they flie so eagerly,
There's no fowle dare him come nie.

Downe there comes a fallow doe,
As great with yong as she might goe.

She lift up his bloudy hed,
And kist his wounds that were so red.

She got him up upon her backe,
And carried him to earthen lake.

She buried him before the prime,
She was dead herselfe ere even-song time.

God send every gentleman
Such haukes, such hounds, and such a leman.

The Lament of the Border Widow

My love he built me a bonny bower,
And clad it a wi lilye flower.
A brawer bower ye ne'er did see
Than my true love he built for me.

There came a man by middle day,
He spied his sport and went away,
And brought the king that very night,
Who brake my bower, and slew my knight.

He slew my knight to me sae dear.
He slew my knight and poind his gear.
My servants all for life did flee
And left me in extremitie.

I sew'd his sheet, making my mane,
I watched the corpse myself alane,
I watched his body night and day.
No living creature came that way.

I took his body on my back,
And whiles I gaed, and whiles I sat.
I digg'd a grave and laid him in,
And happ'd him with the sod sae green.

But think na ye my heart was sair
When I laid the moul on his yellow hair?
O think na ye my heart was wae
When I turn'd about, away to gae?

Nae living man I'll love again,
Since that my lovely knight is slain.
Wi ae lock of his yellow hair
I'll chain my heart for evermair.

Robin Hood and Allen a Dale

Come listen to me, you gallants so free,
    All you that loves mirth for to hear,
And I will you tell of a bold outlaw,
    That lived in Nottinghamshire.

As Robin Hood in the forrest stood,
    All under the green-wood tree.
There was he ware of a brave young man,
    As fine as fine might be.

The youngster was clothed in scarlet red,
    In scarlet fine and gay,
And he did frisk it over the plain,
    And chanted a roundelay.

As Robin Hood next morning stood,
    Amongst the leaves so gay,
There did he espy the same young man
    Come drooping along the way.

The scarlet he wore the day before,
    It was clean cast away;
And every step he fetcht a sigh,
    Alack and a well a day.

Then stepped forth brave Little John,
    And Nick the millers son,
Which made the young man bend his bow,
    When as he see them come.

Stand off, stand off, the young man said,
    What is your will with me?
You must come before our master straight,
    Under yon green-wood tree.

And when he came bold Robin before,
    Robin askt him courteously,
O hast thou any money to spare
    For my merry men and me?

I have no money, the young man said,
    But five shillings and a ring;
And that I have kept this seven long years,
    To have it at my wedding.

Yesterday I should have married a maid,
    But she is now from me tane,
And chosen to be an old knights delight,
    Whereby my poor heart is slain.

What is thy name? then said Robin Hood,
    Come tell me, without any fail.
By the faith of my body, then said the young man,
    My name it is Allen a Dale.

What wilt thou give me, said Robin Hood,
    In ready gold or fee,
To help thee to thy true-love again,
    And deliver her unto thee?

I have no money, then quoth the young man,
    No ready gold nor fee,
But I will swear upon a book
    Thy true servant for to be.

How many miles is it to thy true-love?
    Come tell me without any guile.
By the faith of my body, then said the young man,
It is but five little mile.

Then Robin he hasted over the plain,
    He did neither stint nor lin,
Until he came into the church
    Where Allen should keep his wedding.

What dost thou do here? the bishop he said,
    I prethee now tell to me:
I am a bold harper, quoth Robin Hood,
    And the best in the north countrey.

O welcome, O welcome, the bishop he said.
    That musick best pleaseth me.
You shall have no musick, quoth Robin Hood,
    Till the bride and the bridegroom I see.

With that came in a wealthy knight,
    Which was both grave and old.
And after him a finikin lass,
    Did shine like glistering gold.

This is no fit match, quoth bold Robin Hood,
    That you do seem to make here;
For since we are come unto the church,
    The bride she shall chuse her own dear.

Then Robin Hood put his horn to his mouth,
    And blew blasts two or three,
When four and twenty bowmen bold
    Came leaping over the lee.

And when they came into the church-yard,
    Marching all on a row,
The first man was Allen a Dale,
    To give bold Robin his bow.

This is thy true-love, Robin he said;
    Young Allen, as I hear say,
And you shall be married at this same time,
    Before we depart away.

That shall not be, the bishop he said,
    For thy word shall not stand;
They shall be three times askt in the church,
    As the law is of our land.

Robin Hood pulled off the bishops coat,
    And put it upon Little John;
By the faith of my body, then Robin said,
    This cloath doth make thee a man.

When Little John went into the quire,
    The people began for to laugh;
He askt them seven times in the church,
    Least three times should not be enough.

Who gives me this maid, then said Little John;
    Quoth Robin, That do I,
And he that doth take her from Allen a Dale
    Full dearly he shall her buy.

And thus having ended this merry wedding,
    The bride lookt as fresh as a queen,
And so they returned to the merry green wood,
    Amongst the leaves so green.

Bonnie George Campbell

Hie upon Hielands and laigh upon Tay
Bonnie George Campbell rode out on a day.
He saddled, he bridled, and gallant rode he,
And hame cam his guid horse, but never cam he.

Out cam his mother dear greeting fu' sair,
And out cam his bonnie bryde riving her hair.
My meadow lies green and my corn is unshorn,
My barn is to build and my baby's unborn.

Saddled and bridled and booted rode he,
A plume in his helmet, a sword at his knee.
But toom cam his saddle all bloody to see;
Oh hame cam his guid horse, but never cam he.

Song of the Murdered Child Whose Bones grew into a Milk-white Dove

Pew, pew,
My minny me slew,
My daddy me chew,
My sister gathered my banes,
And put them between twa milk-white stanes,
And I grew and I grew
To a milk-white doo,
And I took to my wings
And away I flew.

The Lady Isabella's Tragedy

There was a lord of worthy fame
    and a hunting he would ride;
Attended by a noble train
    of gentry by his side.

And whilst he did in chase remain,
    to see both sport and play,
His lady went, as she did feign,
    unto the church to pray.

This lord he had a daughter fair,
    whose beauty shin'd so bright,
She was belov'd both far and near,
    of many a lord and knight.

Fair Isabella was she call'd,
    a creature fair was she;
She was her father's only joy,
    as you shall after see.

But yet her cruel step-mother,
    did envy her so much,
That day by day she sought her life,
    her malice it was such.

She bargain'd with the Master Cook,
 to take her life away,
And taking of her daughter's book,
 she thus to her did say:

Go home, sweet daughter, I thee pray,
 go hasten presently,
And tell unto the Master Cook,
 these words that I tell thee.

And bid him dress to dinner straight,
 that faire and milk white doe,
That in the park doth shine so bright,
 there's none so fair to show.

This lady fearing of no harm,
 obey'd her mother's will,
And presently she hasted home,
 her mind for to fulfil.

She straight into the kitchen went,
 her message for to tell;
And there the Master Cook she spy'd
 who did with malice swell.

You Master Cook, it must be so,
 do that which I thee tell,
You needs must dress the milk white doe,
 which you do know full well.

Then straight his cruel bloody hands,
 he on the lady laid,
Who quivering and shaking stands,
 whilst thus to her he said:

Thou art the doe that I must dress,
 see, here behold my knife,
For it is pointed presently,
 to rid thee of thy life.

O then cry'd out the scullion boy
    as loud as loud might be,
O save her life, good Master Cook,
    and make your pies of me.

For pity sake, do not destroy
    my lady with your knife,
You know she is her father's joy,
    for Christ's sake save her life.

I will not save her life, he said,
    nor make my pies of thee,
But if thou dost this deed bewray,
    thy butcher I will be.

But, when this lord, he did come home,
    for to sit down and eat,
He called for his daughter dear,
    to come and carve his meat.

Now sit you down, his lady said,
    O sit you down to meat.
Into some nunnery she is gone,
    your daughter dear forget.

Then solemnly he made a vow,
    before the company,
That he would neither eat nor drink,
    until he did her see.

O then bespoke the scullion boy,
    with a loud voice so high,
If that you will your daughter see,
    my lord, cut up that pie.

Wherein her flesh is minced small,
    and parched with the fire,
All caused by her step-mother,
    who did her death desire.

And cursed be the Master Cook,
    O cursed may he be,
I proffered him my own heart's blood,
    from death to set her free.

Then all in black this lord did mourn,
    and for his daughter's sake
He judged for her step-mother
    to be burnt at a stake.

Likewise he judg'd the Master Cook,
    in boiling oil to stand,
And made the simple scullion boy
    the heir to all his land.

Brennan on the Moor

It's of a famous highwayman a story I will tell,
His name was Willie Brennan and in Ireland he did dwell,
And on the Kilworth mountains he commenced his wild career,
And many a wealthy gentleman before him shook with fear.
   Brennan on the Moor, Brennan on the Moor,
    A brave undaunted robber bold was Brennan on the Moor.

A brace of loaded pistols he carried night and day,
He never robbed a poor man upon the king's highway,
But what he'd taken from the rich, like Turpin and Black Bess,
He always did divide it with the widow in distress.

One night he robbed a packman by the name of Pedlar Bawn,
They travelled on together till day began to dawn.
The pedlar seeing his money gone, likewise his watch and
    chain,
He at once encountered Brennan and he robbed him back again.

One day upon the highway, as Willie he went down,
He met the Mayor of Cashel a mile outside the town.
The Mayor he knew his features. 'I think, young man,' said he,
'Your name is Willie Brennan, you must come along with me.'

As Brennan's wife had gone to town, provisions for to buy,
And when she saw her Willie she began to weep and cry.
He says, 'Give me that tenpenny.' As soon as Willie spoke,
She handed him a blunderbuss from underneath her cloak.

Then with his loaded blunderbuss, the truth I will unfold,
He made the Mayor to tremble, and robbed him of his gold.
One hundred pounds was offered for his apprehension there,
So he with horse and saddle to the mountains did repair.

Then Brennan being an outlaw upon the mountains high,
When cavalry and infantry to take him they did try,
He laughed at them with scorn, until at length, 'tis said,
By a false-hearted young man he basely was betrayed.

In the country of Tipperary, in a place they call Clonmore,
Willie Brennan and his comrade that day did suffer sore.
He lay amongst the fern which was thick upon the field,
And nine deep wounds he did receive before that he did yield.

When Brennan and his comrade found that they were betrayed,
They with the mounted cavalry a noble battle made.
He lost his foremost finger, which was shot off by a ball,
So Brennan and his comrade they were taken after all.

So they were taken prisoners, in irons they were bound,
And both conveyed to Clonmel jail, strong walls did them
    surround.
They were tried and there found guilty, the judge made this
    reply,
'For robbing on the king's highway you're both condemned to
    die.'

Farewell unto my dear wife and to my children three,
Likewise my aged father, he may shed tears for me,
And to my loving mother, who tore her locks and cried,
Saying, 'I wish, my Willie Brennan, in your cradle you had
    died.'
    Brennan on the Moor, Brennan on the Moor,
    A brave undaunted robber bold was Brennan on the Moor.

The Boys of Mullaghbawn

On a Monday morning early as my wand'ring steps did lead me
Down by a farmer's station through meadow and green lawn
I heard great lamentation as the small birds they were
    warbling,
Saying, 'We'll have no more engagements with the Boys of
    Mullaghbawn.'

Esquire Jackson he's unequalled for honour and for reason,
He never turned traitor nor betrayed the rights of man,
But now we are in danger by a vile deceiving stranger
Who has ordered transportation for the Boys of Mullaghbawn.

As those heroes crossed the ocean I'm told the ship in motion
Would stand in wild commotion as if the seas ran dry,
The trout and salmon gaping as the *Cuckoo* left the station,
Saying, 'Farewell to lovely Erin and the hills of Mullaghbawn.'

To end my lamentation, we are all in consternation,
For want of education I here must end my theme,
None cares for recreation since without consideration
We are sent for transportation from the hills of Mullaghbawn.

The Lincolnshire Poacher

When I was bound apprentice, in famous Lincolnsheer,
Full well I served my master for more than seven year,
Till I took up with poaching, as you shall quickly hear.
    Oh, 'tis my delight of a shiny night, in the season of the year.

As me and my comrades were setting of a snare,
'Twas then we seed the gamekeeper – for him we did not care,
For we can wrestle and fight, my boys, and jump o'er
    everywhere.
    Oh, 'tis my delight of a shiny night, in the season of the year.

As me and my comrades were setting four or five,
And taking on 'em up again, we caught the hare alive;
We caught the hare alive, my boys, and through the woods
    did steer.
    Oh, 'tis my delight of a shiny night, in the season of the year.

I threw him on my shoulder, and then we trudged home,
We took him to a neighbour's house and sold him for a crown,
We sold him for a crown, my boys, but I did not tell you where.
    Oh, 'tis my delight of a shiny night, in the season of the year.

Bad luck to every magistrate that lives in Lincolnsheer;
Success to every poacher that wants to sell a hare;
Bad luck to every gamekeeper that will not sell his deer.
    Oh, 'tis my delight of a shiny night, in the season of the year.

Jim Jones at Botany Bay

O listen for a moment, lads,
    And hear me tell my tale,
How o'er the sea from England's shore
    I was compelled to sail.

The jury says, He's guilty, sir,
    And says the judge, says he,
For life, Jim Jones, I'm sending you
    Across the stormy sea.

And take my tip before you ship
    To join the Iron Gang,
Don't be too gay at Botany Bay,
    Or else you'll surely hang.

Or else you'll hang, he says, says he,
    And after that, Jim Jones,
High up upon the gallows tree
    The crows will peck your bones.

You'll have no chance for mischief then,
  Remember what I say,
They'll flog the poaching out of you
  Out there at Botany Bay.

The winds blew high upon the sea,
  And the pirates came along,
But the soldiers on our convict ship
  Were full five hundred strong.

They opened fire and somehow drove
  That pirate ship away.
I'd rather have joined that pirate ship
  Than come to Botany Bay.

For night and day the irons clang,
  And like poor galley slaves
We toil and toil, and when we die
  Must fill dishonoured graves.

But bye and bye I'll break my chains,
  Into the bush I'll go
And join the brave bushrangers there –
  Jack Donohoo and Co.

And some black night when everything
  Is silent in the town
I'll kill the tyrants, one and all,
  And shoot the floggers down.

I'll give the law a little shock,
  Remember what I say,
They'll yet regret they sent Jim Jones
  In chains to Botany Bay.

Waltzing Matilda

Once a jolly swagman camped by a billabong,
 Under the shade of a coolabah tree;
And he sang as he watched and waited till his billy boiled,
 'You'll come a-waltzing Matilda with me!'

 'Waltzing Matilda, Waltzing Matilda,
  You'll come a-waltzing Matilda with me,'
 And he sang as he watched and waited till his billy boiled,
  'You'll come a-waltzing Matilda with me.'

Down came a jumbuck to drink at the billabong,
 Up jumped the swagman and grabbed him with glee;
And he sang as he shoved that jumbuck in his tucker-bag,
 'You'll come a-waltzing Matilda with me.'

 'Waltzing Matilda, Waltzing Matilda,
  You'll come a-waltzing Matilda with me,'
 And he sang as he shoved that jumbuck in his tucker-bag,
  'You'll come a-waltzing Matilda with me,'

Up rode the squatter mounted on his thoroughbred;
 Down came the troopers – one, two and three.
'Whose the jolly jumbuck you've got in your tucker-bag?
 'You'll come a-waltzing Matilda with me.'

 'Waltzing Matilda, Waltzing Matilda,
  You'll come a-waltzing Matilda with me,
 Whose the jolly jumbuck you've got in your tucker-bag?
  You'll come a-waltzing Matilda with me.'

Up jumped the swagman, sprang into the billabong,
 'You'll never catch me alive,' said he.
And his ghost may be heard as you pass by that billabong
 'Who'll come a-waltzing Matilda with me?'

 'Waltzing Matilda, Waltzing Matilda,
  You'll come a-waltzing Matilda with me,'
 And his ghost may be heard as you pass by that billabong,
  'Who'll come a-waltzing Matilda with me?'

She was Poor, but She was Honest

She was poor, but she was honest,
    Victim of the squire's whim.
First he loved her, then he left her,
    And she lost her honest name.

Then she ran away to London,
    For to hide her grief and shame,
There she met another squire,
    And she lost her name again.

See her riding in her carriage,
    In the Park and all so gay,
All the nibs and nobby persons
    Come to pass the time of day,

See the little old-world village
    Where her aged parents live,
Drinking the champagne she sends them,
    But they never can forgive.

In the rich man's arms she flutters,
    Like a bird with broken wing,
First he loved her, then he left her,
    And she hasn't got a ring.

See him in the splendid mansion,
    Entertaining with the best,
While the girl that he has ruined,
    Entertains a sordid guest.

See him in the House of Commons,
    Making laws to put down crime,
While the victim of his passions
    Trails her way through mud and slime.

Standing on the bridge at midnight,
    She says: Farewell, blighted Love.
There's a scream, a splash—Good Heavens!
    What is she a-doing of?

Then they drag her from the river,
   Water from her clothes they wrang,
For they thought that she was drownded,
   But the corpse got up and sang:

It's the same the whole world over,
   It's the poor that gets the blame,
It's the rich that get the pleasure.
   Isn't it a blooming shame?

The Night before Larry was Stretched

The night before Larry was stretched,
   The boys they all paid him a visit;
A bait in their sacks, too, they fetched;
   They sweated their duds till they riz it,
For Larry was ever the lad
   When a boy was condemned to the squeezer,
Would fence all the duds that he had
   To help a poor friend to a sneezer,
      And warm his gob 'fore he died.

The boys they came crowding in fast,
   They drew all their stools round about him,
Six glims round his trap-case were placed,
   He couldn't be well waked without 'em.
When one of us asked could he die
   Without having duly repented?
Says Larry, 'That's all in my eye;
   And first by the clergy invented,
      To get a fat bit for themselves.'

'I'm sorry, dear Larry,' says I,
   'To see you in this situation,
And blister my limbs if I lie,
   I'd as lieve it had been my own station.'
'Ochone! it's all over,' says he,
   'For the neckcloth I'll be forced to put on,
And by this time to-morrow you'll see
   Your poor Larry as dead as a mutton,
      Because, why, his courage was good.

'And I'll be cut up like a pie,
    And my nob from my body be parted.'
'You're in the wrong box, then,' says I,
    'For blast me if they're so hard-hearted:
A chalk on the back of your neck
    Is all that Jack Ketch dares to give you;
Then mind not such trifles a feck,
    For why should the likes of them grieve you?
        And now, boys, come tip us the deck.'

The cards being called for, they played
    Till Larry found one of them cheated;
A dart at his napper he made
    (The boy being easily heated):
'O, by the hokey, you thief,
    I'll scuttle your nob with my daddle!
You cheat me because I'm in grief,
    But soon I'll demolish your noddle,
        And leave you your claret to drink.'

Then the clergy came in with his book,
    He spoke him so smooth and so civil;
Larry tipped him a Kilmainham look,
    And pitched his big wig to the devil.
Then sighing he threw back his head
    To get a sweet drop of the bottle,
And pitiful sighing he said,
    'O the hemp will be soon round my throttle,
        And choke my poor windpipe to death.'

'Though sure it's the best way to die,
    O the devil a better a-livin'!
For when the gallows is high
    Your journey is shorter to heaven.
But what harasses Larry the most,
    And makes his poor soul melancholy,
Is that he thinks of the time when his ghost
    Will come in a sheet to sweet Molly.
        O sure it will kill her alive!'

So moving these last words he spoke,
    We all vented our tears in a shower.
For my part, I thought my heart broke,
    To see him cut down like a flower.
On his travels we watched him next day;
    O the throttler, I thought I could kill him.
But Larry not one word did say,
      Nor changed till he came to 'King William,'
          Then, musha, his colour grew white.

When he came to the numbing chit,
    He was tucked up so neat and so pretty,
The rumbler jogged off from his feet,
    And he died with his face to the city.
He kicked, too – but that was all pride,
    For soon you might see 'twas all over.
Soon after the noose was untied,
      And at darkee we waked him in clover,
          And sent him to take a ground sweat.

The Gaol Song

Step in, young man, I know your face,
It's nothing in your favour;
A little time I'll give to you,
Six months unto hard labour.
    To me hip! fol the day, hip! fol the day,
    To my hip! fol the day, fol the digee, oh!

At six o'clock our turnkey comes in
With a bunch of keys all in his hand:
Come, come, my lads, step up and grind,
Tread the wheel till breakfast time.

At eight o'clock our skilly comes in,
Sometimes thick and sometimes thin,
But devil a word we must not say –
It's bread and water all next day.

At half-past eight the bell doth ring,
Into the chapel we must swing,
Down on our bended knees to fall,
The Lord have mercy on us all.

At nine o'clock the jangle rings,
All on the trap, boys, we must spring.
Come, come, my lads, step up in time,
The wheel to tread and the corn to grind.

Now Saturday's come, I'm sorry to say,
Sunday is our starvation day.
Our hobnail boots and tin mugs too,
They are not shined nor they will not do.

Now six months long are over and past
I will return to my bonny bonny lass,
I'll leave the turnkeys all behind,
The wheel to tread and the corn to grind.

Birmingham Jail

Down in the valley, valley so low,
Hang your head over, hear the wind blow.
Hear the wind blow, dear, hear the wind blow,
Hang your head over, hear the wind blow.

If you don't love me, love whom you please,
Throw your arms round me, give my heart ease.
Give my heart ease, dear, give my heart ease,
Throw your arms round me, give my heart ease.

Write me a letter, send it by mail,
And back it in care of Birmingham Jail,
Birmingham Jail, dear, Birmingham Jail,
And back it in care of Birmingham Jail.

Writing this letter, containing these lines,
Answer my question, Will you be mine?
Will you be mine, dear, Will you be mine?
Answer my question, Will you be mine?

Go build me a castle, forty feet high,
So I can see her as she goes by,
As she goes by, as she goes by,
So I can see her as she goes by.

Roses love sunshine, violets love dew,
Angels in heaven know I love you,
Know I love you, dear, know I love you,
Angels in heaven know I love you.

The Workhouse Boy

The cloth was laid in the Vorkhouse hall,
The great-coats hung on the white-wash'd wall,
The paupers all were blithe and gay,
Keeping their Christmas holiday,
When the Master he cried with a roguish leer,
'You'll all get fat on your Christmas cheer!'
When one by his looks did seem to say,
'I'll have some more soup on this Christmas-day.'
    Oh the Poor Vorkhouse Boy.

At length, all on us to bed vos sent,
The boy vos missing – in search ve vent.
Ve sought him above, ve sought him below,
Ve sought him with faces of grief and woe.
Ve sought him that hour, ve sought him that night,
Ve sought him in fear, and ve sought him in fright,
Ven a young pauper cried 'I knows ve shall
Get jolly vell vopt for losing our pal.'
    Oh the Poor Vorkhouse Boy.

Ve sought in each corner, each crevice ve knew
Ve sought down the yard, ve sought up the flue,
Ve sought in each kettle, each saucepan, each pot,
In the water-butt look'd, but found him not.
And veeks roll'd on; – ve vere all of us told
That somebody said, he'd been burk'd and sold.
Ven our master goes out, the Parishioners vild
Cry 'There goes the cove that burk'd the poor child.'
    Oh the Poor Vorkhouse Boy.

At length the soup copper repairs did need,
The Coppersmith came, and there he seed,
A dollop of bones lay a-grizzling there,
In the leg of the breeches the poor boy did vear!
To gain his fill the boy did stoop,
And dreadful to tell, he was boil'd in the soup!
And ve all of us say, and ve say it sincere,
That he was push'd in there by an overseer.
    Oh the Poor Workhouse Boy.

Cocaine Lil and Morphine Sue

Did you ever hear about Cocaine Lil?
She lived in Cocaine town on Cocaine hill,
She had a cocaine dog and a cocaine cat,
They fought all night with a cocaine rat.

She had cocaine hair on her cocaine head.
She had a cocaine dress that was poppy red:
She wore a snowbird hat and sleigh-riding clothes,
On her coat she wore a crimson, cocaine rose.

Big gold chariots on the Milky Way,
Snakes and elephants silver and gray.
Oh the cocaine blues they make me sad,
Oh the cocaine blues make me feel bad.

Lil went to a snow party one cold night,
And the way she sniffed was sure a fright.
There was Hophead Mag with Dopey Slim,
Kankakee Liz and Yen Shee Jim.

There was Morphine Sue and the Poppy Face Kid,
Climbed up snow ladders and down they skid;
There was the Stepladder Kit, a good six feet,
And the Sleigh-riding Sister who were hard to beat.

Along in the morning about half past three
They were all lit up like a Christmas tree;
Lil got home and started for bed,
Took another sniff and it knocked her dead.

They laid her out in her cocaine clothes:
She wore a snowbird hat with a crimson rose;
On her headstone you'll find this refrain:
'She died as she lived, sniffing cocaine.'

John Cherokee

Oh, this is the tale of John Cherokee,
 Alabama, John Cherokee,
The Indian man from Miramashee,
 Alabama, John Cherokee,
With a hauley high, and a hauley low,
 Alabama, John Cherokee.

They made him a slave down in Alabam,
 Alabama, John Cherokee,
He run away every time he can,
 Alabama, John Cherokee,
With a hauley high, and a hauley low,
 Alabama, John Cherokee.

267

They shipped him aboard of a whaling ship,
 Alabama, John Cherokee,
Again and again he gave 'em the slip,
 Alabama, John Cherokee,
With a hauley high, and a hauley low,
 Alabama, John Cherokee.

But they cotched him again and they chained him tight,
 Alabama, John Cherokee,
Kept him in the dark without any light,
 Alabama, John Cherokee,
With a hauley high, and a hauley low,
 Alabama, John Cherokee.

They gave him nothing for to eat or drink,
 Alabama, John Cherokee,
All of his bones began to clink,
 Alabama, John Cherokee,
With a hauley high, and a hauley low,
 Alabama, John Cherokee.

And now his ghost is often seen,
 Alabama, John Cherokee,
Sitting on the main-truck all wet and green,
 Alabama, John Cherokee,
With a hauley high, and a hauley low,
 Alabama, John Cherokee.

At the break of dawn he goes below,
 Alabama, John Cherokee,
That is where the cocks they crow,
 Alabama, John Cherokee,
With a hauley high, and a hauley low,
 Alabama, John Cherokee.

Captain Hall

My name is Captain Hall, Captain Hall, Captain Hall,
My name is Captain Hall, Captain Hall,
My name is Captain Hall and I only have one ball,
But it's better than none at all,
Damn your eyes, blast your soul,
But it's better than none at all, damn your eyes.

They say I killed a man, killed a man, killed a man,
They say I killed a man, killed a man.
I hit him on the head with a bloody lump of lead,
And now the fellow's dead,
Damn his eyes, blast his soul,
And now the fellow's dead, damn his eyes.

And now I'm in a cell, in a cell, in a cell,
And now I'm in a cell, in a cell,
And now I'm in a cell and on my way to hell,
Perhaps it's just as well,
Damn your eyes, blast your soul,
Perhaps it's just as well, damn your eyes.

The Chaplain he will come, he will come, he will come,
The Chaplain he will come, he will come,
The Chaplain he will come and he'll look so bloomin' glum,
As he talks of Kingdom come,
Damn his eyes, blast his soul,
As he talks of Kingdom come, damn his eyes.

Now this is my last knell, my last knell, my last knell,
Now this is my last knell, my last knell,
Now this is my last knell, and you've had a sell,
For I'll meet you all in hell,
Damn your eyes, blast your soul,
For I'll meet you all in hell, damn your eyes.

Now I feel the rope, feel the rope, feel the rope,
Now I feel the rope, feel the rope,
Now I feel the rope, and I've lost all earthly hope,
Nothing but the Chaplain's soap,
Damn his eyes, blast his soul,
Nothing but the Chaplain's soap, damn his eyes.

Now I am in hell, am in hell, am in hell,
Now I am in hell, am in hell.
Now I am in hell, and it's such a sell,
Because the Chaplain's here as well,
Damn his eyes, blast his soul,
Because the Chaplain's here as well, damn his eyes.

Willy the Weeper

Hark to the story of Willie the Weeper,
Willie the Weeper was a chimney sweeper,
He had the hop habit and he had it bad,
O listen while I tell you 'bout a dream he had.

He went to the hop joint the other night,
When he knew the lights would all be burning bright,
I guess he smoked a dozen pills or more,
When he woke up, he was on a foreign shore.

Queen o' Bulgaria was the first he met,
She called him her darlin' and her lovin' pet,
She promised him a pretty Ford automobile
With a diamond headlight an' a silver steerin' wheel.

She had a million cattle, she had a million sheep,
She had a million vessels on the ocean deep,
She had a million dollars, all in nickels and dimes,
She knew 'cause she counted them a million times.

Willie landed in New York one evenin' late,
He asked his sugar for an after-date,
Willie he got funny, she began to shout,
BIM BAM BOO! – an' the dope gave out.

Hanging Johnny

They call me Hanging Johnny,
Away-i-oh,
They call me Hanging Johnny,
So hang, boys, hang.

First I hung my mother,
Away-i-oh,
First I hung my mother,
So hang, boys, hang.

Then I hung my brother,
Away-i-oh,
Then I hung my brother,
So hang, boys, hang.

A rope, a beam, a ladder,
Away-i-oh,
A rope, a beam, a ladder,
So hang, boys, hang.

I'll hang you all together,
Away-i-oh,
I'll hang you all together,
So hang, boys, hang.

Mary Arnold the Female Monster

Of all the tales was ever told,
I now will you impart,
That cannot fail to terror strike,
To every human heart.
The deeds of Mary Arnold,
Who does in a jail deplore,
Oh! such a dreadful tale as this,
Was never told before.
This wretched woman's dreadful deed,
Does every one affright.
With black beetles in walnut shells
She deprived her child of sight.

271

Now think you, tender parents,
What must this monster feel,
The heart within her breast must ten
Times harder be than steel.
The dreadful crime she did commit
Does all the world surprise,
Black beetles placed in walnut shells
Bound round her infant's eyes.

The beetles in a walnut shell
This monster she did place,
This dreadful deed, as you may read,
All history does disgrace,
The walnut shell, and beetles,
With a bandage she bound tight,
Around her infant's tender eyes,
To take away its sight.

A lady saw this monster
In the street when passing by,
And she was struck with terror
For to hear the infant cry.
The infant's face she swore to see,
Which filled her with surprise,
To see the fatal bandage,
Tied round the infant's eyes.

With speed she called an officer,
Oh! shocking to relate,
Who beheld the deed, and took the wretch
Before the Magistrate.
Who committed her for trial,
Which did the wretch displease,
And she's now transported ten long years,
Across the briny seas.

Is there another in the world,
Could plan such wicked deed,
No one upon this earth before,
Of such did ever see.
To take away her infant's sight,
'Tis horrible to tell,
Binding black beetles round its eyes
Placed in walnut shells.

13 · The Supernatural

Riddles Wisely Expounded

There was a knicht riding frae the east,
   Sing the Cather banks, the bonnie brume
Wha had been wooing at monie a place.
   And ye may beguile a young thing sune.

He came unto a widow's door.
And speird whare her three dochters were.

The auldest ane's to the washing gane,
The second's to a baking gane.

The youngest ane's to a wedding gane,
And it will be nicht or she be hame.

He sat him doun upon a stane,
Till thir three lasses came tripping hame.

The auldest ane's to the bed making,
And the second ane's to the sheet spreading.

The youngest ane was bauld and bricht,
And she was to lye wi' this unco knicht.

Gin ye will answer me questions ten,
This morn ye sall be made my ain.

O what is heigher nor the tree?
And what is deeper nor the sea?

Or what is heavier nor the lead?
And what is better nor the breid?

O what is whiter nor the milk?
Or what is safter nor the silk?

Or what is sharper nor a thorn?
Or what is louder nor a horn?

Or what is greener nor the grass?
Or what is waur nor a woman was?

O heaven is higher nor the tree,
And hell is deeper nor the sea.

O sin is heavier nor the lead,
The blessing's better than the bread.

The snaw is whiter nor the milk,
And the down is safter nor the silk.

Hunger is sharper nor a thorn,
And shame is louder nor a horn.

The pies are greener nor the grass,
And Clootie's waur nor a woman was.

As sune as she the fiend did name,
He flew awa in a blazing flame.

The Twa Magicians

The lady stands in her bower door,
   As straight as willow wand,
The blacksmith stood a little forebye,
   Wi hammer in his hand.

Weel may ye dress ye, lady fair,
   Into your robes o red,
Before the morn at this same time
   I'll gain your maidenhead.

Awa, awa, ye coal-black smith,
   Woud ye do me the wrang
To think to gain my maidenhead,
   That I hae kept sae lang

Then she has hadden up her hand,
   And she sware by the mold,
I wudna be a blacksmith's wife
   For the full o a chest o gold.

I'd rather I were dead and gone,
   And my body laid in grave,
Ere a rusty stock o coal-black smith
   My maidenhead shoud have.

But he has hadden up his hand,
   And he sware by the mass,
I'll cause ye be my light leman
   For the hauf o that and less.

> *O bide, lady, bide,*
>   *And aye he bade her bide*
> *The rusty smith your leman shall be*
>   *For a' your muckle pride.*

Then she became a turtle dow,
   To fly up in the air,
And he became another dow,
   And they flew pair and pair.
     O bide, lady, bide, &c.

She turned hersell into an eel,
   To swim into yon burn,
And he became a speckled trout,
   To gie the eel a turn.
     O bide, lady, bide, &c.

Then she became a duck, a duck,
   To puddle in a peel,
And he became a rose-kaimd drake,
   To gie the duck a dreel.
     O bide, lady, bide, &c.

She turnd hersell into a hare,
  To rin upon yon hill,
And he became a gude grey-hound,
  And boldly he did fill.
    O bide, lady, bide, &c.

Then she became a gay grey mare,
  And stood in yonder slack,
And he became a gilt saddle,
  And sat upon her back.
    Was she wae, he held her sae,
     And still he bade her bide,
    The rusty smith her leman was,
    For a' her muckle pride.

Then she became a het girdle,
  And he became a cake,
And a' the ways she turnd hersell,
  The blacksmith was her make.
    Was she wae, &c.

She turnd hersell into a ship,
  To sail out ower the flood.
He ca'ed a nail intill her tail,
  And syne the ship she stood.
    Was she wae, &c.

Then she became a silken plaid,
  And stretchd upon a bed,
And he became a green covering,
  And gaind her maidenhead.
    Was she wae, &c.

Clerk Colvill

Clerk Colvill and his lusty dame
  Were walking in the garden green,
The belt around her stately waist
  Cost Clerk Colvill of pounds fifteen.

O promise me now, Clerk Colvill,
    Or it will cost ye muckle strife,
Ride never by the wells of Slane,
    If ye wad live and brook your life.

Now speak nae mair, my lusty dame,
    Now speak nae mair of that to me.
Did I neer see a fair woman
    But I wad sin with her body?

He's taen leave o his gay lady,
    Nought minding what his lady said,
And he's rode by the wells of Slane,
    Where washing was a bonny maid.

Wash on, wash on, my bonny maid,
    That wash sae clean your sark of silk.
It's a' for you, ye gentle knight,
    My skin is whiter than the milk.

He's taen her by the milk-white hand,
    And likewise by the grass-green sleeve,
And laid her down upon the green,
    Nor of his lady speer'd he leave.

Then loud, loud cry'd the Clerk Colvill,
    O my head it pains me sair.
Then take, then take, the maiden said,
    And frae my sark you'll cut a gare.

Then she's gied him a little bane-knife,
    And frae her sark he cut a share.
She's ty'd it round his whey-white face,
    And ay his head it aked mair.

Then louder cry'd the Clerk Colvill,
    O sairer, sairer akes my head.
And sairer, sairer ever will,
    The maiden cries, till you be dead.

Out then he drew his shining blade,
    Thinking to stick her where she stood,
But she was vanished to a fish,
    And swam far off, a fair mermaid.

O mother, mother, braid my hair,
    My lusty lady, make my bed.
O brother, take my sword and spear,
    For I have seen the false mermaid.

Grey Goose and Gander

Grey goose and gander,
    Weft your wings together,
And carry the King's fair daughter
    Over the one-strand river

The Great Silkie of Sule Skerrie

An eartly nourris sits and sings,
    And aye she sings, Ba, lily wean,
Little ken I my bairnis father,
    Far less the land that he staps in.

Then ane arose at her bed-fit,
    An a grumly guest I'm sure was he:
Here am I, thy bairnis father,
    Although that I be not comelie.

I am a man, upo the lan,
    An I am a silkie in the sea,
And when I'm far and far frae lan,
    My dwelling is in Sule Skerrie.

It was na weel, quo the maiden fair,
    It was na weel, indeed, quo she,
That the Great Silkie of Sule Skerrie
    Suld hae come and aught a bairn to me.

Now he has taen a purse of goud,
    And he has pat it upo her knee,
Sayin, Gie to me my little young son,
    An tak thee up thy nourris-fee.

An it sall come to pass on a simmer's day,
    When the sin shines het on evera stane,
That I will tak my little young son,
    An teach him for to swim the faem.

An thu sall marry a proud gunner,
    An a proud gunner I'm sure he'll be,
An the very first schot that ere he schoots,
    He'll schoot baith my young son and me.

The Padda Song

(from the Tale o' the Well o' the Warld's End, in which the
Widow's Daughter promises to marry the Frog in exchange for
a dish of water when the well was dry)

Oh, open the door, my hinnie, my heart,
Oh, open the door, my ain true love.
Remember the promise that you and I made,
Doun i' the meadow, where we twa met.

Oh, gie me my supper, my hinnie, my heart,
Oh, gie me my supper, my ain true love.
Remember the promise that you and I made,
Doun i' the meadow, where we twa met.

Oh, put me to bed, my hinnie, my heart,
Oh, put me to bed, my ain true love.
Remember the promise that you and I made,
Doun i' the meadow, where we twa met.

Oh, come to your bed, my hinnie, my heart,
Oh, come to your bed, my ain true love.
Remember the promise that you and I made,
Doun i' the meadow, where we twa met.

Come, tak me to your bosom, my hinnie, my heart,
Come, tak me to your bosom, my hinnie, my heart.
Remember the promise that you and I made,
Doun i' the meadow, where we twa met.

Now fetch me an aix, my hinnie, my heart,
Now fetch me an aix, my ain true love.
Remember the promise that you and I made,
Doun i' the meadow, where we twa met.

Now chap aff my head, my hinnie, my heart,
Now chap aff my head, my ain true love.
Remember the promise that you and I made,
Doun i' the meadow, where we twa met.

(And – 'She had na weel chappit aff his head, as he askit her to
do, before he starts up, the bonniest young prince that ever
was seen. And, of course, they leeved happy a' the rest o' their
days.')

Song of the Cauld Lad of Hylton

Wae's me, wae's me,
The acorn is not yet
Fallen from the tree
That's to grow the wood
That's to make the cradle
That's to rock the bairn
That's to grow to a man
That's to lay me.

The Hobthrush

Hobthrush Hob, wheer is thoo?
I's tryin' on my left foot shoe,
An' I'll be wi' thee – noo.

284

The Elfin Knight

My plaid awa, my plaid awa,
    And ore the hill and far awa,
And far awa to Norrowa,
    My plaid shall not be blown awa.

The elfin knight sits on yon hill,
    Ba, ba, lilli ba.
He blaws his horn both lowd and shril.
    The wind hath blown my plaid awa.

He blowes it east, he blowes it west,
He blowes it where he lyketh best.

I with that horn were in my kist,
Yea, and the knight in my armes two.

She had no sooner these words said,
When that the knight came to her bed.

Thou art over young a maid, quoth he,
Married with me thou il wouldst be.

I have a sister younger than I,
And she was married yesterday.

Married with me if thou wouldst be,
A courtesie thou must do to me.

For thou must shape a sark to me,
Without any cut or heme, quoth he.

Thou must shape it knife-and-sheerlesse,
And also sue it needle-threadlesse.

If that piece of courtesie I do to thee,
Another thou must do to me.

I have an aiker of good ley-land,
Which lyeth low by yon sea-strand.

For thou must eare it with thy horn,
So thou must sow it with thy corn.

And bigg a cart of stone and lyme,
Robin Redbreast he must trail it hame.

Thou must barn it in a mouse-holl,
And thrash it into thy shoes' soll.

And thou must winnow it in thy looff,
And also seek it in thy glove.

For thou must bring it over the sea,
And thou must bring it dry home to me.

When thou hast gotten thy turns well done,
Then come to me and get thy sark then.

I'l not quit my plaid for my life,
It haps my seven bairns and my wife.
  The wind shall not blow my plaid awa.

My maidenhead I'l then keep still,
Let the elphin knight do what he will.
  The wind's not blown my plaid awa.

The Wee Wee Man

As I was walking all alone
  Between the water and the green,
There I spied a wee wee man,
  The least wee man that ever was seen.

His legs were scarce an effet's length,
　　But thick his arms as any tree.
Between his brows there was a span,
　　Between his shoulders there were three.

He took up a boulder stone,
　　And flung it as far as I could see.
Though I had been a miller's man,
　　I could not lift it to my knee.

O wee wee man, but thou art strang!
　　O tell me where thy haunt may be.
My dwelling's down by yon bonny bower,
　　O will you mount and ride with me?

On we leapt, and off we rode,
　　Till we came to far away,
We lighted down to bait our horse,
　　And out there came a bonny may.

Four and twenty at her back,
　　And they were all dressed out in green,
And though King Harry had been there,
　　The worst o' them might be his queen.

On we leapt, and off we rode,
　　Till we came to yon bonny hall.
The roof was o' the beaten gold,
　　Of gleaming crystal was the wall.

When we came to the door of gold,
　　The pipes within did whistle and play,
But ere the tune of it was told,
　　My wee wee man was clean away.

Harpkin

Harpkin gaed up to the hill,
And blew his horn loud and shrill,
And by came Fin.
What for stand you there? quo' Fin.
Spying the weather, quo' Harpkin.
What for had you your staff on your shouther? quo' Fin.
To haud the cauld frae me, quo' Harpkin.
Little cauld will that haud frae you, quo' Fin.
As little will it win through me, quo' Harpkin.
I came by your door, quo' Fin.
It lay in your road, quo' Harpkin.
Your dog barkit at me, quo' Fin.
It's his use and custom, quo' Harpkin.
I flang a stane at him, quo' Fin.
I'd rather it had been a bane, quo' Harpkin.
Your wife's lichter, quo' Fin.
She'll clim the brae brichter, quo' Harpkin.
Of a braw lad bairn, quo' Fin.
There'll be the mair men for the king's wars, quo' Harpkin.
There's a strae at your beard, quo' Fin.
I'd rather it had been a thrave, quo' Harpkin.
The ox is eating at it, quo' Fin.
If the ox were i' the water, quo' Harpkin.
And the water were frozen, quo' Fin.
And the smith and his fore-hammer at it, quo' Harpkin.
And the smith were dead, quo' Fin.
And another in his stead, quo' Harpkin.
Giff, gaff, quo' Fin.
Your mou's fou o' draff, quo' Harpkin.

The False Knight upon the Road

O whare are ye gaun?
    Quo the fause knicht upon the road.
I'm gaun to the scule,
    Quo the wee boy, and still he stude.

What is that upon your back?
    Quo the fause knicht upon the road.
Atweel it is my bukes,
    Quo the wee boy, and still he stude.

What's that ye've got in your arm?
    Quo the fause knicht upon the road.
Atweel it is my peit,
    Quo the wee boy, and still he stude.

Wha's aucht they sheep?
    Quo the fause knicht upon the road.
They are mine and my mither's,
    Quo the wee boy, and still he stude.

How monie o them are mine?
    Quo the fause knicht upon the road.
A' they that hae blue tails,
    Quo the wee boy, and still he stude.

I wiss ye were on yon tree,
    Quo the fause knicht upon the road.
And a gude ladder under me,
    Quo the wee boy, and still he stude.

And the ladder for to break,
    Quo the fause knicht upon the road.
And you for to fa down,
    Quo the wee boy, and still he stude.

I wiss ye were in yon sie,
    Quo the fause knicht upon the road.
And a gude bottom under me,
    Quo the wee boy, and still he stude.

And the bottom for to break,
    Quo the fause knicht upon the road.
And ye to be drowned,
    Quo the wee boy, and still he stude.

Witch's Broomstick Spell

Horse and hattock,
Horse and go,
Horse and pelatis, Ho, ho!

Witch's Milking Charm

Meares' milk, and deers' milk,
And every beast that bears milk
Between St. Johnston and Dundee,
Come a' to me, come a' to me.

Against Witches

Black luggie, lammer bead,
Rowan-tree, and red thread,
Put the witches to their speed.

Cushy Cow, Bonny

Cushy cow, bonny, let down thy milk,
And I will give thee a gown of silk,
A gown of silk and a silver tee
If thou wilt let down thy milk to me.

The Strange Visitor

A wife was sitting at her reel ae night,
    And aye she sat, and aye she reeled, and aye she wished for
        company.

In came a pair o' braid braid soles, and sat down at the fireside,
    And aye she sat, and aye she reeled, and aye she wished for
        company.

In came a pair o' sma' sma' legs, and sat down on the braid
    braid soles,
  And aye she sat, and aye she reeled, and aye she wished for
    company.

In came a pair o' muckle muckle knees, and sat down on the
    sma' sma' legs,
  And aye she sat, and aye she reeled, and aye she wished for
    company.

In came a pair o' sma' sma' thees, and sat down on the muckle
    muckle knees,
  And aye she sat, and aye she reeled, and aye she wished for
    company.

In came a pair o' muckle muckle hips, and sat down on the sma'
    sma' thees,
  And aye she sat, and aye she reeled, and aye she wished for
    company.

In came a sma' sma' waist, and sat down on the muckle muckle
    hips,
  And aye she sat, and aye she reeled, and aye she wished for
    company.

In came a pair o' braid braid shouthers, and sat down on the
    sma' sma' waist,
  And aye she sat, and aye she reeled, and aye she wished for
    company.

In came a pair o' sma' sma' arms, and sat down on the braid
    braid shouthers,
  And aye she sat, and aye she reeled, and aye she wished for
    company.

In came a pair o' muckle muckle hands, and sat down on the
    sma' sma' arms,
  And aye she sat, and aye she reeled, and aye she wished for
    company.

In came a sma' sma' neck, and sat down on the braid braid
    shouthers,
  And aye she sat, and aye she reeled, and aye she wished for
    company.

In came a great big head, and sat down on the sma' sma' neck.

What way hae ye sic braid braid feet? quo' the wife.
Muckle ganging, muckle ganging.
What way hae ye sic sma' sma' legs?
Aih-h-h! – late – and wee-e-e moul.
What way hae ye sic muckle muckle knees?
Muckle praying, muckle praying.
What way hae ye sic sma' sma' thees?
Aih-h-h! – late – and wee-e-e – moul.
What way hae ye sic big big hips?
Muckle sitting, muckle sitting.
What way hae ye sic a sma' sma' waist?
Aih-h-h! – late – and wee-e-e – moul.
What way hae ye sic braid braid shouthers?
Wi' carrying broom, wi' carrying broom.
What way hae ye sic sma' sma' arms?
Aih-h-h! – late – and wee-e-e – moul.
What way hae ye sic muckle muckle hands?
Threshing wi' an iron flail, threshing wi' an iron flail.
What way hae ye sic a sma' sma' neck?
Aih-h-h! – late – and wee-e-e – moul.
What way hae ye sic a muckle muckle head?
Muckle wit, muckle wit.
What do you come for?
For YOU!

Unfortunate Miss Bailey

I

A captain bold in Halifax, that dwelt in country quarters,
Seduced a maid who hanged herself one morning in her
    garters:
His wicked conscience smited him: he lost his stomach daily;
He took to drinking ratafia, and thought upon Miss Bailey.
        Oh, Miss Bailey! unfortunate Miss Bailey!

II

One night betimes he went to rest, for he had caught a fever.
Says he, 'I am a handsome man, but I'm a gay deceiver.'
His candle just at twelve o'clock began to burn quite palely;
A ghost stepped up to his bedside, and said, 'Behold Miss
    Bailey!'
        Oh, Miss Bailey! unfortunate Miss Bailey!

III

'Avaunt, Mis Bailey!' then he cried. 'Your face looks white and
    mealy!'
'Dear Captain Smith,' the ghost replied, 'you've used me
    ungenteelly.
The crowner's quest goes hard with me because I've acted
    frailly,
And Parson Biggs won't bury me, though I am dead Miss
    Bailey.'
        Oh, Miss Bailey! unfortunate Miss Bailey!

IV

'Dear corpse,' says he, 'since you and I accounts must once for
    all close,
I've got a one-pound note in my regimental small-clothes;
'Twill bribe the sexton for your grave.' The ghost then
    vanished gaily,
Crying, 'Bless you, wicked Captain Smith! remember poor
    Miss Bailey.'
        Oh, Miss Bailey! unfortunate Miss Bailey!

14 · The Christian Supernatural

New Year's Water

Here we bring new water from the well so clear,
For to worship God with, this happy New Year.
Sing levy dew, sing levy dew, the water and the wine,
With seven bright gold wires, and bugles that do shine.
Sing reign of fair maid, with gold upon her toe,
Open you the west door, and turn the Old Year go.
Sing reign of fair maid, with gold upon her chin,
Open you the east door, and let the New Year in.

The Moon Shines Bright

The moon shines bright, and the stars give a light:
    A little before it was day
Our Lord, our God he called on us,
    And bid us awake and pray.

Awake, awake, good people all,
    Awake, and you shall hear,
Our Lord, our God, died on the cross,
    For us whom he loved so dear.

O fair, O fair Jerusalem,
    When shall I come to thee?
When shall my sorrows have an end,
    Thy joy that I may see?

The fields were green as green could be,
    When from his glorious seat
Our Lord, our God, he watered us,
    With his heavenly dew so sweet.

And for the saving of our souls
    Christ died upon the cross.
We ne'er shall do for Jesus Christ
    As he has done for us.

The life of man is but a span,
And cut down in its flower,
We are here to-day and to-morrow are gone,
We are all dead in an hour.

O pray teach your children, man,
The while that you are here.
It will be better for your souls
When your corpse lies on the bier.

To-day you may be alive, dear man,
Worth many a thousand pound,
To-morrow may be dead, dear man,
And your body be laid under ground.

With one turf at your head, O man,
And another at your feet,
Thy good deeds and thy bad, O man,
Will all together meet.

My song is done, I must be gone,
I can stay no longer here.
God bless you all, both great and small,
And send you a happy new year.

The White Paternoster

Matthew, Mark, Luke, and John,
Bless the bed that I lie on.
Four corners to my bed,
Four angels at my head,
One to watch, and one to pray,
And two to bear my soul away.

Now I lay me down to Sleep

Now I lay me down to sleep,
I pray the Lord my soul to keep.
If I should die before I wake,
I pray the Lord my soul to take.

If You Want to go to Heben

If you want to go to heben,
Let me tell you what to do:
Grease your hand with de muttin sue,
Take St. Peter by de hand,
Slide right over in de Promise Land.

The Cherry-Tree Carol

Joseph was an old man,
    And an old man was he,
When he wedded Mary
    In the land of Galilee.

Joseph and Mary walked
    Through an orchard good,
Where was cherries and berries
    So red as any blood.

Joseph and Mary walked
    Through an orchard green,
Where was berries and cherries
    As thick as might be seen.

O then bespoke Mary
    So meek and so mild,
Pluck me one cherry, Joseph,
    For I am with child.

O then bespoke Joseph
    With words most unkind,
Let him pluck thee a cherry
    That brought thee with child.

O then bespoke the Babe
    Within his Mother's womb,
Bow down then the tallest tree
    For my Mother to have some.

Then bowed down the highest tree
    Unto his Mother's hand.
Then she cried, See, Joseph,
    I have cherries at command.

O then bespake Joseph,
    I have done Mary wrong,
But cheer up, my dearest,
    And be not cast down.

Then Mary plucked a cherry
    As red as the blood,
Then Mary went home
    With her heavy load.

Then Mary took her Babe
    And sat him on her knee,
Saying, My dear Son, tell me
    What this world will be.

O I shall be as dead, Mother,
    As the stones in the wall,
O the stones in the streets, Mother,
    Shall mourn for me all.

Upon Easter-day, Mother,
    My uprising shall be,
O the sun and the moon, Mother,
    Shall both rise with me.

Sunny Bank

As I sat on a sunny bank,
    A sunny bank, a sunny bank,
As I sat on a sunny bank
    On Christmas Day in the morning.

I saw three ships come sailing in,
    Come sailing in, come sailing in,
I saw three ships come sailing in
    On Christmas Day in the morning.

I asked them what they had in,
    What they had in, what they had in,
I asked them what they had in
    On Christmas Day in the morning.

They said they had the Saviour in,
    The Saviour in, the Saviour in,
They said they had the Saviour in
    On Christmas Day in the morning.

I asked them where they found him,
    Where they found him, where they found him.
I asked them where they found him
    On Christmas Day in the morning.

They said they found him in Bethlehem,
    In Bethlehem, in Bethlehem,
They said they found him in Bethlehem
    On Christmas Day in the morning.

Now all the bells on earth shall ring,
    On earth shall ring, on earth shall ring,
Now all the bells on earth shall ring
    On Christmas Day in the morning.

And all the angels in heaven shall sing,
    In heaven shall sing, in heaven shall sing,
And all the angels in heaven shall sing
    On Christmas Day in the morning.

The Holly and the Ivy

The holly and the ivy,
    When they are both full grown,
Of all the trees that are in the wood,
    The holly bears the crown.
The rising of the sun
    And the running of the deer,
The playing of the merry organ,
    Sweet singing in the choir.

The holly bears a blossom
　　As white as the lily flower,
And Mary bore sweet Jesus Christ
　　To be our sweet saviour.

The holly bears a berry
　　As red as any blood,
And Mary bore sweet Jesus Christ
　　To do poor sinners good.

The holly bears a prickle
　　As sharp as any thorn,
And Mary bore sweet Jesus Christ
　　On Christmas day in the morn.

The holly bears a bark
　　As bitter as any gall,
And Mary bore sweet Jesus Christ
　　For to redeem us all.

The holly and the ivy,
　　When they are both full grown,
Of all the trees that are in the wood
　　The holly bears the crown.

How Grand and how Bright

How grand and how bright that wonderful night
　　When angels to Bethlehem came,
They burst forth like fires and they shot their loud lyres
　　And mingled their sound with the flame.

The Shepherds were amazed, the pretty lambs gazed
　　At darkness thus turned into light,
No voice was there heard, from man, beast nor bird,
　　So sudden and solemn the sight.

And then when the sound re-echoed around,
    The hills and the dales awoke,
The moon and the stars stopt their fiery cars
    And listened while Gabriel spoke.

I bring you, said he, from that glorious tree
    A message both gladsome and good,
Our Saviour is come to the world as his home,
    But he lies in a manger of wood.

At mention of this, the source of all bliss,
    The angels sang loudly and long,
They soared to the sky beyond mortal eye,
    But left us the words of their song.

All glory to God, who laid by his rod
    To smile on the world by his son,
And peace be on earth, for this wonderful birth
    Most wonderful conquest has won.

And goodwill to man, though his life's but a span,
    And his soul all sinful and vile.
Then pray, Christians, pray, and let Christmas Day
    Have a tear as well as a smile.

The Virgin

At a spring well under a thorn
There was bote of bale a little here aforn.
There beside stant a maid,
Full of love i-bound.
Whoso wol seche true love
In her it shall be found.

The Bitter Withy

As it befell on a bright holiday
Small hail from the sky did fall.
Our Saviour asked his mother dear
If he might go play at ball.

At ball, at ball, my own dear son,
It's time that you were gone,
But don't let me hear of any mischief
At night when you come home.

So up the hill and down the hill
Our sweet young Saviour run,
Until he met three rich young lords –
Good morning to each one.

Good morn, good morn, good morn, said they,
Good morning, then said he,
And which of you three rich young lords
Will play at ball with me?

We are all lords and ladies' sons
Born in our bower and hall,
And you are nothing but a poor maid's child
Born in an ox's stall.

It's if I'm nothing but a poor maid's child,
Born in an ox's stall,
I'll make you believe in your latter end
I'm an angel above you all.

So he made him a bridge of the beams of the sun,
And over the water run he,
The rich young lords chased after him,
And drowned they were all three.

So up the hill and down the hill
Three rich young mothers run,
Crying, Mary mild, fetch home your child,
For ours he's drowned each one.

So Mary mild fetched home her child,
And laid him across her knee,
And with a handful of willow twigs
She gave him slashes three.

Ah bitter withy, ah bitter withy,
You have caused me to smart,
And the willow shall be the very first tree
To perish at the heart.

The Holy Well

As it fell out one May morning,
    And upon one bright holiday,
Sweet Jesus asked of his mother dear,
    If he might go to play.

To play, to play, sweet Jesus shall go,
    And to play pray get you gone,
And let me hear of no complaint
    At night when you come home.

Sweet Jesus went down to yonder town,
    As far as the Holy Well,
And there did see as fine children
    As any tongue can tell.

He said, God bless you every one,
    And your bodies Christ save and see:
Little children, shall I play with you,
    And you shall play with me.

But they made answer to him, No:
    They were lords' and ladies' sons;
And he, the meanest of them all,
    Was but a maiden's child, born in an ox's stall.

Sweet Jesus turned him around,
    And he neither laugh'd nor smil'd,
But the tears came trickling from his eyes
    Like water from the skies.

Sweet Jesus turned him about,
    To his mother's dear home went he,
And said, I have been in yonder town,
    As far as you may see.

I have been down in yonder town
    As far as the Holy Well,
There did I meet as fine children
    As any tongue can tell.

I bid God bless them every one,
    And their bodies Christ save and see:
Little children, shall I play with you,
    And you shall play with me.

But they made answer to me, No:
    They were lords' and ladies' sons,
And I, the meanest of them all,
    Was but a maiden's child, born in an ox's stall.

Though you are but a maiden's child,
    Born in an ox's stall,
Thou art the Christ, the King of Heaven,
    And the Saviour of them all.

Sweet Jesus, go down to yonder town
    As far as the Holy Well,
And take away those sinful souls,
    And dip them deep in Hell.

Nay, nay, sweet Jesus said,
    Nay, nay, that may not be;
For there are too many sinful souls
    Crying out for the help of me.

Me Rueth, Mary

Now goth son under wod,
Me rueth, Mary, thy fair rode.
Now goth son under tree,
Me rueth, Mary, thy son and thee.

The Elder, or Bourtree

Bourtree, bourtree, crookit rung,
Never straight, and never strong,
Ever bush, and never tree
Since our Lord was nail'd t' ye.

Never Said a Mumbalin' Word

Oh, dey whupped him up de hill, up de hill, up de hill,
Oh, dey whupped him up de hill, an' he never said a mumbalin'
  word,
Oh, dey whupped him up de hill, an' he never said a mumbalin'
  word,
He jes' hung down his head, an' he cried.

Oh, dey crowned him wid a thorny crown, thorny crown,
  thorny crown,
Oh, dey crowned him wid a thorny crown, an' he never said a
  mumbalin' word,
Oh, dey crowned him wid a thorny crown, an' he never said a
  mumbalin' word,
He jes' hung down his head, an' he cried.

Well, dey nailed him to de cross, to de cross, to de cross,
Well, dey nailed him to de cross, an' he never said a mumbalin'
  word,
Well, dey nailed him to de cross, an' he never said a mumbalin'
  word,
He jes' hung down his head, an' he cried.

Well, dey pierced him in de side, in de side, in de side,
Well, dey pierced him in de side, an' de blood come a-twinklin'
  down,
Well, dey pierced him in de side, an' de blood come a-twinklin'
  down,
Den he hung down his head, an' he died.

The Corpus Christi Carol

Lully, lulley, lully, lulley,
The fawcon hath born my mak away.

He bare him up, he bare him down,
He bare him into an orchard brown.

In that orchard there was an hall
That was hangid with purpill and pall.

And in that hall ther was a bed.
It was hangid with gold so red.

And in that bed ther lythe a knight,
His woundes bleeding day and night.

By that bedes side ther kneeleth a may,
And she weepeth both night and day.

And by that bedes side ther stondeth a ston,
'Corpus Christi' wretyn theron.

The Corpus Christi Carol

(from Staffordshire)

Over yonder's a park, which is newly begun,
   All bells in Paradise I heard them a-ring,
Which is silver on the outside, and gold within,
   And I love sweet Jesus above all things.

And in that park there stands a hall,
Which is covered all over with purple and pall.

And in that hall there stands a bed,
Which is hung all round with silk curtains so red.

And in that bed there lies a knight,
Whose wounds they do bleed by day and by night.

At that bed side there lies a stone,
Which is our blessed Virgin Mary then kneeling on.

At that bed's foot there lies a hound,
Which is licking the blood as it daily runs down.

At that bed's head there grows a thorn,
Which was never so blossomed since Christ was born.

The Corpus Christi Carol

(from Scotland)

The heron flew east, the heron flew west,
The heron flew to the fair forest;
She flew o'er streams and meadows green,
And a' to see what could be seen:
And when she saw the faithful pair,
Her breast grew sick, her head grew sair;
For there she saw a lovely bower,
Was a' clad o'er wi' lilly-flower;
And in the bower there was a bed
With silken sheets, and weel down spread:
And in the bed there lay a knight,
Whose wounds did bleed both day and night;
And by the bed there stood a stane,
And there was set a leal maiden,
With silver needle and silken thread,
Stemming the wounds when they did bleed.

An ABC

In Adam's Fall
We sinned all.

Thy life to mend,
This Book attend.

The Cat doth play,
And after slay.

A Dog will bite
A thief at night.

An Eagle's flight
Is out of sight.

The idle Fool
Is whipt at school.

As runs the Glass,
Man's life doth pass.

My book and Heart
Shall never part.

Job feels the rod,
Yet blesses God.

Kings should be good,
No men of blood.

The Lion bold
The Lamb doth hold.

The Moon gives light
In time of night.

Nightingales sing
In time of spring.

Young Obadias,
David, Josias,
All were pious.

Peter denies
His Lord, and cries.

Queen Esther sues
And saves the Jews.

Rachel doth mourn
For her first-born.

Samuel anoints
Whom God appoints.

Time cuts down all,
Both great and small.

Uriah's beauteous wife
Made David seek his life.

Whales in the sea
God's voice obey.

Xerxes the great did die
And so must you and I.

Youth forward slips,
Death soonest nips.

Zaccheus he
Did climb the tree
His Lord to see.

The Seven Virgins

All under the leaves, the leaves of life,
  I met with virgins seven,
And one of them was Mary mild,
  Our Lord's mother from heaven.

'O what are you seeking, you seven fair maids,
  All under the leaves of life?
Come tell, come tell me what seek you
  All under the leaves of life.'

'We're seeking for no leaves, Thomas,
    But for a friend of thine,
We're seeking for sweet Jesus Christ,
    To be our guide and thine.'

'Go you down, go you down to yonder town,
    And sit in the gallery,
And there you'll find sweet Jesus Christ
    Nailed to a big yew-tree.'

So down they went to yonder town
    As fast as foot could fall,
And many a grievous bitter tear
    From the virgins' eyes did fall.

'O peace, mother, O peace, mother,
    Your weeping doth me grieve.
O I must suffer this,' he said,
    'For Adam and for Eve.'

'O how can I my weeping leave
    Or my sorrows undergo
Whilst I do see my own son die,
    When sons I have no mo'?'

'Dear mother, dear mother, you must take John,
    All for to be your son,
And he will comfort you sometimes,
    Mother, as I have done.'

'O come, thou John Evangelist,
    Thou'rt welcome unto me,
But more welcome my own dear son
    That I nursed upon my knee.'

Then he laid his head on his right shoulder,
    Seeing death it struck him nigh:
'The Holy Ghost be with your soul,
    I die, mother dear, I die.'

Oh the rose, the rose, the gentle rose,
    And the fennel that grows so green,
God give us grace in every place
    To pray for our king and queen.

Furthermore for our enemies all
    Our prayers they should be strong.
Amen, Good Lord. Your charity
    Is the ending of my song.

By a Chapel as I Came

Merry it is in May morning
Merry ways for to gone.

And by a chapel as I came
Met I wyhte Jesu to churchward gone,
Peter and Paul, Thomas and John,
And his disciples everyone.
                    Merry it is.

Saint Thomas the bells gan ring,
And Saint Collas the mass gan sing,
Saint John took that sweet offering,
And by a chapel as I came.
                    Merry it is.

Our Lord offered what he wolld,
A chalice all of rich red gold,
Our Lady the crown off her mould,
The sun out of her bosom shone.
                    Merry it is.

Saint George that is Our Lady knight,
He tend the tapers fair and bright,
To mine eye a seemly sight,
And by a chapel as I came.
                    Merry it is.

Brown Robyn's Confession

It fell upon a Wodensday
  Brown Robyn's men went to sea,
But they saw neither moon nor sun,
  Nor starlight wi their ee.

We'll cast kevels us amang,
  See wha the unhappy man may be.
The kevel fell on Brown Robyn,
  The master-man was he.

It is nae wonder, said Brown Robyn,
  Altho I dinna thrive,
For wi my mither I had twa bairns,
  And wi my sister five.

But tie me to a plank o wude,
  And throw me in the sea,
And if I sink, ye may bid me sink,
  But if I swim, just lat me be.

They've tied him to a plank o wude,
  And thrown him in the sea.
He didna sink, tho they bade him sink,
  He swimd, and they bade lat him be.

He hadna been into the sea
  An hour but barely three
Till by it came Our Blessed Lady,
  Her dear young son her wi.

Will ye gang to your men again,
  Or will ye gang wi me?
Will ye gang to the high heavens,
  Wi my dear son and me?

I winna gang to my men again,
  For they would be feared at me,
But I woud gang to the high heavens,
  Wi thy dear son and thee.

It's for nae honour ye did to me, Brown Robyn,
   It's for nae guid ye did to me,
But a' is for your fair confession
   You've made upon the sea.

The Royal Fisherman

As I walked out one May morning,
   When May was all in bloom,
O there I spied a bold fisherman,
   Come fishing all alone.

I said to this bold fisherman,
   'How come you fishing here?'
'I'm fishing for your own sweet sake
   All down the river clear.'

He drove his boat towards the side,
   Which was his full intent,
Then he laid hold of her lily-white hand
   And down the stream they went.

Then he pulled off his morning gown
   And threw it over the sea,
And there she spied three robes of gold
   All hanging down his knee.

Then on her bended knees she fell:
   'Pray, sir, pardon me
For calling you a fisherman
   And a rover down the sea.'

'Rise up, rise up, my pretty fair maid,
   Don't mention that to me,
For not one word that you have spoke
   Has the least offended me.

'Then we'll go to my father's hall,
    And married we shall be,
And you shall have your fisherman
    To row you on the sea.'

Then they went to his father's house,
    And married now they be;
And now she's got her fisherman
    To row her down the sea.

In Dessexshire as it Befel

In Dessexshire as it befel
A farmer there as I knew well
On a Christmas day as it happened so
Down in the meadows he went to plough.

As he was a ploughing on so fast
Our Saviour Christ came by at last;
He said, O man, why dost thou plough
So hard as it do blow and snow?

The man he answered the Lord with speed,
For to work we have great need,
If we wasn't to work all on that day
We should want some other way.

For his hands did tremble and pass to and fro,
He ran so fast that he could not plough;
And the ground did open and let him in
Before he could repent his sin.

His wife and children were out at play;
And all the world consumed at last.
And his beasts and cattle all died away
For breaking of the Lord's birthday.

15 · Old Age and Death

Sair Fyel'd, Hinny

Aw was young and lusty,
  Aw was fair and clear,
Aw was young and lusty
  Mony a lang year.
     Sair fyel'd, hinny,
      Sair fyel'd now,
     Sair fyel'd, hinny,
      Sin' aw ken'd thou.

When aw was young and lusty,
  Aw cud lowp a dyke,
But now aw'm awd an' stiff
  Aw can hardly step a syke.
     Sair fyel'd, hinny,
      Sair fyel'd now,
     Sair fyel'd, hinny,
      Sin' aw ken'd thou.

When aw was five an' twenty,
  Aw was brave and bauld,
Now at five and sixty
  Aw'm byeth stiff and cauld.
     Sair fyel'd, hinny,
      Sair fyel'd now,
     Sair fyel'd, hinny,
      Sin' aw ken'd thou.

Thus said the awd man
  To the oak tree,
Sair fyel'd is aw
  Sin' aw ken'd thee.
     Sair fyel'd, hinny,
      Sair fyel'd now,
     Sair fyel'd, hinny,
      Sin' aw ken'd thou.

Wedding and Funeral

Blest is t' bride at t' sun shines on,
An' blest is t' deead at t' rain rains on.

The Tod's Hole

Now be ye lords or commoners
    Ye needna laugh nor sneer,
For ye'll be a' i' the tod's hole
    In less than a hunner year.

The Duke of Grafton

As two men were a-walking, down by the sea-side
O the brave Duke of Grafton they straightway espied,
Said the one to the other, and thus did they say,
It is the brave Duke of Grafton that is now cast away.

They brought him to Portsmouth, his fame to make known,
And from thence to fair London, so near to the Crown,
They pull'd out his bowels, and they stretch'd forth his feet,
They embalm'd his body with spices so sweet.

All things were made ready, his funeral for to be,
Where the royal Queen Mary came there for to see,
Six lords went before him, six bore him from the ground,
Six Dukes walk'd before him in black velvet gowns.

So black was their mourning, so white were their bands!
So yellow were the flamboys they carried in their hands!
The drums they did rattle, the trumpets sweetly sound,
While the muskets and cannons did thunder all around.

In Westminster Abbey 'tis now call'd by name,
There the great Duke of Grafton does lie in great fame;
In Westminster Abbey he lies in cold clay
Where the royal Queen Mary went weeping away.

The Cowboy's Lament

As I walked out in the streets of Laredo,
As I walked out in Laredo one day,
I spied a poor cowboy wrapped up in white linen,
Wrapped up in white linen as cold as the clay.

Oh beat the drum slowly and play the fife lowly,
Play the Dead March as you carry me along;
Take me to the green valley, there lay the sod o'er me,
For I'm a young cowboy and I know I've done wrong.

I see by your outfit that you are a cowboy —
These words he did say as I boldly stepped by.
Come sit down beside me and hear my sad story,
I am shot in the breast and I know I must die.

Let sixteen gamblers come handle my coffin,
Let sixteen cowboys come sing me a song.
Take me to the graveyard and lay the sod o'er me,
For I'm a poor cowboy and I know I've done wrong.

My friends and relations they live in the Nation,
They know not where their boy has gone.
I first came to Texas and hired to a ranchman.
Oh I'm a young cowboy and I know I've done wrong.

It was once in the saddle I used to go dashing,
It was once in the saddle I used to go gay
First to the dram-house and then to the card-house,
Got shot in the breast and I am dying to-day.

Get six jolly cowboys to carry my coffin,
Get six pretty maidens to bear up my pall.
Put bunches of roses all over my coffin,
Put roses to deaden the sods as they fall.

Then swing your rope slowly and rattle your spurs lowly,
And give a wild whoop as you carry me along,
And in the grave throw me and roll the sod o'er me,
For I'm a young cowboy and I know I've done wrong.

Oh bury beside me my knife and six-shooter,
My spurs on my heel, as you sing me a song,
And over my coffin put a bottle of brandy
That the cowboys may drink as they carry me along.

Go bring me a cup, a cup of cold water
To cool my parched lips, the cowboy then said;
Before I returned his soul had departed,
And gone to the round-up, the cowboy was dead.

We beat the drum slowly and played the fife lowly,
And bitterly wept as we bore him along;
For we all loved our comrade, so brave, young, and handsome,
We all loved our comrade although he'd done wrong.

The Lyke-Wake Dirge

This ean night, this ean night,
    Every night and awle,
Fire and fleet and candle-light,
    And Christ receive thy sawle.

When thou from hence doest pass away,
    Every night and awle,
To Whinny-moor thou comest at last,
    And Christ receive thy sawle.

If ever thou gave either hosen or shoon,
    Every night and awle,
Sit thee down and put them on,
    And Christ receive thy sawle.

But if hosen or shoon thou never gave nean,
    Every night and awle,
The whinnes shall prick thee to the bare beane,
    And Christ receive thy sawle.

From Whinny-moor that thou mayst pass,
    Every night and awle,
To Brig o' Dread thou comest at last,
    And Christ receive thy sawle.

From Brig of Dread that thou mayest pass
    Every night and awle,
To Purgatory fire thou com's at last,
    And Christ receive thy sawle.

If ever thou gave either milke or drinke,
    Every night and awle,
The fire shall never make thee shrink,
    And Christ receive thy sawle.

But if milk nor drink thou never gave nean,
    Every night and awle,
The fire shall burn thee to the bare bene,
    And Christ receive thy sawle.

This ean night, this ean night,
    Every night and awle,
Fire and fleet and candle-light,
    And Christ receive thy sawle.

Two Riddles

i

There was a man made a thing,
And he that made it did it bring,
But he 'twas made for did not know
Whether 'twas a thing or no.

(A coffin)

I sat wi' my love, and I drank wi' my love,
  And my love she gave me light.
I'll give any man a pint o' wine
  That'll read my riddle right.

> (*I sat in a chair made of my
> love's bones, drank out of her
> skull, and was given light by a
> candle made of her fat.*)

The Blue-tail Fly

When I was young I used to wait
On master and give him the plate
And pass the bottle when he got dry,
And brush away the blue-tail fly.
  *Jimmy crack corn and I don't care,
  Old massa's gone away.*

And when he'd ride in the arternoon
I'd follow after with a hickory broom,
The pony being very shy,
When bitten by the blue-tail fly.

One day when ridin' round the farm
The flies so num'rous they did swarm
One chanced to bite him on the thigh,
The devil take the blue-tail fly.

The pony jump, he run, he pitch,
He threw my master in the ditch,
He died and the jury wondered why,
The verdict was the blue-tail fly.

We laid him under a 'simmon tree,
His epitaph was there to see,
Beneath this stone I'm forced to lie,
Victim of a blue-tail fly.

Ole massa's dead and gone to rest,
They say all things is for the best.
I never shall forget till the day I die
Old massa and the blue-tail fly.

The hornet gets in eyes and nose,
The skeeter bites you through your clothes,
The gallinipper flies up high,
But wusser yet, the blue-tail fly.

The Undertakers' Club

One night, being pressed by his old friend Chubb,
To go to an Undertakers' Club,
I'll furnish you all, if that I dare,
With a mournful account of this grave affair.
For such a black looking lot is this Club of
Undertakers, such a black looking set
   You never did see.

This selfsame Club, and House of Call,
Was held at Blackheath, or else Blackwall,
The landlord's name it was Blackmore,
And an African chief hung over the door.

The Undertakers had all met.
They were dress'd in black a dingey set,
The picture frames black, and so were the walls,
And the window curtains were made of palls.

The stove black leaded not long had been,
On the table was laid Blackwood's magazine,
The carpet was black and so was each chair,
The chairman'd black whiskers and raven hair.

The supper was laid, there were lots of black game,
With polonies in mourning to match with the same,
There were blackbird pies, and nothing but good 'uns,
And a quantity of good black puddings.

The knives were black, and so were the forks,
Black strap in black bottles, with black sealed corks,
The rules of the club were done in black figures,
And the waiters and cooks were all of them niggers.

The dessert was black grapes, and black heart cherries,
Blackcurrants and mulberries and blackberries.
Prunes and elder wine were there,
Which just made up this black bill of fare.

Mr. Sable sang first, and what should he choose on
But the favourite ballad of Black eyed Susan,
The Coal Black Steed Mr. Hatband chose,
And Mr. Merryhell sang Coal Black Rose.

The best that was sung, and that all did confess,
Was the favourite song of My bonny Black Bess,
The Chairman then whistled, when his throat was clear,
The fav'rite grand march that is played in Black Beard.

Hold the Wind

You may talk about me just as much as you please,
    Hold the wind, don't let it blow,
I'm gonna talk about you on the bendin' of my knees,
    Hold the wind, hold the wind,
    Hold the wind, don't let it blow.
    Hold the wind, hold the wind,
    Hold the wind, don't let it blow.

If you don't believe I have been redeemed,
Just follow me down to the Jordan stream.

My soul got wet in the midnight dew,
And the mornin' star was a witness too.

When I get to Heaven, gwine walk and tell,
Three bright angels go ring them bells.

When I get to Heaven, gwine be at ease,
Me and my God gonna do as we please.

Gonna chatter with the Father, argue with the Son,
Tell um 'bout the world I just come from.

Swing Low, Sweet Chariot

I ain't never been to heaven but Ah been told,
   Comin' fuh to carry me home,
Dat de streets in heaben am paved with gold,
   Comin' fuh to carry me home.
     Swing low, sweet chariot,
     Comin' fuh to carry me home,
     Swing low, sweet chariot,
     Comin' fuh to carry me home.

Dat ain't all, I got mo' besides –
Ah been tuh de ribber an' Ah been baptize'.

Lemme tell yuh whut's a mattah o' fac',
Ef yuh evah leaves de debbil, yuh nevah go back.

Yuh see dem sisters dress so fine?
Well, dey ain't got Jesus on dey min'.

Ef salvation wuz a thing money could buy,
Den de rich would live an' de po' would die.

But Ah'm so glad God fix it so,
Dat de rich mus' die jes' as well as de po'!

Pie in the Sky

Long-haired preachers come out ev'ry night,
And they tell you what's wrong and what's right,
When you ask them for something to eat,
They will answer in voices so sweet:

> 'You will eat, bye and bye,
> In that glorious land above the sky,
> Work and pray, live on hay,
> You'll get pie in the sky when you die.'

Holy Rollers and Jumpers, come out,
And they holler, they jump and they shout.
'Give your money to Jesus,' they say,
'He will cure all diseases today.'

If you fight hard for children and wife,
Try to get something good in this life,
You're a sinner and a bad man, they tell,
When you die you will sure go to Hell.

Working men of all countries, unite,
Side by side we for freedom will fight,
When the world and its wealth we have gained
To the grafter we will sing this refrain:

O the starvation army they play,
And they sing and they clap and they pray,
Till they get all your coin on the drum,
Then they'll tell you when you're on the bum.

> You will eat bye and bye
> When you've learned how to cook and fry,
> Chop some wood, 'twill do you good,
> And you'll eat in the sweet bye and bye.

No Hiding Place Down There

A sinner man sat on the gates of hell,
A sinner man sat on the gates of hell,
A sinner man sat on the gates of hell,
The gates fell in and down he fell,
No hiding place down there.

I thought I heard my sister yell,
I thought I heard my sister yell,
I thought I heard my sister yell,
Way down deep in the middle of hell,
No hiding place down there.

I went to the rock to hide my face,
I went to the rock to hide my face,
I went to the rock to hide my face,
The rock called out, Go wash your face:
No hiding place down there.

Notes and Sources

Abbreviations

Ashton	John Ashton, *Modern Street Ballads*, 1888
Bell	John Bell, *Rhymes of Northern Bards*, 1812
Botkin	B. A. Botkin, *Treasury of American Folklore*, 1944
Chambers	Robert Chambers, *Popular Rhymes of Scotland*, 3rd edition, 1858.
Chappell	William Chappell, *Popular Music of the Olden Time*, 1859
Child	Francis James Child, *The English and Scottish Popular Ballads*, 1882–1898
Gomme, 1894	Alice Gomme, *Traditional Games of England, Scotland and Ireland*, Vol. I.
Gomme, 1898	Ibid. Vol. 2.
Graves	Robert Graves, *The Less Familiar Nursery Rhymes*, 1927
Greene	R. L. Greene, *The Early English Carols*, 1935
Henderson	W. Henderson, *Victorian Street Ballads*, 1937
Herd	David Herd, *Ancient and Modern Scottish Songs*, 1776
Hugill	Stan Hugill, *Shanties of the Seven Seas*, 1966
J.F.S.S.	*Journal of the Folk Song Society*
J.E.F.D.S.S.	*Journal of the English Folk Dance & Song Society*
J.O.H.	James Orchard Halliwell, *The Nursery Rhymes of England*, various editions from 1842
Joyce	P. W. Joyce, *Old Irish Folk Music and Songs*, 1909
Lomax, 1934	J. A. and Z. Lomax, *American Ballads and Folk Songs*, 1934
Lomax, 1960	A. Lomax, *Folk Songs of North America*, 1960
Marshall	John J. Marshall, *Popular Rhymes of Ireland*, 1931
Moorman	F. W. Moorman, *Yorkshire Dialect Poems*, 1917
N. and Q.	*Notes and Queries*
Northall	G. F. Northall, *English Folk-Rhymes*, 1892
O.D.N.R.	Iona & Peter Opie, *Oxford Dictionary of Nursery Rhymes*, 1952
Opie, 1969	Iona and Peter Opie, *Children's Games in Street and Playground*, 1969

Ritson   Joseph Ritson, *Gammer Gurton's Garland* (1783)
Robbins   R. H. Robbins, *Secular Lyrics of the XIVth and XVth Centuries*, 1952
Robert Bell   Robert Bell, *Poems, Ballads & Songs of the Peasantry of Scotland*, 1861
Sandburg   Carl Sandburg, *The American Song-bag*, 1927
Taylor   Archer Taylor, *English Riddles from Oral Tradition*, 1951
White   N. I. White, *American Negro Folk Songs*, 1928
Williams   Alfred Williams, *Folk-Songs of the Upper Thames*, 1923
Wright   E. W. Wright, *Rustic Speech and Folklore*, 1913

page

15. HUSH-A-BA, BURDIE. A. L. J. Gosset, *Lullabies of the Four Nations* [1915].

15. HUSH AND BALOO. Chambers.

15. BONNY AT MORN. *Songs and Ballads of Northern England*, Newcastle, 1949.

16. THE MILLER'S WIFE'S LULLABY. Viking Society, Old Lore Miscellany. Vol. 4, 1911.

17. GO TO BED FIRST. Personal recollection. Also J.O.H., 1844 (with 'pheasant' in line 4).

17. DON'T CARE. Graves.

17. SOME RIDDLES (i) *O.D.N.R.* (ii) J.O.H., 1846. (iii) Gutch and Peacock, *County Folklore, Lincolnshire*, Folk-Lore Society, 1908. (iv) J.O.H., 1842.

18. JACK THE PIPER. J.O.H., 1853

18. THE NUT-TREE. *The Newest Christmas Box, c.* 1797. (*O.D.N.R.*) This seems to be a polite derivative of the fifteenth century *Pear-Tree* (page 140).

19. WHAT'S IN THE CUPBOARD. *N. and Q.*, 7. iv. 1887.

19. COME, LET'S TO BED. Ritson.

19. CROSSPATCH. Ritson.

19. FIRE, FIRE. *Mother Goose's Nursery Rhymes*, 1890.

20. DIPS, OR COUNTING OUT RHYMES. (i) from Dylan Thomas, who knew it in his Swansea childhood. (ii) Opie, 1969. (iii) Ibid. *lum:* chimney. (iv) Gregor, *Notes on the Folk-Lore of the North-East of Scotland*, 1881. *doo:* woodpigeon (dove). *ban:* neckband, collar. *fite:* white. (v) *Nicht at Eeenie*, Samson Press, 1932. This begins with Brittonic number words of the 'shepherd's score'.

The King o'Heazle Peasil: the Man in the Moon. (vi) Opie, 1969. (vii) Ibid. (viii) Sandburg.

22. STARTING RHYMES. Both from Opie, 1969.

22. THE MERRY-MA-TANZIE. Chambers. Chambers describes the action of the dancing game in which this was sung.

23. HOW MANY MILES TO BABYLON? J.O.H., 1842. From the children's catching game most commonly known as 'Running Across' (see *O.D.N.R.* and Opie, 1969).

24. WHO GOES ROUND MY PINFOLD WALL. S. O. Addy, *Sheffield Glossary*, 1888. The pinfold is the village pound, in which stray animals were impounded.

24. LONDON BRIDGE. Ritson. Gomme, 1894.

25. GREEN GRASS. Gomme, 1894. Scotch version of song for a game recorded from many parts of Britain.

26. WE ARE THREE BRETHREN COME FROM SPAIN. Chambers. (see also Gomme, 1898, and Walter de la Mare's *Come Hither*, 1923.) One of many versions of a game song.

27. TO-MORROW'S THE FAIR. Northall.

27. LEMONADE. Botkin.

28. HE THAT NE'ER LEARNS HIS ABC. *New England Primer*, late seventeenth century.

28. THE SCHOOLMASTER. Carswell, *The Scots Week-End*, 1936. *skelp:* beat.

28. THE DILLY SONG. Baring-Gould and Sheppard, *Songs of the West*. 1892. By origin this famous song is a late medieval mnemonic to the realms of God and man — often learnt, one may suppose, by schoolchildren. This is made clear by comparing it with three less lyrical and less mysterious parallels, one of them called 'Man's Duty; or, Meditation for the Twelve Hours of the Day', printed by Sandys, *Christmas Carols*, 1833.

Number one, the root of all things, is one God, one faith, one truth, one baptism. The Lily-white boys of two are the New and Old Testaments, in the persons of Christ and John the Baptist. Three, the three rivals, i.e. three rivalling each other, or being co-equal, in power, are the Trinity (cf. in the Athanasian creed, 'And in this Trinity none is afore, or after other: none is greater, or less than another'). The four Gospelmakers are Matthew, Mark, Luke and John. Five can be identified with a painted symbol of the Five Senses of Man (cf. the symbolical wheel of the Five Senses in the painted chamber, early fourteenth century, of Longthorpe Tower, Northants).

According to 2 out of the 3 parallel poems, six, the six proud walkers, should be man labouring on the six working days of the week (a confusion of walk and work?). Other versions of *The Dilly Song* have 'waters' for 'walkers' (e.g. in Chambers, 'Six the echoing waters'), to be equated, as in the third of Sandys' parallels, with the Six Ages of the history of the world, commonly symbolized in the six waters, i.e. water-pots, of the marriage in Cana (Luke 2, 6–8).

The 'seven stars in the sky' are the Seven Planets, Sun, Moon, Mercury, Mars, Jupiter, Venus and Saturn, apparently standing for one of the groups of seven, The Seven Liberal Arts, or Sciences (the trivium and quadrivium of medieval education), which were God's ennobling gifts to man.

The eight bold rangers (or 'rainers') are the Eight Souls, the eight forefathers of mankind, who survived in the Ark (or the eight groups of the blessed – Matthew 5, 3–10). The 'nine bright shiners' stand either for the Nine Orders of Angels, or – following 2 of the poems printed by Sandys – for the Nine Muses, whose harmonious voices sing the praise of the Redeemer.

Ten explains itself. Eleven has two interpretations, either it is eleven out of the Twelve apostles of the final number, eleven in Heaven (with Judas in the flames), or it is shorthand for the Eleven Thousand Virgins of the legend of St. Ursula, doing duty in this not, after all, so mysterious *Dilly Song* for the whole army of saints and martyrs.

The symbolic paintings in Longthorpe Tower include the Seven Ages of Man and man at his divinely ordained work (Labours of the Months), as well as the Five Senses.

35. THE ZODIAC RHYME. Graves.

35. WASSAIL SONG. Percy Papers, Harvard (*J.E.F.D.S.S.*, Vol. 7, 1952). Written down by Thomas Percy *c.* 1760, when he was vicar of Easton Maudit, Northants.

36. SNOW. Moorman.

36. FEATHERS OF SNOW. Northall.

36. RIDDLES OF THE WEATHER. (i) *O.D.N.R.*, cf. Taylor 368–9. (ii) *N. and Q.*, 1855, a riddle discussed at length by Taylor, pp. 115–23. (iii) Chambers (Taylor 762a). (iv) Chambers (Taylor 1651). *nieves:* hands. (v) Taylor 487, from Bermuda. (vi) *A Booke of merrie Riddles*, 1631.

37. MISTY-MOISTY WAS THE MORN. Graves. A version of the first stanza of 'The Wiltshire Wedding', an otherwise dull broadside ballad of the late seventeenth century (*Roxburghe Ballads*, Vol. VII; O.D.N.R., No. 359).

38. MARCH. R. Inwards, *Weather Lore*, 1893. From Northumberland. *yeans:* gives birth to.

38. THE BORROWING DAYS. Chambers. *hoggs:* young sheep. *hirpling:* limping.

38. WHICH IS THE BOW? Ireson, *Faber Book of Nursery Verse.*

39. MORE RIDDLES. (i) Withers, *Rocket in my Pocket*, 1948. (See *O.D.N.R.* No. 425; Taylor 1570). (ii) Taylor 391. (iii) Other versions from North America in Taylor, 391. (iv) Marshall, cf. Taylor 392.

39. I SEE THE MOON. Harland, *Lancashire Legends*, 1867.

40. SUMER IS ICUMEN IN. Robbins. Early thirteenth century.

40. THE RURAL DANCE ABOUT THE MAYPOLE. *Westminster Drollery, the Second Part*, 1672.

42. THE MAYERS' SONG. Hone, *Every-Day Book*, 1825.

43. THE PADSTOW NIGHT SONG. Wright and Jones, *British Calendar Customs*, Folk-Lore Society, 1938.

44. THE PRETTY PLOUGHBOY. Kidson, *Traditional Tunes*, 1891.

44. UNDER THE GREENWOOD TREE. Bodleian Library, MS. Ashmole fol. 294.

46. HOLLIN, GREEN HOLLIN. R. and A. C. Macleod, M. Lawson and H. Boulton, *Songs of the North* [1895–97].

46. THE RIPE AND BEARDED BARLEY. Williams.

47. THE YULE DAYS. Chambers. *papingo-aye:* popinjay, parrot.

49. YULE'S COME, AND YULE'S GANE. Chambers.

53. THE HART LOVES THE HIGH WOOD. *The Pinder of Wakefield, Being the Merry History of George a Greene . . . full of pretty Histories, Songs, Catches, Iests, and Ridles*, 1632.

53. I HAVE TWELVE OXEN. Robbins. Fifteenth century.

53. CAT AT THE CREAM. Chambers.

53. THE CAT'S SONG. Chambers.

54. MY FATHER KEPT A HORSE. Henderson.

54. OLD GRAY MARE. Sandburg.

55. THE FALSE FOX. Robbins. Fifteenth century. *shrove:* confessed. *assoyled:* absolved. *rok:* distaff.

56. THE GOOSE AND THE GANDER. Kidson, *Traditional Tunes*, 1891.

56. WHEN THE RAIN RAINETH. By John Skelton (1460?–1529); in *Garlande of Laurell*. (Graves).

57. THE OLD GRAY GOOSE. Lomax, 1934.

58. THE FIVE HENS. J.O.H., 1842.

58. HEN AND COCK. J.O.H., 1849.

58. RIDDLES. (i) *O.D.N.R.* (see Taylor 1476–95 for variants). (ii) J.O.H., 1844; Taylor 1136.

59. THE BONNY GREY. J.F.S.S. II, (Vaughan Williams & A. L. Lloyd, *Penguin Book of English Folk Songs*, 1959). According to Harland's *Ballads and Songs of Lancashire*, 1875, the Lord Derby of 'The Bonny Grey', was the 12th earl, Edward, who died in 1834.

60. THE KOOCOO. In *John Heywoodes woorkes*, 1576.

60. THE CUCKOO. Cecil Sharp, *English Folk Songs*, 1959.

60. THE LARK. Gregor, *Folk-Lore of the North-East of Scotland*, 1881.

61. CROW'S DITTY. Folk Lore (v), 1894. Yorkshire variant of rhyme with German, Irish, Gaelic and other equivalents.

61. AGAINST THE MAGPIE. Moorman.

61. THE DOVE. Swainson, *Folk Lore of British Birds*, 1886.

61. A MAGPIE RHYME. Wright.

62. HOP'T SHE. *Wiseheart's Merry Songster*, No. 3 (1832).

62. THE ROOKS. Chambers. *croupin:* cawing. *craws:* rooks.

62. BLACKBIRD'S SONG. Gosset, *Lullabies of the Four Nations*.

62. THE SEA-GULL. Chambers.

63. MALISON OF THE STONE-CHAT. Chambers.

63. ROBIN, WREN, MARTIN. Hone, *Every-Day Book*, 1825.

63. THE CUTTY WREN. *Manners and Customs of the People of Tenby*, 1858. Song of the wren hunters who carried a live wren in a box, on a pole, from house to house on Twelfth Night.

65. BIRD RIDDLES. (i) Gutch & Peacock, *County Folklore, Lincolnshire*, 1908. The hanged man was said to be Tom Otter, executed at Saxilby, Lincolnshire in 1806. (ii) *A Book of merrie Riddles*, 1631. (iii) Ibid. (iv) Taylor 1237b (from Tennessee).

66. ROBIN REDBREAST'S TESTAMENT. Herd. One of several songs of the pugnacious conceit of the robin and his relationship with the wren. *neb:* beak. *steer:* stir. *cutty:* wicked little. *quean:* whore. *coll:* haycock. *gled:* kite.

67. THE FROG AND THE CROW. *N. and Q.*, 1850.

68. THE PUDDY AND THE MOUSE. K. Sharpe, *Ballad Book*, 1824 (*O.D.N.R.*, No. 175). An Elizabethan version with a spinning refrain appears in Ravenscroft's *Melismata*, 1611, but is evidently incomplete. *puddy:* frog. *wonne:* dwelling. *rottan:* rat. *gar busk:* make ready. *jimp:* slender. *sola:* dirty. *but:* outside. *gart:* caused to.

69. THE SNAIL. Ritson. *Kyloe:* small shaggy race of cattle with long horns, from the Highlands and Islands.

70. THE LADYBIRD. Northall. *colly:* Midland adjective of endearment for cows.

70. INSECT RIDDLES. (i) *Miscellanies of the Rymour Club*, 1911 (*O.D.N.R.*, p. 406; Taylor 887–904). *nick nackit:* naked necked. (ii) Chambers; Taylor 1597–1627. *rock:* distaff. *reel:* winder for spinning. (iii) Taylor 672 (Tupper, *The Holme Riddles*, *PMLA*, XVIII, 1903).

71. THE PERSIMMON TREE. White.

71. FRUIT, FLOWER AND TREE RIDDLES. (i) *A Booke of merrie Riddles*, 1631. (ii) *O.D.N.R.* No. 474 (see Taylor 1269–72). (iii) Tupper, *The Holme Riddles*, *PMLA*, XVIII, 1903. (iv) *N. and Q.*, 1858 (see Taylor 601–3). (v) Taylor 1572b (from the Antilles. Versions are known from England and North America). (vi) Taylor 1391, an Illinois version of an English riddle.

72. THE FISHES. Shanty for capstan & pumps. Many versions (see Hugill, *Shanties from the Seven Seas*, 1966), deriving from a fisherman's song of Northumberland & Scotland.

73. FISH RIDDLES. (i) similar version in Ashton, *Chap-Books of the Eighteenth Century*, 1882. (ii) Chambers (see Taylor 906).

74. THE ANIMALS IN THE ARK. *Chester Play of the Deluge*, sixteenth century.

75. IN COME DE ANIMULS TWO BY TWO. White.

76. THE KIRK OF THE BIRDS, BEASTS AND FISHES. Chambers. *coft:* bought. *kirtle:* gown. *big:* build. *moupit:* nibbled. *doo:* dove (i.e. wood pigeon). *gled:* kite. *rackled up:* rattled up, hurriedly built. *pyat:* magpie (the devil's bird). *hirpling:* limping. *knowe:* hill. *hurcheon:* hedgehog.

81. THE DERBY RAM. Williams. One of many versions of a folksong still happily sung with ribald stanzas. *O.D.N.R.* mentions a reference to *The Derby Ram* in 1739.

82. THE ONE-HORNED EWE. *J.F.S.S.* 11. 79. In Lincolnshire speech, *pindar:* keeper of the village pound, in which stray animals were held.

83. A MAN IN THE WILDERNESS. The earliest form quoted in *O.D.N.R.* p. 318, from a manuscript addition dated 1744 in a book in the Municipal Library at Bath.

83. HEY-HO KNAVE. *The Pindar of Wakefield, being the Merry History of George a Green*, 1632.

84. THE TOKENS OF LOVE: 1. Robbins. Earlier fifteenth century. *drowries:* tokens of love. *brer:* briar. *rind:* branch. *lemman:* lover. *ey:* egg. *onbred:* unbred (still a seed).

85. THE TOKENS OF LOVE: 2. Walter Crane, *The Baby's Bouquet* (1878), with restoration of the two questioning stanzas and change of order in stanza 6. One of several versions (see *O.D.N.R.*, pp. 386–88) recorded in the last century and a half. Some increase the sisters of the fifteenth century poem, 'I had four sisters', etc. One version from Scotland begins 'I had a true love', and retains the sense of 'drowrys' if not the word, 'And many a love token he sends to me'.

86. THERE WERE THREE JOVIAL WELSHMEN. J.O.H., 1853. (*O.D.N.R.*, No. 525). A song of fools. Three stanzas approximating to the first and the two final stanzas occur in a broadside of 1632, in which three men of Gotham go hunting on St. David's Day. So they become Welsh Gothamites, the song turning into one of raillery about the Welsh.

87. I WILL HAVE THE WHETSTONE. Greene. Sixteenth century. To be given the whetstone was to be accorded the prize for lying (for sharpening a sharp tongue). *urchin:* hedgehog. *shape:* cut out (cloth). *burdensbind:* tie up loads. *clewens:* balls of yarn. *kyrchers:* kerchiefs. *plash:* lay and interweave.

88. THE COW ATE THE PIPER. Colm O Lochlainn, *More Irish Street Ballads*, 1965. *ninety-eight:* i.e. 1798. *Milesian:* Irishman (descendant of legendary King Milesius). *Hessians:* German mercenaries. *cant her:* auction her. *luck-penny:* portion of a price given back for luck. *gommach:* fool. *grá:* love.

90. I SAW A PEACOCK. *Westminster Drollery*, 1671 (J.O.H., 1853).

91. I SAW A FISHPOND. *Folk-Lore*, 1889 (*O.D.N.R.*, No. 167).

91. RIDDLE. Ashton. *Chap-Books of the Eighteenth Century*, 1882 (from *The True Trial of the Understanding*, by S.M.).

91. IF ALL THE WORLD WERE PAPER. *Witts Recreation Augmented*, 1641, as 'Interrogativa Cantilena', a song in questions. A poem of medieval descent – the common memory retaining only the first stanza – touched with the kind of irony which marks some of Ralegh's verse.

92. RATS, DUCKS, DOGS, CATS, PIGS. Ernest Rhys, *Land of Nursery Rhyme*, 1932 (*O.D.N.R.*, No. 437). *flats:* hats.

93. WE'RE ALL IN THE DUMPS. J.O.H., 1842.

93. THERE WAS A MAN OF DOUBLE DEED. Ritson.

93. THERE WAS A MAN AND HE WAS MAD. Personal recollection. A version is also in *Nonsense Verses*, ed. Langford Reed [1925].

97. THERE GOWANS ARE GAY. Herd. *gowans:* spring flowers. *halst:* embraced. *speir:* ask. *syne:* then. *ware:* spend. *know:* hill. *my lane:* alone. *bedeen:* anon. *pansand:* thinking, wondering.

98. THE HAWTHORN. Robbins. Fourteenth century. *everykune:* every kind of. *leman:* lover.

98. WHISTLE O'ER THE LAVE O'T. Herd. *the lave o't:* the rest of it.

99. TOM, HE WAS A PIPER'S SON. The first two stanzas of the song in late eighteenth and early nineteenth century chapbooks called *Tom the Piper's Son*. The remaining four stanzas – if not the second stanza as well – look like awkward additions made for the chapbook publisher (see *O.D.N.R.*, No. 508). Tom seems to have been the stock sobriquet for a bagpiper. The 'tune' Tom the Piper's son played was apparently the burden of the girl in danger of losing her virginity which introduces the ballad of 'The Elfin Knight' (p. 285), the northern plaid having been changed to the top-knot girls wore in their hair.

99. JOHNNIE CAM TO OUR TOUN. R. Chambers, *Scottish Song*, 1829. *tye:* tie-wig. *kittled:* tickled.

100. COCKEREL. Robbins. Fifteenth century. A poem of double entendre. *gentle:* well born. *of gret:* of great (ancestry). *of kinde:* of good family. *inde:* indigo. *asor:* azure. *wortewale:* skin at the root of the spur. *eynen:* eyes. *loken:* set.

100. CAME YOU NOT FROM NEWCASTLE. Hales and Furnivall, *Bishop Percy's Folio Manuscript*, 1867.

101. THE YELLOW-HAIRED LADDIE. Allan Ramsay, *Tea-Table Miscellany*, 1724 (Chambers, *Scottish Songs*, 1829). *brae:* hillside. *yowes:* ewes. *cleadin:* clothing. *bucht:* fold. *butt, ben:* outside, inside. *kirn:* churn.

101. KISS'D YESTREEN. Allan Cunningham, *Songs of Scotland*, 1825. *Gallowgate:* in Glasgow. *mool'd, mell'd:* made love. *carles:* rough common men. *cairds:* tinkers. *sark:* chemise.

101. GREEN GROWS THE RASHES. Herd.

102. GREEN SLEEVES. A song recorded by Robert Burns, printed in *The Merry Muses of Caledonia*, ed. J. Burke & S. G. Smith, 1965.

102. MAY NO MAN SLEEP IN YOUR HALL. Robbins. *tent:* a surgeon's probe. *clogs:* blocks. *bogs:* pangs. *knaps:* knobs. *swaps:* blows. *byes:* bees (i.e. rings, hoops). *swyes:* sways.

103. O MY BONNY, BONNY MAY. Herd. *ae:* one. *a cast:* all cast. *lown:* mistress.

104. BOBBY SHAFTOE. Bell.
The Shaftoe family belongs to Northumberland (Bavington Hall and Benwell) and to Co. Durham (Whitworth Park). The song appears to have been adapted from an earlier Shafto song to serve the parliamentary candidature in 1761 of Robert Shafto of Whitworth Park.

104. MERRY MAY THE KEEL ROW. James Hogg, *Jacobite Relics of Scotland*, 2nd series, 1821. Robert Chambers in his *Scottish Songs*, 1829, calls it a song sung by the Jacobite ladies of the Canongate of Edinburgh. *keel:* a coal boat as used on the Tyne.

105. CAM YE BY THE SALMON FISHERS. Gomme, 1898. Recorded from Moray, from the singing of children in a game. *roperee:* rope-walk.

106. THE FRIAR AND THE NUN. (Richard Kele) *Christmas carolles newely Imprynted*, *c.* 1550. (Greene. No. 461.)
The Latin (*ne nos*) *inducas in tentationem*, lead us not into temptation, from the Lord's Prayer.

106. A MAID OF BRENTEN ARSE. (Richard Keele) *Christmas carolles newely Imprynted. c.* 1550 (Greene. No. 460). *brenten arse:* burnt arse, i.e. a hot number. *iwis:* indeed. *vice:* screw.

107. THERE WAS A MAID WENT TO THE MILL. From Richard Brome's play *A Joviall Crew*, 1652 (Chappell).

107. THE LADY'S SONG IN LEAP YEAR, *O.D.N.R.* No. 299, explaining the descent of this and other versions from a longish broadside of the late seventeenth century.

108. HOGYN. Robbins. Fifteenth century. *awent:* thought. *worshipped:* favoured, honoured. *iwis:* indeed. *leman:* love.

109. KATE DALRYMPLE. By William Watt (1792–1859). *pease-weeps:* lapwings. *plovers:* golden plovers. *whaups:* curlews. *tapsalterie:* topsy-turvy. *surkin':* shirting. *skellie:* squinting.

110. APPLES BE RIPE. Prefixed by Llewelyn Powys (1884–1939) to his novel *Apples be Ripe* (1930), and presumably Powys's own parody of country or nursery rhyme.

110. BLOW THE WINDS, I-HO. Robert Bell. A version of 'The Baffled Knight' (Child, 112) known in many parts of Europe.

112. IF YOU DON'T LIKE MY APPLES. Botkin.

112. THE GARDENER. Child, 219 B. *pingo:* pink. *cammovine:* camomile. *seel o downs:* celandines. *mary mild:* marigold. *lockerin:* curling. *blavers:* cornflowers. *snell:* bitter.

115. THE BROKEN-HEARTED GARDENER. Ashton: *Modern Street Ballads*, 1858.

116. THE DRYNAUN DHUN. Joyce – less one stanza which seems interpolated. *Drynaun Dhun:* blackthorn.

116. BLACKBIRDS AND THRUSHES. Colm O Lochlainn, *More Irish Street Ballads*, 1965 (from Samuel Lover's novel, *Rory O'More*, 1837, but probably, as O Lochlainn says, an older song touched up).

117. O GIN MY LOVE WERE YON RED ROSE. Herd.

117. I KNOW WHERE I'M GOING. Padraic Colum, *Broad-Sheet Ballads*, 1914.

118. BLACK IS THE COLOUR. Sharp & Karpeles, *English Folk Songs of the Southern Appalachian Mountains*, 1932.

118. WESTERN WIND. Chambers & Sidgwick, *Early English Lyrics*, 1907. First half of the sixteenth century. A fragment of a song, and not a poem complete in itself, which makes it none the less moving. The first line has its counterpart in 'Waly, Waly, Gin Love be Bonny' in Allan Ramsay's *Tea-Table Miscellany:*

> Martinmas wind, when wilt thou blaw
> And shake the green leaves off the tree

(see Child, notes to 204). A night-visit song recorded in Dorset early in this century, related to 'The Gray Cock' (Child 248), may descend from the lost original (A. L. Lloyd, *Folk Song in England*, 1967). The man and the girl make love, she sleeps the latter part of the night in his arms, then the cock crows too soon and the girl hastens him away:

> The wind it did blow and the cocks they did crow,
> As I tripped over the plain, plain so very, plain so very, plain,
> So I wished myself back in my true love's arms
> And she in her bed again.

The song is printed, No. 59A, in *The Everlasting Circle*, ed. James Reeves, 1960.

119. SHACKLEY-HAY. Chappell.

119. THE VALIANT SEAMAN'S HAPPY RETURN. C. Stone, *Sea Songs & Ballads*, 1906, from a broadsheet.

124. THE WATERS OF TYNE. Bell.

124. SOURWOOD MOUNTAIN. Sandburg. One of many versions. *jenny:* donkey.

125. SUCKING CIDER THROUGH A STRAW. Sandburg.

126. A KISS IN THE MORNING EARLY. Colm O Lochlainn, *More Irish Street Ballads*, 1965.

131. THE UNQUIET GRAVE. Child 78A. Many versions are still current.

132. LOWLANDS AWAY. Hugill, – who calls it a pumping song, which was later used at windlass and capstan.

133. RARE WILLIE DROWNED IN YARROW. Child, 215A.

133. MAW BONNIE LAD. *Songs and Ballads of Northern England*, Newcastle, 1949. *keel:* coal boat on the Tyne.

134. A MINER COMING HOME ONE NIGHT. Harry Morgan, *More Rugger Songs*, 1968. C.f. 'Go Bring me Back my Blue-Eyed Boy' and 'London City' in Carl Sandburg's *The American Songbag*, 1927.

134. THE RATCATCHER'S DAUGHTER. Ashton.

136. NEDDY NIBBLE'M AND BIDDY FINN. *Wisehart's Merry Songster*, No. 8 (1832).

137. THE SEEDS OF LOVE. Robert Bell. According to T. D. Whitaker's *History of Whalley*, 1801, this famous song, often printed in broadsides, was written by Mrs. Fleetwood Habergham, of Habergham Hall, Padiham, Lancashire, who died in 1703, ruined and disgraced by her husband.

139. FALSE LUVE. Herd (see also Child 218).

139. WHITTINGHAM FAIR. D. D. Dixon, *The Vale of Whittingham*, 1887. The location of the fair changed, according to the locality of the singer.

140. THE PEAR-TREE. Robbins. Fifteenth century. *peryr:* pear tree. *pear Jennet:* a pear ripening at midsummer, St. John's Day (French *poire de Saint-Jean*). *griffin:* graft. *up in her home:* ?right inside her skin (see 'hame' in O.E.D.). *pear Robert:* a pear of the devil who is often known as Robert or Sir Robert. This song appears to be the ancestor of 'I had a little nut-tree' (p. 18).

141. JOLLY JANKIN. Greene. Earlier fifteenth century. *Yol:* Christmas. *have I sel:* have I good fortune. *on a knot:* i.e. at once. *wortes:* green vegetables.

142. THE WAKE AT THE WELL. Greene. Fifteenth century. According to Greene's note the girl is caught by the priest either at a midsummer wake at the holy well (a common locale for such parish wakes or feasts), or when she went to 'wake the well' by

herself. That children are born nine months after the parish feast is still proverbial (cf. 'The Virgin', p. 303). *croke:* crook. *burne:* stream. *rofe my bell-y:* pierced my womb, – but also a pun, plucked away my bell, my treasure. *copious:* well furnished (with presents). *shrew:* curse.

143. BIRD IN A CAGE. A. L. Lloyd, *The Singing Englishman* 1944.

144. O WALY, WALY UP THE BANK. Allan Ramsay, *Tea-Table Miscellany*, 1729. Traditionally occasioned by the separation – for reasons described in the ballad of *Jamie Douglas* (Child 204) – of Lady Barbara Douglas and her husband James, Marquis of Douglas, in 1681. *waly:* woe, alas. *cramasie:* crimson. *fyl'd:* defiled.

Arthur's Seat is the mountain-like hill rising above the palace of Holyrood, Edinburgh. St. Anton's Well (i.e. St. Anthony's Well) is on the side of the hill.

145. UP I AROSE IN VERNO TEMPORE. J. E. Stevens, *Music & Poetry in the Early Tudor Court*, 1961. *in verno tempore:* in the spring time. *sub quadam arbore:* under a certain tree. *in suo pectore:* deep inside her (in her heart). *puerum movere:* a child move.

antiquo tempore: from time past. *solebam ludere:* I used to play. *mihi deridere:* jeer at me. *incipeo flere:* I begin to cry.

meis parentibus: to my parents. *quidam clericus:* a certain cleric. *cum virgis ac fustibus:* with birches and cudgels. *chast:* chastise. *coram omnibus:* in front of everyone.

quid faciam: what shall I do. *vel interficiam:* or kill it. *quo loco fugiam:* what place shall I fly to. *et vitam aeternam:* and life everlasting.

146. O MY BELLY. Northall.

146. NOW JENTIL BELLY DOWN. Ritson, *Ancient Songs*, 1790.

147. THE FOGGY, FOGGY DEW. Sharp & Karpeles, *Folk Songs of the South Appalachians*, 1932.

148. TO KNOW WHOM ONE SHALL MARRY. John Aubrey, *Miscellanies*, 1696. A longer version of this divinatory formula will be found in Chambers.

151. MARRIAGE. Chambers.

151. I HAVE BEEN A FOSTER. J. E. Stevens, *Music & Poetry in the Early Tudor Court*, 1961. One of many forester songs of double meaning. *foster:* forester. *bigg:* build.

151. THERE WAS A LADY LOVED A SWINE. J.O.H., 1842. A song (see *O.D.N.R.*, No. 294) which can be traced back to the early seventeenth century.

152. HARRY PARRY. Ritson.

152. SUPPER IS NA READY. J. Barke & S. G. Smith's edition of *The Merry Muses of Caledonia*, 1965. From a French sixteenth century song. *hinnie:* honey.

152. BLYTHSOME BRIDAL. Herd. It has been attributed to the ballad poet Francis Sempill (?1616–1682). For many of the dishes in this Bruegel-like poem, see F. M. McNeill, *The Scots Kitchen*, 1929. *lilting:* gay singing (to the pipes). *langkail:* kail with the leaves cooked whole. *sawt:* salt. *cogue:* wooden cup. *soutar:* cobbler. *blutter:* ?gabbler, ? (O.E.D.) dirty. *tinkler:* tinker. *sowlibber:* gelder of sows. *plucky-fac'd:* pimply-faced. *capper-nos'd:* copper-nosed. *wons:* dwells. *how:* hollow. *mool:* make love. *stool:* of repentance in the kirk. *buckled:* i.e. married to. *coft:* bought. *gleed:* squinting. *wame:* belly. *Mons Meg:* fifteenth century cannon at Edinburgh Castle. *flea-lugged:* flea eared. *sharney-fac'd:* cowpat-faced. *shangy-mou'd:* with a mouth like a cleft stick. *halucket:* giddy, foolish. *happer-arsed:* with arse like a hopper. *girn-again:* grin-again. *glaiket:* flighty. *measly-shin'd:* spotty-legged. *pearlings:* gowns edged with thread-lace. *sybows, risarts, carlings:* chives, radishes, parched pease. *sodden:* boiled. *fadges:* rolls of bread. *brochen:* oatmeal with water, honey and butter. *fouth:* plenty. *gabbocks:* mouth-fuls. *powsowdie:* sheep's head soup. *drammock and crowdie:* oatmeal mixed in either case with water. *caller nowtfeet:* fresh cow's feet. *partens:* crabs. *buckies:* whelks. *whytens:* whitings. *spaldings:* split and dried fish. *scadlips* (scald lips): hot barley broth. *lapper'd milk kebbucks:* curdled milk cheeses. *sowens:* soured and fermented oatmeal. *farles:* oatcakes cut in quarters. *baps:* flour and yeast rolls. *swats:* small ale. *caps:* drinking bowls. *mealkale:* soup of oatmeal and vegetables. *castocks:* (kale stocks) cabbage stems. *skink:* beef and vegetable soup. *rive:* burst. *brander:* gridiron. *flowkes:* flatfish. *dulse, tangles:* kinds of edible sea-weeds. *snishing:* snuff. *prie:* try.

155. MA CANNY HINNY. Bell. The scene is Newcastle. *canny:* nice, pleasant, winsome. *hinny:* honey. *pick night:* pitch dark. *hing on the girdle:* hang on the griddle. *singin hinny:* i.e. a griddle cake, a 'singing honey' singing or sizzling as it cooks.

156. ROBERTIN TUSH. M. A. Mason, *Nursery Rhymes & Country Songs*, 1877. The hard cheeses of Banbury, sold round the market cross, were famous from the sixteenth century to the end of the eighteenth century.

156. KISSING OF MY DAME. J.O.H., 1842.

157. THE HUNT IS UP. Ritson, *Ancient Songs*, 1790.

157. LITTLE BILLY. Bell. A version of a folk tale (Aarne and Thompson's Type 1735 A) known also in France and other countries.

157. OH LUCKY JIM! Ahlstrand, *Anthology of Anglo-Saxon Songs*, 1951. From the United States.

158. THE OLD FARMER AND HIS YOUNG WIFE. Williams (Child 274). The versions given by Child from Scotland and a broadside are less good.

160. MY AULD WIFE. John Buchan, *The Northern Muse*, 1924. *sturt:* quarrelling. *the maut's aboon the meal:* the malt's above the meal, phrase used of being drunk. *the nicht:* tonight. *baff:* biff, beat. *greet:* weep.

163. THE ENGLISH. Robert Fabyan's *Prima Pars Cronecarum*, 1516, where it is given as a Scottish comment made when the Scots met English courtiers in 1328, for the marriage of Edward III's sister to David Bruce, afterwards David II of Scotland.

163. A SCOT, A WELSH AND AN IRISH MAN. *Witts Recreations Augmented*, 1641.

163. SHON A MORGAN. J.O.H., 1849.

163. TAFFY WAS A WELSHMAN. J.O.H., 1842. (See also *O.D.N.R.*, No. 495.)

164. I AM OF IRELAND. Robbins. Fourteenth century. Jotted down without line division on a strip of vellum in a Bodleian manuscript, it is supposed to have been part of a carol, the first three lines being taken as the burden. Possibly the couplet about Shropshire in the much later 'The Properties of the Shires of England' (p. 168) may have belonged to the original poem, making an apt answer:

> I am of Ireland and of the holy land of Ireland.
> Good sir, pray I thee for of saint charity
> Come and dance with me for Ireland.
>
> I am of Shropshire, my shins be sharp:
> Lay wood to the fire and dress me my harp –

i.e. I have nimble shins, make up the fire and let's have music, and dance we will.

164. BRYAN O'LYNN. Williams. One of many versions of what appears by origin to have been a sixteenth century nonsense song adapted to insult the Scotch ('Tommy Linn is a Scotchman born') and then the Irish. See *O.D.N.R.*, No. 514.

165. HO, BROTHER TEIG. Marshall.
Tory – 'In the 17th century one of the dispossest Irish, who became outlaws, subsisting by plundering and killing the

English settlers and soldiers; a bog-trotter, a rapparee'. *Oxford English Dictionary*.

166. YANKEE DOODLE. Lomax, 1934. It seems to have been, first of all, an English song ridiculing the country bumpkins of New England, at the time of the American War of Independence.

166. THE ISLE OF MAN. *Denham Tracts*, Folk-Lore Society, 1891.

166. HOW THE FIRST HIELANDMAN OF GOD WAS MADE. The Bannatyne MS. (sixteenth century) National Library, Edinburgh. *sport word:* joking word. *pykit:* pointed. *draff:* rubbish. *leuch:* laughed. *lap:* leaped. *gully:* large knife. *fast:* carefully. *braid roun:* breadth, or space, around. *plaid neuk:* nook or corner of his plaid.

168. JOHN HIELANDMAN. Maclagan, *Games and Diversions of Argyleshire*, 1901. Descended from the poem above on the creation of the Highlander.

168. THE PROPERTIES OF THE SHIRES OF ENGLAND. Thomas Hearn's edition of *The Itinerary of John Leland*, Vol. 5, with part of a line from the version in Harleian MS. 7371, and substitution (last word) of 'I' for 'we'. *wring pear:* press pear, i.e. maker of perry. *bere:* barley. *resortere:* ?resetter, harbourer of thieves. *make:* mate. *thwakkere:* thatcher. *tot for sote:* hill indeed. *Pinnokshire:* Pinnock in Gloucestershire. *goote and kene:* goat and kine.

169. BUCKINGHAMSHIRE. Chambers.

169. LANCASHIRE BORN. Ritson; but there, with differences, referring to Lincolnshire. Lancashire was for long the poorest of English counties.

170. THE MERCHANTS OF LONDON. J.O.H., 1844. Chappell prints the song 'London is a Fine Town', from Playford's *The Dancing Master*, 1665, which begins 'Oh London is a fine town, and a gallant city;/'Tis govern'd by the scarlet gown. . . .'

170. A, U, HINNY BURD. Stokoe, *Songs and Ballads of Northern England*, 1892. A Northumbrian nurse's song. *hinny:* honey. *ragin':* raking. *Keelers:* men working a keel or coal boat. *trolly bags:* trollops. *seut:* soot.

171. STRAND ON THE GREEN. Northall. On the edge of the Thames, Twickenham.

171. WINWICK, LANCASHIRE. Northall.

171. ERITH, ON THE THAMES. Graves. ? A modern literary piece. Erith was formerly an anchorage for East Indiamen.

172. AT BRILL ON THE HILL. J.O.H., 1853.

172. I WENT TO NOKE. Graves. Noke, Thame, Burford, Beckley, all in Oxfordshire; Brill, in Buckinghamshire, near Thame.

172. THE RIVER DART. R. L. Tongue, *Somerset Folklore*, Folk-Lore Society, 1965.

172. THE DART. Murray's *Handbook for Travellers in Devonshire*, 1879.

172. HORSEY GAP. Walter Rye, *Recreations of an Antiquary*, 1920. Horsey Gap on the coast of Norfolk near Hickling Broad, opening the way in to Horning and the fens of the Bure.

173. THE POWTE'S COMPLAINT. Chambers, *Book of Days*, 1869. A longer version in Sir William Dugdale's *History of Imbanking and Draining*, 1772. *powte:* the freshwater fish now better known as the burbot — 'The river wezell or eele poult is to be found in Norwich river and in the broads . . . as also in marsh land, a delicate dish.' (Sir Thomas Browne, *Notes on the Natural History of Norfolk.*) *boots:* i.e. leather waders. *skatches:* stilts. *Twopenny Jack:* the stickleback or Jack Sharp. *whirligigs:* windmills for pumping. *mean thee:* destine thee.

174. BOSTON, LINCOLNSHIRE. Wright. Other versions add a line after steeple — 'A proud, conceited, ignorant people'. This is said to have been made up out of disappointment with the effects of the Grand Sluice, opened in 1766 (Gutch & Peacock, *County Folklore, Lincolnshire*, 1908).

174. LEGSBY, LINCOLNSHIRE. North, *Church Bells of Lincoln*, 1882. *thack:* thatched.

174. ACTON BEAUCHAMP. Northall.

175. HOO, SUFFOLK. Forby's *Vocabulary of East Anglia*, 1830. A small village in a small parish.

175. THE PEOPLE OF BLAKENEY. Harvey, *Ballads, Songs & Rhymes of East Anglia*, 1935. Blakeney in Norfolk.

175. THE RIVER DON. Moorman.

175. PRESTON. Wright. East Preston, on the Suffolk coast.

175. THE PENTLAND HILLS. *Nicht at Eenie*, Samson Press, 1932. The Pentland Hills, s.w. of Edinburgh. Sir William Forbes (1739–1806), Edinburgh banker. *corbies:* rooks.

175. DURHAM OLD WOMEN. Bell.

176. PIGS O'PELTON. Sir Cuthbert Sharp, *Bishoprick Garland*, 1834. Pelton, a village in Co. Durham. A lonin is a village pasture separated from ploughland by a dyke or wall.

176. THE WIVES OF SPITTAL. *The Denham Tracts*, Folk-Lore Society, 1891. Spittal, in Northumberland, near Berwick-upon-Tweed. *kail:* cabbage. *broo':* broth.

176. TWEED AND TILL. Chambers. These lines, Chambers wrote, 'when I first heard them pronounced by the deep voice of Sir Walter Scott, seemed to me to possess a solemnity approaching to poetry'.

176. PONT AND BLYTH. *Denham Tracts*, Folk-Lore Society, 1891.

177. CAULD CORNWOOD. *Denham Tracts*, Folk-Lore Society, 1891. Cornwood is a small district of bleak, high moorland near Alston, Cumberland, within sight of Cross Fell, 2930 feet.

177. TINTOCK. Chambers. Tinto Hill, rising to 2335 feet out of flattish country near Lanark. The cup, according to Chambers, was a hole, usually full of water, in a huge stone impossible to lift.

177. GIN I WERE A DOO. *Nicht at Eenie*, Samson Press, 1932. *gin:* if. *doo:* pigeon (dove). *neb:* beak. *fit:* foot. *ilka:* every. *lums:* chimneys.

177. LITTLE DUNKELD. Chambers, *Scottish Songs*. Traditional stanza, to which other stanzas were added. Little Dunkeld, on the Tay, in Perthshire, is the parish which contains Birnam Wood. *stickit:* stabbed. *dung down:* knocked down.

178. JOHNSHAVEN. Chambers. Johnshaven, a fishing village in Kincardineshire.

178. BUCHLYVIE. Chambers. Buchlyvie, a village in Stirlingshire.

178. MANOR WATER. Chambers. Manor Water, in south Peeble-shire, flows into the Tweed. Posso is in the Manor valley. *cleugh:* glen. *bere:* barley.

178. IDAHO. Lomax, *Our Singing Country*, 1941.

179. THE CODFISH SHANTY. One of many versions (see Hugill).

183. THE WARS OF THE ROSES. Graves. And by him?

183. THE NORFOLK REBELLION. Both rhymes, *Harvey's Ballads, Songs & Rhymes of East Anglia*, 1935.
 Robert Kett's agrarian rebellion, 1549, was ended with great slaughter in Dussyn's Dale outside Norwich. The rhyme about the country gnoffes was said to have been a prophecy[*] which

persuaded Kett to leave his encampment on Mousehold Heath, and give battle in the open ground where the Earl of Warwick's mercenaries had the advantage.

184. A LAMENT FOR THE PRIORY OF WALSINGHAM. Bodleian Library, MS. Rawl. Poet. 219. The Augustinian priory of Walsingham, one of the three great pilgrimage centres of England, was suppressed in 1538. *peers:* company, companions. *palmers:* pilgrims.

185. SIR FRANCIS DRAKE; OR EIGHTY-EIGHT. *Roxburghe Ballads*, Vol. VI, 1889, from a broadside of 1670. *Knight of the Sun:* from *The Mirrour of Princely Deedes and Knighthood wherein is shown the worthiness of the Knight of the Sun*, the first part of which was translated (1578) from the Spanish of Diego Ortunez de Calahorra.

186. BAD BISHOP JEGON. *Norfolk and Norwich Annual*, 1889. John Jegon (1550–1618), Master of Corpus Christi, Cambridge, Vice-Chancellor of Cambridge University and Bishop of Norwich, a man short, fat, ugly, severe, miserly, and witty. *Luddom:* Ludham, where Jegon built a palace, destroyed by fire. *devine:* ?divine office. *strop and waste:* legal term, strip and waste (estrepement). *Alsome:* Aylsham. *glossing:* glozing, smooth talk. *oserie:* usury. *gear:* goings on.

188. KING CHARLES THE FIRST. J.O.H., 1843. Hubert le Sueur's bronze equestrian statue of Charles I was set up after the Restoration at Charing Cross, some 200 yards from its present site. *O.D.N.R.* calls this quatrain 'a Puritan jingle satirizing the unhibited emotions of the Royalists.' It seems unlikely.

189. THE PARLIAMENT SOLDIERS. *O.D.N.R.*, No. 395. A vengeful song of the Restoration.

189. THE BATTLE OF SOLE BAY. W. A. Dutt, *Highways and Byways of East Anglia*, 1901. The Battle of Sole (i.e. Southwold Bay), May 28, 1672, in the Third Dutch War – fierce and prolonged, but indecisive and far from 'the rarest victory since the Armada'. The cliff top at Dunwich must have afforded a good view.

190. O WHAT'S THE RHYME TO PORRINGER. Hogg, *Jacobite Relics of Scotland*, 1819. On William of Orange's succession to James II, whose daughter he had married.

191. THE BONNY MOORHEN. Hogg, *Jacobite Relics of Scotland*, 1819. A song of the Jacobite rising of 1715, the moorhen (capercaillie, from the description) being the Old Chevalier. *butt:* in the direction of the kitchen. *ben:* in direction of the parlour.

191. THE ORANGE LILY. O Lochlainn, *Irish Street Ballads*, 1939. A Belfast song of the Orangemen.

192. OLD ORANGE FLUTE. O Lochlainn, *Irish Street Ballads*, 1939.

193. THE WEARING OF THE GREEN. Sparling, *Irish Minstrelsy*, 1887. A street ballad of 1798. *Napper Tandy:* James Napper Tandy (1740–1803), Irish revolutionary patriot, co-founder of the United Irishmen.

194. THE SHAN VAN VOCHT. A street ballad of 1797, when the French fleet reached Bantry Bay, printed with variants in *The Nation*, 29.x.1842. *Shan van Vocht:* the Poor Old Woman, i.e. Ireland. *Lord Edward:* Lord Edward Fitzgerald (1763–1798), Irish patriot and rebel leader, died in Newgate prison.

196. LORD WATERFORD. A different but equally racy version of this derivative from the 'Shan van Vocht' is printed by Colm O Lochlainn in *More Irish Street Ballads*, from a ballad-sheet of about 1906. Colm O Lochlainn says it may have been written by a journalist Michael A. Moran.

197. WHAT WILL WE DO FOR LINEN? Marshall.

197. I AM THE DUKE OF NORFOLK. *Suffolk Garland*, 1818.
The words were sung at Suffolk harvest suppers, one man kneeling and offering ale to another crowned with a cushion, who had to drink the ale without spilling a drop or allowing the cushion to fall. *I am the Duke of Norfolk* was the name of a dance tune familiar in the early seventeenth century, and given by Chappell. The ceremony, with all the words, is described in A. S. Harvey's *Ballads, Songs & Rhymes of East Anglia*, 1935.

197. THE GRAND OLD DUKE OF YORK. See *O.D.N.R.*, No. 550, for the many versions of this rhyme, adapted to Frederick Duke of York (1763–1827), who tops the column in Waterloo Place, in London. He commanded the English troops in Flanders, 1793–1795 and was then commander-in-chief through most of the Napoleonic Wars, and after Waterloo until his death.

198. THE VICAR OF BRAY. *Edinburgh Musical Miscellany*, 1788, slightly different from other printings, e.g. in the *British Musical Miscellany*, 1734. The actual vicar of Bray, Berkshire, adapted to the Georgian era in the ballad, was Simon Aleyn, who kept his cure under Henry VIII, Edward VI, Mary, and Elizabeth I. Chappell quotes a statement that the ballad was written by a soldier in Colonel Fuller's dragoons in the reign of George I.

200. ENGLAND FOREVER AND DO IT NO MORE. Henderson.

201. THE DODGER. Botkin.

205. LABOURS OF THE MONTHS. Robbins. *delfe:* dig. *thynge:* seeds. *inow:* enough.

205. JOG ON, JOG ON, THE FOOTPATH WAY. *An Antidote against Melancholy*, 1601. The first four lines quoted by Shakespeare in *A Winter's Tale* (IV. 3). The song & music are discussed by Chappell.

206. JOHN GRUMLIE. Cunningham, *Songs of Scotland*, 1825. Derived from 'The Wife of Auchtermuchty' in the sixteenth century Bannatyne MS., National Library, Edinburgh. J.O.H. prints an English version, 'The Old Man and his Wife.' *maut:* malt. *reel the tweel:* roll the twill. *hawkit:* white-spotted. *crummie:* cow with a crumple horn. *kirned:* churned. *knowe:* hill. *stots:* steers, oxen. *kep:* keep, care.

207. A WOMAN IS A WORTHY THING. Greene. Early sixteenth century.

208. CHAMBER-POT RHYME. Often inscribed, together with an eye, inside chamber-pots.

208. THE BLACKSMITH'S SONG. Williams.

209. TURKEY IN THE STRAW. Sandburg. A song of the 1830's. 'This is the classical American rural tune. . . . It has been sung at horses and mules from a million wagons. It has a thousand verses if all were collected.' *day-day:* bye-bye. *wagon tongue:* the wagon pole. *tuckahaw:* the truffle-like 'Indian Bread'.

210. RIDDLE. *Booke of Meery Riddles*, 1629. Taylor 1632–1641. *O.D.N.R.* pp. 435–46.

210. DRUMDELGIE. J. Ord, *Bothy Ballads and Songs*, 1930. *toon:* farmstead. *brose:* hot milk and oatmeal. *neeps:* turnips. *owsen:* oxen. *strae raips:* straw ropes. *queet:* the lower part of the ox's leg, the cannon bone. *saiddler:* ? saddle horse.

211. THE PLOUGHMAN. Bell. *dyke:* fence, hedge, wall.

212. THE BANKS OF THE CONDAMINE. D. Stewart and N. Keesing, *Old Bush Songs*, 1957. *ringer:* highest scoring sheep shearer in a shed. *squatter:* sheep station owner. *selection:* piece of land selected and taken up under Australian Land Law. *jumbucks:* sheep.

213. THE WAGGONER. Bell. *gang:* go(ing). *poke:* bag, sack. *pock brocken:* pock-marked. *staithe:* coal wharf. *posey:* flowered, posy-embroidered.

214. THE MILLER OF DEE. Williams.

215. THE BONNY KEEL LADDIE. Bell. *keel:* coal boat on the Tyne. *huddock:* small cabin on a keel. *canny:* nice, good, agreeable.

215. WE'LL GO TO SEA NO MORE. Iliffe, *Songs of the Seaports*, 1861. Less four lines of refrain which seem a clerical sententious addition (Iliffe was a clergyman at North Shields). *low:* blaze.

216. THE FISHER'S LIFE. Iliffe, *Songs of the Seaports*, 1861.

217. RHYME OF THE FISHERMEN'S CHILDREN. Moorman.

217. THE GREENLAND WHALE. Edward Thomas, *Pocket Book of Poems and Songs*, 1907. There are many broadside versions, the first known dating from the early eighteenth century. (See R. Vaughan Williams and A. L. Lloyd, *Penguin Book of English Folksongs*, 1959.)

219. THE BANKS OF NEWFOUNDLAND. A. L. Lloyd, *Folk Song in England*, 1967.

220. THE BUFFALO SKINNERS. Lomax, 1934. *croton coffee:* ?nasty-tasting like croton oil. *gray-backs:* lice. *six and needle gun:* the Dreyse rifle.

221. DRIVING THE MULE. Botkin.

222. THE GRINDERS. A. L. Lloyd, *Folk Song in England*, 1967. (From the *Sheffield Daily Telegraph*, 18. xi. 1865.)

223. THE BLACKLEG MINERS. A. L. Lloyd, *Folk Song in England*, 1967. From Co. Durham. *dorty:* dirty. *toon-raw:* town-row. *hoy:* heave.

224. DE BLACK GIRL. Lomax, 1934.

225. THE GRESFORD DISASTER. A. L. Lloyd, *Come All Ye Bold Miners*, 1952. The colliery disaster at Gresford, in the Denbighshire coalfield, in 1934, cost 268 lives.

226. AN INVITATION TO LUBBERLAND. Ashton, *Humour, Wit and Satire of the Seventeenth Century*, 1883, from a broadside published between 1684 and 1688; which descends from the medieval fancy of a Land of Cockaigne, which in turn has classical analogues. Cf. Bruegel's great picture at Munich, and the Anglo-Irish poem, 'The Land of Cokaygne', of the fourteenth century —

> Ther beth rivers gret and fine
> Of oile, melk, honi and wine. . . .

> Ther beth bowres and halles,
> Al of pasteies beth the walles.

(in Bennett & Smithers, *Early Middle English Verse and Prose*, 1966). *powder'd beef:* salted and spiced beef (*The Land of Cokaygne* offers larks 'pudrid' with cloves and cinnamon).

228. THE BEGGARS ARE COMING TO TOWN. Ritson.

228. THE BIG ROCK CANDY MOUNTAINS. Botkin. Descended from the English ballad above, p. 226. *hamming:* showing off. *handouts:* food given to a hobo. *box-car:* freight-car on railway. *rock-and-rye:* ice and rye-whisky. *whangdoodle:* imaginary bird. *shacks:* tramps. *bulls:* policemen.

230. CRAIGBILLY FAIR. Richard Hayward, *Ulster Songs and Ballads*, 1925, probably from a broadside. *Ball-o'-Wax:* polite alteration of Ballocks.

231. HALLELUJAH, BUM AGAIN. M. Lomax, 1934.

232. SHOVELLING IRON ORE. Sandburg.

232. REASON I STAY ON JOB SO LONG. Lomax, 1934.

235. WE BE SOLDIERS THREE. Ravenscroft's *Deuteromelia*, 1609.

235. THE FORTY-SECOND. *Nicht at Eenie*, Samson Press, 1932. *waupinschaw:* ('weapon show') muster of arms. *chappit tatties:* chipped potatoes. *the Broomie-Law:* the quay along the Clyde at Glasgow. *ava:* at all.

236. DO LI A. Bell. *Black Cuffs:* the York Militia. *Green Cuffs:* 23rd or Western Dragoons. *sark:* chemise.

236. ARTHUR MCBRIDE. Joyce.

238. THE GRENADIER. J.O.H., 1842 (see also *O.D.N.R.*).

238. CAPTAIN BOVER. Bruce and Stokoe, *Northumbrian Minstrelsy*, 1882. John Bover, 'regulating officer', Port of Newcastle upon Tyne, d. 1782 (A. L. Lloyd, *Folk Song in England*). *canny hinny:* dear honey.

238. HERE'S THE TENDER COMING. A. L. Lloyd, *Folk Song in England*, 1967 (Bruce and Stokoe, *Northumbrian Minstrelsy*, 1882, and the John Bell MS.).

238. OH CRUEL WAS THE PRESS-GANG. *A Collection of Nursery Rhymes*, Poetry Bookshop, 1922.

239. DEATH OF ADMIRAL BENBOW. Halliwell, *Early Naval Ballads*, 1841. Vice-Admiral Benbow, d. 1702, from chain-shot wounds after an engagement with the French, in which he was deserted by his captains, Kirkby and Wade, who were tried and hanged.

241. JOHNNY, I HARDLY KNEW YE. Sparling, *Irish Minstrelsy*, 1887. According to Sparling, it dates from the beginning of the nineteenth century 'when Irish regiments were so extensively raised for the East Indian service.'

242. SOLDIERS. N. Rosten, *The Big Road*, 1945. Found written up in a U.S. army latrine.

245. THE THREE RAVENS. Ravenscroft's *Melismata*, 1611 (Child 36). *leman:* lover.

246. **THE LAMENT OF THE BORDER WIDOW.** Scott's *Minstrelsy of the Scottish Border.* The occasion of this coronach or lament is said by Scott to have been the execution by James V of Cockburn of Henderland, a free-booter in the border country. *poin'd:* seized and sold. *mane:* moan. *happ'd:* covered. *moul:* mould. *ae:* one.

247. **ROBIN HOOD AND ALLEN A DALE.** Child, 138, from a broadside of the second half of the seventeenth century. *stint nor lin:* stop nor cease.

250. **BONNY GEORGE CAMPBELL.** Child, 210C. *toom:* empty.

251. **SONG OF THE MURDERED CHILD.** Chambers. From the story (given in Chambers) of the boy who was cooked in the pot by his mother. *doo:* dove.

251. **THE LADY ISABELLA'S TRAGEDY.** Ashton, *A Century of Ballads,* 1887, from a broadside of the late seventeenth century. Cf. the version in Percy's *Reliques.* Without much humour Child (*Popular Ballads,* V, p. 34) called it 'perhaps the silliest ballad that ever was made'. It was very popular. On the edge of parody, doesn't it recall the verse tales of Southey – or Wordsworth?

254. **BRENNAN ON THE MOOR.** Joyce. From a broadside. Brennan was hanged in 1804.

256. **THE BOYS OF MULLAGHBAWN.** Joyce, *c.* 1798. Mullaghbawn is in Co. Armagh.

256. **THE LINCOLNSHIRE POACHER.** Robert Bell, with the fourth stanza added. Eighteenth century.

257. **JIM JONES AT BOTANY BAY.** MacAlister, *Old Pioneering Days in the Sunny South,* Goulburn, 1907. Jack Donohoo, also the subject of a ballad (W. R. Mackenzie's *Ballads and Sea Songs of Nova Scotia,* 1928) was transported to Australia in 1823. He escaped, and was killed by the police in 1830.

259. **WALTZING MATILDA.** As first published in 1903 to go with an advertisement for Billy Tea, *Australian Encyclopaedia,* 1958, Vol. 9. Supposedly written by the poet A. B. Patterson (1864–1941). Russel Ward's article on 'Waltzing Matilda", in *Australian Signpost,* ed. T. A. G. Hungerford, 1956, intimates that earlier versions were known and repeats a suggestion that 'Waltzing Matilda' derives from an English song 'The Bold Fusilier':

> A gay fusilier was marching down through Rochester,
>   Bound for the wars in the Low Country,
> And he cried as he tramped through the dear streets of
>   Rochester –
>   'Who'll be a sojer for Marlbro' with me?'

Australian accounts only give the first stanza and chorus of
'The Bold Fusilier', which appears otherwise unknown.
swagman: tramp with his swag or bedding-roll. *billabong:* loop
or blind channel of a river. *coolabah tree:* a species of gum-tree.
Matilda: a swag. *waltzing Matilda:* carrying a swag. *jumbuck:*
sheep. *tucker-bag:* food bag. *squatter:* owner of a sheep station.

260. SHE WAS POOR, BUT SHE WAS HONEST. Many versions exist of
this Victorian music-hall song. This from W. H. Auden, *Oxford
Book of Light Verse*, 1938.

261. THE NIGHT BEFORE LARRY WAS STRETCHED. H. H. Sparling,
Irish Minstrelsy, 1887. Early nineteenth century. *glims:*
candles. *trap-case:* coffin. *Jack Ketch:* i.e. the hangman. *waked:*
i.e. given a wake. *daddle:* fist. *rumbler:* cart. *numbing chit:*
gallows. Probably written by one of Dublin wits.

263. THE GAOL SONG. *J.F.S.S.*, VII.

264. BIRMINGHAM JAIL. Botkin.

265. THE WORKHOUSE BOY. Ashton.

266. COCAINE LIL AND MORPHINE SUE. Auden, *Oxford Book of
Light Verse*, 1938 (a richer version than, e.g., in Carl Sandburg's
American Songbag).

267. JOHN CHEROKEE. A hauling or capstan shanty (also known as
Alabama), derived from a negro work-song. See Hugill.

269. CAPTAIN HALL. One of many variants of a song originating
in the broadside ballad on the chimney sweep Jack Hall, who
was hanged for murder.

270. WILLY THE WEEPER. Lomax, 1960.

271. HANGING JOHNNY. John Masefield, *A Sailor's Garland*, 1906.
Masefield wrote of this halyard shanty, with its saddening
melancholy tune, 'I heard it for the first time off the Horn,
in a snowstorm when we were hoisting topsails after heavy
weather. There was a heavy, grey sea running and the decks
were awash. The skies were sodden and oily, shutting in the sea
about a quarter of a mile away. . . . I thought at the time that
it was the whole scene set to music.' In other versions Johnny
hangs father, sister, granny and the whole family.

271. MARY ARNOLD. Ashton.

277. RIDDLES WISELY EXPOUNDED. Child IC. He also prints a
fifteenth century version. *speird:* inquired. *unco:* uncouth.
pies: magpies. *Clootie:* the devil. *waur:* worse.

278. THE TWA MAGICIANS. Child 44. *forebye:* apart. *leman:* lover.
peel: pool. *dreel:* drill, piercing. *fill:* copulate. *slack:* low, wet
ground. *girdle:* griddle. *ca'ed:* drove.

280. **CLERK COLVILL.** Child 42B, with changes from eighteenth century MS., in stanza 5, and addition of stanza 6, as in Friedman, *Viking Book of Ballads*, 1956. The ballad is incomplete; evidently the mermaid is having her own back for desertion. *speer'd:* asked. *gare:* triangle of cloth.

282. **GREY GOOSE AND GANDER.** J.O.H., 1844. A verse from a folktale such as 'The Grey Goose Feathers' (Briggs and Tongue, *Folktales of England*, 1965)?

282. **THE GREAT SILKIE OF SULE SKERRIE.** Child 113. From the Shetlands. Sule Skerry (i.e. seal skerry): ocean reef west of Orkney. *grumly:* fierce looking.

283. **THE PADDA SONG.** Chambers, *Scottish Songs*, 1829. The verses in a cante-fable. *padda:* frog. *hinnie:* honey.

284. **SONG OF THE CAULD LAD OF HYLTON.** Sharp, *Bishoprick Garland*, 1834. The Cauld Lad was a hobthrush or drudging goblin who lived at Hylton Castle, Co. Durham, now a ruin surrounded by council houses.

285. **THE HOBTHRUSH.** Moorman.

285. **THE ELFIN KNIGHT.** Child 2A, from a late seventeenth century broadside. *plaid:* woollen cloak worn over one shoulder. *kist:* chest. *sark:* chemise. *ley-land:* pasture. *eare:* plough. *bigg:* make. *barn it in a mouse-holl:* i.e. put the corn in a mouse hole for a barn. *loof:* palm of the hand.

286. **THE WEE WEE MAN.** Ernest Rhys, *Fairy Gold* [1907]. An English variant of Child 38. *effet:* eft or newt.

288. **HARPKIN.** Chambers. *brae:* hill. *brichter:* more brightly. *strae:* straw. *thrave:* two stooks of corn. *draff:* hog wash.

288. **THE FALSE KNIGHT UPON THE ROAD.** Child 3. For an English version, in which the speakers are Meet-on-the-Road and Child-as-it-Stood, see Pamela Grey, *The White Wallet*, 1928. *atweel:* to be sure, of course. *peit:* peat (a peat carried to school as a contribution to the fire).

290. **WITCH'S BROOMSTICK SPELL.** From Issobel Gowdie's Second Confession, at her trial, 3rd. May, 1662. Dalyell, *Darker Superstitions of Scotland*, 1834.

290. **WITCH'S MILKING CHARM.** Chambers. It was thought that a cow which was being magically (and invisibly) milked, lowed in a peculiar way. One defence was 'to lay a twig of rowan-tree, bound with a scarlet thread, across the threshold of the byre' (Chambers).

290. AGAINST WITCHES. Chambers. *luggie:* wooden vessel for milk. *lammer bead:* amber bead.

290. CUSHY COW, BONNY. *Songs for the Nursery*, 1805. Mentioned in Chambers as a counter charm used by milk-maids. *cushy:* darling, gentle. *tce:* a tie, i.e. rope or halter.

290. THE STRANGE VISITOR. Chambers. *reeled:* wound her yarn.

293. UNFORTUNATE MISS BAILEY. By George Coleman the Younger (1762–1836), from *Broad Grins* (1872). It was sung in his play *Love Laughs at Locksmiths* (Haymarket Theatre, 1803), and was familiar from broadsides and song books.

297. NEW YEAR'S WATER. *Manners & Customs of the People of Tenby*, 1858. In Tenby and elsewhere in South Wales children went round on New Year's morning with a bunch of evergreens and water drawn from a well, and sprinkled householders and everyone in each house, singing this song. The custom is described in T. M. Owen's *Welsh Folk Customs*, 1968. *levy dew:* ? the early form *levedi* or *lavedi*, for (Our) Lady, or French *lever-Dieu*, Elevation of the Host, so that the third line would celebrate the Bread, the Wine, and the Water. *Fair Maid:* ? Our Lady.

297. THE MOON SHINES BRIGHT. Sandys, *Christmas Carols, Ancient & Modern*, 1833, from a broadside. Cf. 'New Year's Water', above.

298. THE WHITE PATERNOSTER. Chambers.

298. NOW I LAY ME DOWN TO SLEEP. *New England Primer*, late seventeenth century.

299. IF YOU WANT TO GO TO HEBEN. N. I. White, *American Negro Folk Songs*, 1928. *sue:* suet.

299. THE CHERRY-TREE CAROL. Sandys, *Christmas Carols, Ancient & Modern*, 1833 (Child 51). Sandys drew attention to the resemblance between the carol and the cherry tree dialogue of Mary and Joseph in one of the two Coventry Mystery Plays (fifteenth century). The cherry tree is a northern substitution for the palm tree in the *Gospel of Pseudo-Matthew*.

300. SUNNY BANK. Broadway and Maitland, *English County Songs*, 1893. Many versions. See *Oxford Book of Carols*, Nos. 3 and 18, and Routley, *The English Carol*, 1966. The carol is said to originate in the translation of the presumed relics of the Three Kings from Milan to Cologne. The relics left Milan in 1162, were taken over the Alps, and were then sailed down the Rhine, reaching Cologne on July 23rd, 1164.

301. THE HOLLY AND THE IVY. *Oxford Book of Carols*, No. 38. For fifteenth century carols of the holly and the ivy, see Greene. The holly symbolized men, in opposition to women, symbolized by the clinging ivy. This contention was thought of particularly at Christmas, when red berries of the holly contrast with the subfusc fruit of the ivy. On Christmas Day it was unlucky for women to be the first to enter a house. The scarlet-berried holly of wintery shine and glow easily became affined to Christ's birth and passion.

302. HOW GRAND AND HOW BRIGHT. Sylvester, *A Garland of Christmas Carols*, 1861. According to Sylvester, from a Birmingham printed broadside of the seventeenth century.

303. THE VIRGIN. Carleton Brown, *Religious Lyrics of the Fourteenth Century*, 1952. A fragment (cf. 'The Wake at the Well', p. 142) to do with village 'feasts' at the holy well. *bote of bale:* remedy of woe. *here a forn:* heretofore. *wol seche:* will seek.

303. THE BITTER WITHY. *N. and Q.*, 1905. From medieval miracle legends akin to the miracles in the apocryphal gospels of the infancy of Christ. The sources are given by G. H. Gerould, 'The Ballad of the *Bitter Withy*', P.M.L.A., 23. 1908.

305. THE HOLY WELL. Sandys, *Christmas Carols, Ancient and Modern*, 1833, from a broadside. Evidently related to 'The Bitter Withy' above, making Mary suggest unChristlike retribution.

306. ME RUETH, MARY. Carleton Brown: *English Lyrics of the Thirteenth Century*, 1932. *wod:* wood (of the Cross). *rode:* complexion (that which is ruddy).

307. THE ELDER, OR BOURTREE. Chambers.

307. NEVER SAID A MUMBALIN' WORD. Lomax, 1934.

308. THE CORPUS CHRISTI CAROL. Greene, from the commonplace book of Richard Hill *c.* 1500–1535, Balliol College, Oxford. It has been over-ingeniously explained as involving the legend of the Grail. The explanation by R. T. Davies (*Medieval English Lyrics*, 1963) seems more sensible – that this is a carol of the familiar Easter ceremony in which an image of Christ, with a cross and the reserved Host, was 'buried' in the chancel on Good Friday in a wooden Easter Sepulchre, richly coloured and decorated. Candles were lit round the Sepulchre, at which a vigil was kept. Then on Easter Day the Christ and the Host were resurrected and carried to the altar. The Easter Sepulchres were sometimes permanent structures in the chancel wall, with carvings of the Three Maries and the Three Roman Soldiers.

One might compare this carol with the intricate Easter Sepulchres at Hawton, Nottinghamshire, or Patrington in the East Riding.

308. THE CORPUS CHRISTI CAROL (Staffordshire). *N. and Q.*, 1862.

309. THE CORPUS CHRISTI CAROL (from Scotland). James Hogg, notes to *The Mountain Bard*, 1840.

309. AN ABC, From the *New England Primer*, late seventeenth century.

311. THE SEVEN VIRGINS. *Oxford Book of Carols*, 1928, No. 43.

313. BY A CHAPEL AS I CAME. Greene. Fifteenth century. *wyhte Jesu:* variously interpreted as 'white Jesu', 'strong Jesu' or 'brave Jesu' or 'with Jesu' – of which the first appeals to one's sense of image and the last is probably correct (best fitting the sound as well). *saint Collas:* St. Nicholas. *off her mould:* off the top of her head.

314. BROWN ROBYN'S CONFESSION. Child 57. *kevels:* lots.

315. THE ROYAL FISHERMAN. *J.F.S.S.*, V.

316. IN DESSEXSHIRE AS IT BEFEL. Alice Gillington, *Songs of the Open Road*, 1911. A corrupted ballad taken down from gypsies.

319. SAIR FYEL'D, HINNY. J. Collingwood Bruce and John Stokoe, *Northumberland Minstrelsy*, 1882.

320. WEDDING AND FUNERAL. Moorman.

320. THE TOD'S HOLE. Chambers. *tod:* fox.

320. THE DUKE OF GRAFTON. *Roxburghe Ballads*, Vol. V, 1884, from a broadside of 1738.

321. THE COWBOY'S LAMENT. Bodkin.

322. THE LYKE-WAKE DIRGE. John Aubrey, *Remaines of Gentilisme and Judaisme*, Folk-Lore Society, 1881. Aubrey's manuscript in the British Museum is possibly the source of all versions (though another Yorkshire version with 2 extra stanzas on falling from the Brig o'Dread into the flames was printed by R. Blakeborough in *Wit, Character, Folklore & Customs of the North Riding of Yorkshire*, 1898). Usually Scott's version, from his *Minstrelsy of the Scottish Border*, is reprinted with 'Fire and sleet', not 'Fire and fleet'. Alas for over-romantic thoughts of the soul flitting through sleet over the moorland of gorse, Aubrey's 'fire and fleet' is certainly right, the expression meaning 'hearth and home'. See O.E.D. under *flet*, where it is explained that 'fire and fleet' was a customary expression in wills. O.E.D. quotes a will of 1539. 'My wife to have . . . fyre

and fleete in my haule and kitchen'. The poem is grim enough without Yorkshire sleet over the gorse.

Aubrey wrote that till about 1616 or 1624 the song was sung in Yorkshire by a woman who came to the dead man's house. Also, from *A Description of Cleveland in a letter addressed by H.Tr. to Sir T. Chaloner* (British Museum, M. S. Cotton. Julius, FVI. 431. printed in the *Topographer and Genealogist*, ii, 1853): 'When any dieth certaine women singe a song to the dead body, recyting the jorney that the partie deceased must goe; and they are of beleife (such is their fondnesse) that once in their lives yt is good to give a payre of newe shoes to a poor man, forasmuch as after this life they are to passe barefoote through a greate launde full of thornes and furzen, excepte by the meryte of the almes aforesaid they have redeemed their forfeyte; for at the edge of the launde an oulde man shall meete them with the same shoes that were given by the partye when he was livinge, and after he hath shodde them he dismisseth them to goe through thicke and thin without scratch or scalle.' *ean:* one. *beane:* bone.

323. TWO RIDDLES. (i) Chambers. (ii) Chambers.

324. THE BLUE-TAIL FLY. Lomax, 1960. Alan Lomax mentions that this song was much liked by Abraham Lincoln.

325. THE UNDERTAKERS' CLUB. Ashton, *Modern Street Ballads*, 1888.

326. HOLD THE WIND. Lomax, 1960. Taken down from a negro blacksmith in Louisiana State Penitentiary, in 1933.

327. SWING LOW, SWEET CHARIOT. Lomax, 1934.

328. PIE IN THE SKY. Lomax, 1960. Written by Joe Hill, executed in Utah, 1914, after being found guilty of murder.

329. NO HIDING PLACE DOWN THERE. Whitney and Bullock, *Folklore from Maryland*, 1925.

Index of Titles and First Lines

365

367